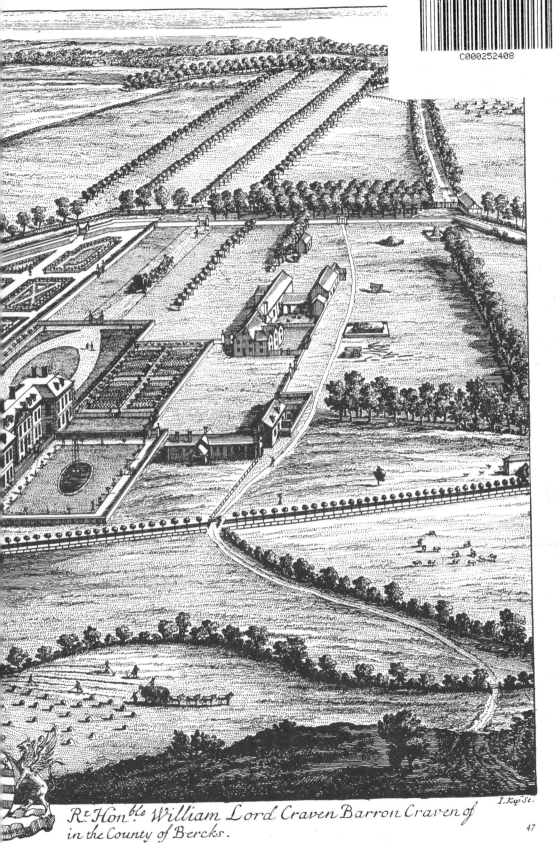

R.t Hon.ble William Lord Craven Barron Craven of
in the County of Bercks.

I. Kip Sc.

47

Combe Abbey from the north-west, from Kip's *Britannia Illustrata* (1707).

WARWICKSHIRE
COUNTRY HOUSES

The bay window in the Saloon of Arbury Hall. The plasterwork, by W. Hanwell, dates from 1795 and was influenced by the Perpendicular Gothic work in Henry VII's Chapel at Westminster Abbey.

English Country Houses Series   *General Editor:* Nicholas Kingsley

WARWICKSHIRE COUNTRY HOUSES

Geoffrey Tyack

Phillimore

1994

Published by
PHILLIMORE & CO. LTD.
Shopwyke Manor Barn, Chichester, Sussex

© Geoffrey Tyack, 1994

ISBN 0 85033 868 9

Colour plates printed in Great Britain by
CHICHESTER PRESS LTD.

Printed and bound in Great Britain by
BIDDLES LTD.
Guildford, Surrey

CONTENTS

List of Illustrations vii
Illustration Acknowledgements xii
Preface and Acknowledgements xiii
Abbreviations xv
Introduction xvii

Part 1
Alscot Park 1
Ansley Hall 6
Arbury Hall 9
Astley Castle 16
Aston Hall 19
Baddesley Clinton 23
Baginton Hall 28
Barrells Hall 30
Billesley Manor 33
Bilton Grange 35
Castle Bromwich Hall 38
Charlecote 42
Chesterton House 48
Clopton House 50
Coleshill Hall 53
Combe Abbey 57
Compton Verney 64
Compton Wynyates 71
Coughton Court 77
Ettington Park 81
Farnborough Hall 88
Four Oaks Hall 92
Foxcote 95
Grove Park 97
Guy's Cliffe 100
Hams Hall 106
Honington Hall 109
Kenilworth Castle 113
Knowle Hall 119
Malvern Hall 122
Maxstoke Castle 125
Merevale Hall 130
Middleton Hall 134
Moreton Hall and Moreton Paddox 138
New Hall 141
Newbold Revel 145

Newnham Paddox 148
Packington Hall 152
Packwood House 158
Radway Grange 162
Ragley Hall 166
Salford Hall 173
Shuckburgh Hall 175
Stoneleigh Abbey 178
Studley Castle 186
Umberslade Hall 189
Upton House 192
Walton Hall 196
Warwick Castle 200
Warwick Priory 209
Welcombe 213
Weston House 216
Wroxall Abbey 220

Part 2

Gazetteer of other houses 223

Index 275

LIST OF ILLUSTRATIONS

Frontispiece: Arbury Hall, the Saloon
Map of the County xvi
1. Alscot Park from the north west 2
2. Alscot Park, south front 3
3. Alscot Park, Entrance Hall 4
4. Ansley Hall, from the south west 6
5. Ansley Hall, north front 7
6. Arbury Hall, drawing by Henry Beighton 9
7. Arbury Hall, Chapel 10
8. Arbury Hall, south front 12
9. Arbury Hall, Dining Room 13
10. Astley Castle 16
11. Astley Castle, stable block 17
12. Aston Hall, view by A.E. Everitt 18
13. Aston Hall, east tower 19
14. Aston Hall, staircase 20
15. Aston Hall, Long Gallery 21
16. Baddesley Clinton, entrance front 23
17. Baddesley Clinton, Hall 25
18. Baddesley Clinton from the north east 26
19. Baginton Hall, south front 28
20. Barrells Hall from the west 31
21. Barrells Hall, Bonomi drawing 32
22. Billesley Manor, south front 34
23. Bilton Grange from the garden 35
24. Bilton Grange, Hall 36
25. Bilton Grange, Library 37
26. Castle Bromwich Hall, view by A.E. Everitt 38
27. Castle Bromwich Hall, foot of Staircase 39
28. Castle Bromwich Hall, Drawing Room 40
29. Charlecote, drawing by Henry Beighton 42
30. Charlecote, porch 43
31. Charlecote, entrance front 45
32. Charlecote, Great Hall 46
33. Charlecote from the south 47
34. Chesterton House, windmill 48
35. Chesterton House, from an 18th-century estate plan 49
36. Clopton House, east front 50
37. Clopton House, west and south fronts 51
38. Coleshill Hall, drawing by Thomas Ward 53
39. Coleshill Hall, loggia 54
40. Combe Abbey from the south 56
41. Combe Abbey, garden porch 57

42. Combe Abbey, Great Chamber 58
43. Combe Abbey, west range 60
44. Combe Abbey, Staircase 60
45. Combe Abbey from the north-west 61
46. Combe Abbey from the south showing Nesfield wing 62
47. Compton Verney in 1656 65
48. Compton Verney, west front 65
49. Compton Verney from the south east 67
50. Compton Verney, Entrance Hall 68
51. Compton Wynyates from the south west 71
52. Compton Wynyates, Hall 72
53. Compton Wynyates, courtyard 73
54. Compton Wynyates from the north-west 75
55. Coughton Court, entrance front 77
56. Coughton Court, south range, from the courtyard 78
57. Coughton Court, courtyard from the east, by A.E. Everitt 80
58. Ettington Park from the south 81
59. Ettington Park, south front 83
60. Ettington Park, design for the west front by Rickman and Hutchinson 83
61. Ettington Park, south end of the west front 85
62. Ettington Park, south front 86
63. Farnborough Hall from the north west 88
64. Farnborough Hall, Dining Room 90
65. Farnborough Hall, garden terrace and obelisk 91
66. Farnborough Hall, oval pavilion 91
67. Four Oaks Hall, view by Henry Beighton 93
68. Four Oaks Hall after rebuilding 94
69. Foxcote, entrance front 95
70. Grove Park, old house 97
71. Grove Park, design for rebuilding by C.S. Smith 99
72. Guys Cliffe from the west in 1788 100
73. Guys Cliffe, courtyard and entrance front 101
74. Guys Cliffe from the river, c.1795 103
75. Guys Cliffe from the river after rebuilding 104
76. Guys Cliffe, west front 105
77. Hams Hall, entrance front 107
78. Honington Hall, bird's-eye view, 1731 (Bodleian Library, MS Gough Drawings) 108
79. Honington Hall, entrance front 108
80. Honington Hall, Entrance Hall 110
81. Honington Hall, Saloon 111
82. Kenilworth Castle, Hall 113
83. Kenilworth Castle from the east in 1620 116
84. Kenilworth Castle, porch to Leicester's Gatehouse 116
85. Kenilworth Castle from the south 117
86. Knowle Hall, drawing by Thomas Ward 119
87. Knowle Hall, Entrance Hall, by Thomas Ward 120
88. Malvern Hall, entrance front 122
89. Malvern Hall, Barn à la Paestum 123
90. Maxstoke Castle, entrance front 125
91. Maxstoke Castle from the north west, by A.E. Everitt 126

 92. Maxstoke Castle, the courtyard 127
 93. Maxstoke Castle, Oak Drawing Room 128
 94. Merevale Hall, *c.*1829 130
 95. Merevale Hall from the south west 131
 96. Merevale Hall, Staircase Hall, by Edward Blore 132
 97. Merevale Hall from the west 133
 98. Middleton Hall, entrance front 134
 99. Middleton Hall, Staircase 135
100. Middleton Hall from the west 136
101. Moreton Hall, garden front 138
102. Moreton Paddox, garden front 139
103. Moreton Paddox, Staircase 140
104. New Hall, entrance front 141
105. New Hall, Hall, by A.E. Everitt 142
106. New Hall from the north west 143
107. Newbold Revel 146
108. Newnham Paddox, *c.*1707 148
109. Newnham Paddox from the south east 150
110. Newnham Paddox, south front 150
111. Packington Hall, late 17th-century drawing 153
112. Packington Hall, stables 154
113. Packington Hall, west front, by Matthew Brettingham 155
114. Packington Hall, Gallery 156
115. Packwood House, 1756 drawing 158
116. Packwood House from the east 159
117. Packwood House, Long Gallery 160
118. Radway Grange, Edge Hill Tower 163
119. Radway Grange from the south east 164
120. Ragley Hall 167
121. Ragley Hall, Great Hall 169
122. Ragley Hall, west front 170
123. Ragley Hall, Red Saloon 171
124. Salford Hall, entrance front 173
125. Shuckburgh Hall, entrance front in the late 18th century 175
126. Shuckburgh Hall, entrance front 176
127. Stoneleigh Abbey, courtyard 178
128. Stoneleigh Abbey, north range in the 1720s 179
129. Stoneleigh Abbey from the south west 180
130. Stoneleigh Abbey, Drawing Room 181
131. Stoneleigh Abbey, Chapel 183
132. Stoneleigh Abbey, stables, *c.*1830 184
133. Studley Castle, garden front 187
134. Umberslade Hall 190
135. Upton House, garden front 193
136. Upton House, entrance front 193
137. Upton House, Gallery 194
138. Walton Hall in the late 18th century 196
139. Walton Hall, Bath House 197
140. Walton Hall, house and grounds 198
141. Warwick Castle from the south east 200

142. Warwick Castle, undercroft 201
143. Warwick Castle, Great Hall 204
144. Warwick Castle, State Bedroom 205
145. Warwick Castle, courtyard 206
146. Warwick Castle, Great Hall 207
147. Warwick Priory, from a 1711 estate plan 209
148. Warwick Priory, hall range 210
149. Warwick Priory, Hall 211
150. Warwick Priory, garden front 212
151. Welcombe House, c.1821 213
152. Welcombe, c.1900 214
153. Weston House, view by Henry Beighton 216
154. Weston House from the south 217
155. Weston House, Dining Room 218
156. Wroxall Abbey, drawing by Thomas Ward 220
157. Wroxall Abbey, entrance front 221
158. Allesley Park 223
159. Barford Hill House 226
160. Old Berry Hall 228
161. Bilton Hall 229
162. Birdingbury Hall 230
163. Blyth Hall 230
164. Brandon Hall 233
165. Brownsover Hall 233
166. Caldecote Hall 235
167. Cawston House 236
168. Claverdon House, Stone Tower 237
169. Clifford Chambers Manor 239
170. Coton House 239
171. Dunchurch Lodge 240
172. Edgbaston Hall 241
173. Elmdon Hall 243
174. Erdington Hall 244
175. Grendon Hall 246
176. Grimshaw Hall 246
177. Haseley Manor 248
178. Lawford Hall 251
179. Little Compton Manor 251
180. Little Kineton House 252
181. Little Wolford Manor 253
182. Loxley Hall 254
183. Moxhull Hall, 1763 drawing 256
184. Moxhull Hall, c.1821 257
185. New House 258
186. Offchurch Bury 259
187. Pooley Hall 261
188. St John's House 262
189. Shrubland House 264
190. Snitterfield House 265
191. Stivichall Hall 266

192.	Weddington Hall	267
193.	Weston-in-Arden Hall	269
194.	Weston-under-Wetherley Hall	269
195.	Whitley Abbey	271
196.	Woodcote	271
197.	Wootton Hall	272
198.	Wormleighton Manor, gatehouse	273
199.	Wormleighton Manor, chamber block	273

Colour

I	Baddesley Clinton from the north west	facing 76
II	Charlecote, the Dining Room	facing 77
III	Compton Wynyates from the south west	facing 77
IV	Coughton Court, gatehouse	facing 92
V	Ettington Park from the south	facing 92
VI	Honington Hall, view of the garden, 1759	facing 93
VII	Kenilworth Castle, gatehouse	facing 93
VIII	Malvern Hall, entrance front, by John Constable	facing 172
IX	Packwood House from the south east	facing 172
X	Ragley Hall from the south east	facing 173
XI	Stoneleigh Abbey, the Saloon	facing 188
XII	Upton House, by Anthony Devis	facing 189
XIII	Warwick Castle from the east, painting by Canaletto	facing 189

Plans

Arbury Hall	11
Aston Hall	18
Baddesley Clinton	25
Combe Abbey	56
Compton Verney	66
Kenilworth Castle	114
Stoneleigh Abbey	179
Walton Hall	197
Warwick Castle	202

ILLUSTRATION ACKNOWLEDGEMENTS

A.F. Kersting: frontispiece, 2, 31-2, 81, 129, 137, 147, II-IV, X, X

Oxfordshire County County Council, Leisure & Arts: 1, 33, 62, 79, 102, 118, 119, 139, 140, 169, 179, 181, 197

Country Life Picture Library: 3, 50

Warwick County Record Office: 4, 10, 20, 23-5, 40-2, 49, 54, 59, 60, 68, 69, 71, 74, 75, 77, 82, 88, 90, 94, 100, 104, 110, 114, 122, 134, 141-4, 147, 149, 151, 153, 158, 161, 173, 183-6, 189, 192, 195

National Monuments Record © Crown Copyright: 5, 37, 46, 48, 51, 53, 63-5, 73, 76, 80, 99, 103, 106, 112, 114, 116, 124, 126, 130-1

National Monuments Record/Marquess of Hertford © Crown Copyright: 121, 123

Birmingham City Libraries, Archives Section, by permission of Birmingham Library Services: 6, 19, 22, 36, 58, 70, 109, 111, 125, 138, 145, 168, 178, 194

Birmingham City Libraries, Local History Section, by permission of Birmingham Library Services: 7-9, 17, 28, 93, 98, 133, 187

Birmingham Museums & Art Gallery: 12, 14, 15, 26, 27, 57, 91, 105, 160, 174, XIII

Royal Institute of British Architects: 21, 164, 169

Shakespeare Birthplace Trust: 35, 83, 132, 152, 168, 175, 191

British Library: 38, 86-7, 96, 156, 162, 180, 190

The Bodleian Library, Oxford: 43, 72, 78

Coventry City Libraries: 44

Victoria and Albert Museum, by permission of the Board of Trustees: 61

The Earl of Aylesford: 113

Michael Fetherston-Dilke: 115

Private Collections: 128, VI

B.F.G. Pardoe (copyright reserved): 150

Mrs. M.H. Warriner: 154, 155

Leamington Spa Courier: 159

The National Trust: I, XII

John Crook: V, VII, IX

Yale Center for British Art, Paul Mellon Collection: VIII

The unacknowledged photographs were taken by the author, mostly in the spring and early summer of 1993.

The plans of Arbury Hall, Combe Abbey and Compton Verney are reproduced by permission of the Warwickshire Local History Society, those of Aston Hall, Baddesley Clinton and Warwick Castle by permission of the Victoria County Histories, that of Kenilworth Castle by permission of the Warwick County Record Office, and that of Stoneleigh Abbey by permission of the Birmingham and Warwick-shire Archaeological Society.

PREFACE AND ACKNOWLEDGEMENTS

Sir William Dugdale dedicated his *Antiquities of Warwickshire* (1656) to the gentry of the county, 'as the most proper Persons to whom it can be presented; wherein you will see very much of your worthy Ancestors, to whose Memory I have erected it, as a <u>Monumental Pillar</u>, and to shew in what Honour they lived in those flourishing Ages past'. This book has been written with a similar aim in mind. Like previous volumes in this series, it is divided into two main parts: a detailed survey of the history of 54 of the larger and best-documented houses in Warwickshire, and a second part in which 98 of the lesser-known houses are described in rather less detail. The division of houses between the two parts of the book is inevitably somewhat arbitrary, as is the choice of which houses to include and which to leave out. The definition of a country house is bound to be less precise than that of other types of building. But I have tried to include all of the houses which, at one time or other, have been at the centre of important landed estates, and for which there is some visual or documentary evidence. I have also included some houses which, though surrounded by relatively small estates, are, or were in their heyday, impressive enough to support a recognisable country-house style of life; the choice of these houses, many of them built in the 19th or 20th centuries, has largely depended on the amount of available information and on their intrinsic architectural interest. In order to make the book of manageable size, I have left out many of the smaller manor houses built between the 16th and the 18th centuries. Most of these houses are poorly documented, but many would repay further investigation, especially by someone with the requisite archaeological skills.

Some of the houses in the book are regularly open to the public; times of opening can be found in *Historic Houses, Castles and Gardens*, published annually by Reed Information Services. Others are open on occasion, as advertised in the local press, and some country-house gardens are open from time to time under the National Gardens Scheme. I have visited all the houses that can be visited in the first part of the book, and, often alas more cursorily, seen most of those in the second part. I owe it to all the owners and occupiers of the houses in the book to state that the inclusion of a house does not mean that it is open to the public, and I hope that no one will feel that his or her privacy has been violated by inclusion. It is a sad fact that those who live or work in country houses have to be concerned about security in a way which was unimaginable even 25 years ago, when I first started taking an interest in the domestic architecture of Warwickshire. Under these circumstances I am especially grateful to those who have kindly allowed me to visit or revisit their houses, and have gone well beyond the call of duty and courtesy in answering my questions and supplying me with information.

The boundaries of Warwickshire have changed from time to time. For the purposes of this book, Warwickshire means the county as it was in 1974, before a large tract of territory between, and including, Coventry and Birmingham, was wrenched out of it to form part of the new county of the West Midlands. Those parts of south Warwickshire which were once in Gloucestershire and Worcestershire have been included in the book, but the area to the north-east of Tamworth, which was transferred to Staffordshire before 1974 has not. Those parts of the Birmingham conurbation to the south and south-east of the city which were in Worcestershire until 1911 — the old parishes of Northfield, Kings Norton, Moseley and Yardley — have not been included either.

I owe a great debt of gratitude to the ever-helpful archivists and their staffs at Warwick, Stratford and Birmingham. I would also like to thank the local history librarians at Birmingham, Coventry, Solihull and Sutton Coldfield, and the staff of the Bodleian Library in Oxford, where I have done the bulk of my research involving printed materials. Howard Colvin has been most generous in supplying me with information on many Warwickshire houses over a long period of time. Others who have generously supplied information, have read sections of the manuscript, or have helped in other ways, are Dr. N.W. Alcock, the Earl of Aylesford, Michael Barbour, Paul Barker, Dr. Robert Bearman, Dr. Steven Brindle, Maxwell Craven, George Demidowicz, Viscount Daventry, Sir William Dugdale, Beryl Ellerslie and the Middleton Hall Trust, Martin Ellis, Dr. Michael Farr, T.W. Ferrers-Walker, Charles and Michael Fetherston-Dilke, Hazel Fryer, Professor Andor Gomme, Keith Goodway, W.R. Hakewill, Lady Elizabeth Hamilton, William Hawkes, Jeffrey Haworth, Peter Henderson, Christine Hodgetts, Mrs. Geoffrey Holbech, C.B. Holman, Mrs. Ives at Wroxall Abbey School, Dr. Joan Lane, S.J. Lowe, Mrs. McLaren-Throckmorton, Peter Meadows, Anna Meredith, Nicholas Moore, Mr. Newton at Bilton Grange School, Caroline Parkes, Jean Powrie, Graham Suggett, Mrs James West, and Lord Willoughby de Broke. I am also grateful to John Crook and A.F. Kersting for supplying colour plates, and to Wilbur Wright for drawing the map of the county. My final thanks are due to Noel Osborne, Managing Director of Phillimore & Co, for supporting the project throughout, and to my wife for her encouragement, criticism, and help in preparing the manuscript.

Oxford, February 1994

To
Paul, Jonathan and Catherine

xiv

Burlington's former assistant Henry Flitcroft, and at Hams Hall (1768) Charles Bowyer Adderley, like Gregory a member of an old Warwickshire family, brought in the Derby builder/architect Joseph Pickford to design another villa of Palladian inspiration. The long-delayed completion of the interior of the west wing of Stoneleigh Abbey was entrusted to Timothy Lightoler, a Lancashire craftsman/architect who settled in Warwick and designed the neo-Elizabethan dining room in the Castle — a forestaste of what was to be a widely-used style in the 19th century.[14] Packington Hall, the most important classical house in late 18th-century Warwickshire, was also designed by a relatively little-known architect from a similar background, Matthew Brettingham, the executant architect at Holkham Hall (Norfolk) and the designer of Norfolk House in London. His design was of unimpeachable Palladian correctness, but the most interesting of the interiors, the Pompeian Galley, was designed in the 1780s by Joseph Bonomi, an Italian who had worked in the office of Robert Adam, in a style modelled on recently-discovered ancient Roman precedents; together with the estate church, also by Bonomi, this ranks as Warwickshire's main contribution to neo-classical architecture and decoration. Bonomi later extended Barrells Hall and designed Springfield House.

As the larger landlords expanded their estates in the 18th and early 19th centuries, there was some attrition among the houses and estates of the lesser gentry. Some of their manor houses, like Berry Hall, Solihull, became farmhouses; others, like Henwood Hall in the same parish, disappeared completely. Whereas, according to one estimate, there were 125 resident gentry and noblemen in 1673, only 63 houses were deemed to be 'seats' in 1815.[15] The Rev. Thomas Ward, who came from a gentry family from Barford, near Warwick, drew attention in 1830 to the 'numerous families of great consequence in this county, who flourished for hundreds of years before, and ... all of them expired nearly at the same time in the last century'.[16] His own cousin sold the manor house at Barford to the 2nd Earl of Warwick, and it was later demolished. Even some of the larger houses disappeared, like Chesterton, demolished in 1802 after the estate came into the hands of Lord Willoughby de Broke.

To some extent the influx of newcomers in the 19th century compensated for the disappearance of old families.[17] Rural Warwickshire began to attract Birmingham businessmen and manufacturers as early as the 1660s, when the iron-master Humphrey Jennens built Erdington Hall. But the wealth of Birmingham did not have a very great effect on Warwickshire landed society until the later 19th century, when agricultural depression forced many of the established landowners to sell off parts, or sometimes all, of their estates. Until then, the political and economic power of the established gentry and nobility remained intact. Their wealth was sometimes reinforced from non-agricultural sources. Coal-mining helped finance the rebuilding of Merevale Hall by William Stratford Dugdale, and the money for the rebuilding of Guy's Cliffe by Bertie Greatheed came partly from the sale of building land in the rapidly growing town of Leamington Spa, and partly from an inheritance from the last Earl of Ancaster. But even in the absence of such windfalls, landed incomes were sufficient to finance the complete rebuilding of Grove Park by the 11th Lord Dormer in 1833-8, Ettington Park by Evelyn Philip Shirley in 1858-62, Walton Hall by Sir Charles Mordaunt at the same time, and Combe Abbey in the 1860s.

Newcomers wishing to establish themselves as landowners in Warwickshire had to rely on the occasional sale of an old estate through profligacy or the failure of heirs, or to carve out new estates by buying smaller concentrations of land, often without an existing house of any size. The first course was adopted by the Lancashire mill-owner Sir George Philips, who bought the Weston estate from the Sheldons in 1817, the second by the Prime Minister Sir Robert Peel, the squire of Drayton, just over the Staffordshire border, who bought 750 acres at Hampton-in-Arden on which his younger son Frederick built the present Hampton Manor in 1855. Both purchases resulted in the building of new houses. Houses of the second type did not confer on their owners the territorial and political influence formerly inseparable from the idea of the country house. In this sense they were closer to the idea of the country villa or 'gentleman's residence' which first made an appearance in the Home Counties in the 17th century, and became popular around the fringes of Birmingham, Leamington and Rugby in the early 19th century, as well as on the banks of the Avon near Stratford. But, so long as there was a sufficient source of outside wealth, the size of the estate did not have to be a constraint on the size or splendour of the house, as can be seen at Bilton Grange, built in 1841-50 on a 390-acre estate in hunting country near Rugby by John Washington Hibbert, the son of a West Indies plantation owner, and one of the largest Warwickshire houses of its date.

The best of Warwickshire's 19th-century country houses bear witness to the Romanticism of the age. Packington Hall was the last major classical house to be built in the county, though several smaller houses (e.g. Edstone Hall, of the 1820s, by an unknown architect, and Fillongley Hall, extended in 1840-1 by James Akroyd of Coventry) show the influence of the Greek Revival, and Shuckburgh Hall was refronted in the Italian Renaissance manner by a London architect, H.E. Kendall, in the 1850s. There were also some compact classically-inspired villas, like Baraset, near Stratford, of 1800, and Barford Hill, designed in by Henry Hakewill, an architect with a successful local practice. But the most engaging early 19th-century villa was the 'cottage' built at Brandon c.1800-10 for Lord Grey de Ruthin to the designs of Robert Lugar, who also rebuilt Weddington Hall in the castellated manner at about the same time. The largest sham castle in Warwickshire was built at Studley in 1834 by another London architect, Samuel Beazley, for Sir Francis Holyoake Goodricke, the inheritor of a large banking fortune, but the presence of two genuine castles of the calibre of Warwick and Kenilworth in the heart of the county may have deterred others from embarking on this risky style.

The main vehicles for the Romantic impulses of the Warwickshire gentry were the Tudor-Gothic and Elizabethan Revival styles. The growing taste for 'Old English' architecture and decoration in the Regency and early Victorian eras led to a rediscovery of houses like Compton Wynyates, Aston Hall and the earlier parts of Combe Abbey, and the cult of Shakespeare drew a steady trickle of visitors to Charlecote, the scene of a legendary escapade in the early years of the dramatist's career. The visitors included Sir Walter Scott, whose *Kenilworth* put that magnificent ruin high on the list of attractions in what was already by the 1820s becoming a popular tourist area, with Stratford and Warwick Castle as the main destinations. No-one proposed restoring Kenilworth Castle, but the interior of Aston Hall was restored by James Watt, the son of the great inventor, after the house had been sold by the last of the Holtes in 1817, with new furniture comissioned to create an 'authentic' atmosphere. Charlecote was also gradually remodelled and enlarged in a neo-Elizabethan style by George Hammond Lucy and his wife, starting in the 1820s, and the interiors are among the finest and best-preserved of their type and date in England. The 'Old English' character of Warwick Castle was also enhanced in a series of restorations, culminating in the rebuilding of the Great Hall by Anthony Salvin after a fire in 1871. Compton Wynyates was restored after a long period of neglect in 1859-60, and the restoration of Baddesley Clinton followed in the 1880s. Meanwhile Warwick craftsmen, like the firm of William Cookes, makers of the massive 'Kenilworth Buffet' in Warwick Castle, the wood-carver James Willcox, who worked at Charlecote and Stoneleigh Abbey, his successor T.H. Kendall, and the decorator and stained-glass manufacturer William Holland, disseminated 'Old English' craftsmanship throughout the county and outside.[18]

The most original reconstruction of a Warwickshire house in the 'Old English' manner took place at Guy's Cliffe, starting c.1810. The alterations here were designed by the owner, Bertie Greatheed, using local builders, and when completed the house represented the quintessence of that sensibility to pictur-esque surroundings and historical associations which characterised the Regency era. An equal sensitivity to site and to the dramatic potential of the 'Old English' styles was shown by Edward Blore at Weston (1827-30) and Merevale (1838-44), both of them 'commanding the prospect' in a way which none of the 16th- or 17th-century houses of Warwickshire achieved, with the exception of Aston Hall. C.S. Smith, the Leamington architect involved in the expansion of Charlecote in the 1820s, employed the Tudor-Gothic idiom at Stoneleigh Abbey, where he designed a new stable block in 1815-20 and remodelled the north range in 1836-8; he also designed the insipid neo-Tudor Grove Park. Later houses in the 'Old English' manner include Welcombe (1866-8), by Blore's pupil Henry Clutton and the Manchester architect Thomas Newby, Woodcote (1861-2), by John Gibson, a pupil of Sir Charles Barry, and Caldecote Hall (1879-80), by the Goddards of Leicester.

By the middle of the 19th century the more adventurous Warwickshire patrons were turning back from the various manifestations of 'Old English' to the Gothic. Bilton Grange was designed by the apostle of Victorian Gothic, A.W.N. Pugin, and in the 1850s George Gilbert Scott, who acknowledged Pugin as his inspiration, designed two houses in the county, Brownsover Hall and Walton Hall, both of them for the representatives of old Warwickshire families who seem to have seen the Gothic style as an embodiment of historical continuity and dynastic pride. But these houses are all outshone by Ettington Park, rebuilt for Evelyn Philip Shirley, to the designs of John Prichard of Llandaff, a deft manipulator of 'constructional polychromy', 'truthful' detailing, much of it taken from Continental sources, vigorous and dramatic outlines, and all the other weapons in the High Victorian armoury. The huge east wing of Combe Abbey, begun in 1863 for the 3rd Earl of Craven to the designs of William Eden Nesfield, was also Gothic in inspiration, but here medieval details were mixed with other motifs to produce a stylistic compromise which was very characteristic of the late 19th century.

Nesfield was the son of the garden designer W.A. Nesfield, who designed new formal gardens at Merevale and also at Combe Abbey. At Stoneleigh Abbey the 18th-century gardens were largely landscaped away by Humphry Repton, but a new formal garden was created near the house in the mid-19th century. Formal gardens were also laid out at Ragley Hall and Warwick Castle by the well-known mid-Victorian designer Robert Marnock. Some country house owners were also assiduous builders of estate cottages like James Roberts West of Alscot and Louisa Ann Ryland, the daughter of a Birmingham manufacturer who had bought the Sherbourne and Barford Hill estates. Gilbert Scott's splendid estate church at Sherbourne is an eloquent memorial to her munificence.

The agricultural depression which set in during the 1870s put an end to large-scale building by the older Warwickshire gentry and nobility. It also set in train a process which led to the shrinking of some of the great estates and the complete extinction of others, a process which gathered momentum as taxes increased after the First World War. Some of the major county seats, like Compton Verney and Combe Abbey, passed out of the hands of the families which had lived in them for many generations; others, like Weston and Hams Hall, were demolished completely. The building of a power station on the site of Hams Hall symbolises the passing of an era.

But country-house life still retained its allure, especially for wealthy businessmen and the building of new country houses and the renovation of old ones continued, at least until the Second World War, when a renewed spate of taxes combined with the shortage of domestic service to prompt a new wave of sales. Most of the new houses were built on what were, by the standards of the early 19th century, relatively small estates: enough to sustain the illusion of squirearchical life, but not too much to be a financial burden. Many of the builders came from Birmingham, like Joseph Gillott, the builder of the new Berry Hall *c.*1875, and Herbert Wade, who built Honiley Hall near the site of a long-vanished house in 1914. Others came from much further afield, attracted by the historical associations of the county and by its sporting potential. The wealth which lay behind the building of Haseley Manor and Dunchurch Lodge derived from coal mining in the North of England, and three of the largest late-Victorian and Edwardian houses, Ashorne Hill, Moreton Hall and Moreton Paddox, were built out of American fortunes. Upton House, a hunting seat of the Earls of Jersey, was sold at the end of the 19th century, and lavishly rebuilt in the 1930s by the 2nd Viscount Bearstead, heir of the Shell oil fortune; it now contains the finest art collection in any Warwickshire house.

The new country-house owners of the late 19th and early 20th centuries liked 'Old English' and Georgian architecture, and their houses reflect their aesthetic preferences. Several owners restored old and neglected houses, like the timber-framed Grimshaw Hall near Knowle, the Jacobean manor house at Little Compton, restored after a fire in 1927, and the late 17th-century Clifford Chambers Manor, where Edwin Lutyens was brought in after a fire in 1918. Their restorations usually involved the formation of new gardens made up 'outdoor rooms' bounded by brick or stone walls sheltering colourful herbaceous borders; at Bourton Hall, remodelled in a Renaissance manner for a new owner, Frederick Shaw, by the Warwick architect Charles Armstrong in 1906-8, the gardens were designed in an Italianate style by Harold Peto. But the finest examples of this kind of restoration are Packwood House, where the new owner Graham Baron Ash, a discriminating collector, carried out a complete remodelling of the old and much-mauled Elizabethan house, and Upton, where Lord Bearstead employed Percy

Morley Horder to create what was in effect a new neo-Georgian interior within the walls of the old house, and to improve the gardens.

The new houses followed the same rather predictable pattern. Several are in the Norman Shaw manner (e.g. Upper Skilts, by J.A. and P.B. Chatwin of Birmingham with gardens by Thomas Mawson) and in the 'free style' of the Edwardian era (e.g. Moor Hall, Sutton Coldfield, by the Birmingham architects Henman and Cooper). Others, like Ashorne Hill (by E. Goldie 1895-8) and Honiley Hall (by C.E. Bateman of Birmingham, 1914), show the influence of the Arts and Crafts movement. Two luxurious Edwardian houses by W.H. Romaine-Walker, Moreton Hall and Moreton Paddox, aspired to, and even surpassed, the grandeur of the larger Warwickshire houses in their heyday before the onset of the agricultural depression. But in general it is fair to say that the creative energy of the best domestic architects in late 19th- and 20th-century Warwickshire was chanelled not into country houses, many of which became anachronisms soon after they were built, but into smaller houses, of which there are some excellent examples in the smarter suburbs of Birmingham and other towns.

Despite the huge social and political upheavals of the last hundred years, the country houses of Warwickshire have shown a remarkable ability to survive. To some extent this is the result of the tenacity of some of the owners of the larger estates, reduced though these estates are in size. A Marquess of Northampton still lives at Compton Wynyates, a Marquess of Hertford at Ragley and an Earl of Aylesford at Packington. There are still Fetherston-Dilkes at Maxstoke, Dugdales at Merevale, Newdigates at Arbury and Shuckburghs at Shuckburgh Hall. The Throckmortons still live at Coughton, the Holbechs at Farnborough and the Fairfax-Lucys at Charlecote, though the houses are now owned by the National Trust. Some houses are no longer lived in by their owners, like Walton Hall and Ettington Park, though the family still owns the land. Several houses have become hotels, others are schools or institutions, others are flats, and yet more are conference and training centres. Most of these houses are well looked after, and they give pleasure and employment to more people than probably at any time in their history. There has, it is true, been some irreparable damage. Combe Abbey was quite unnecessarily mutilated in the 1920s, Guys Cliffe was allowed to fall into ruin after the Second World War, and some houses, like Newnham Paddox, have gone completely. But, for all the fashionable jeremiads of those who deplore the decline and fall of the English country house, it is impossible not to feel a guarded sense of optimism for the future of the houses of Warwickshire, even in the straitened and pessimistic 1990s.

A Note on Sources

Warwickshire is rewarding territory for the topographically minded historian. William Dugdale's *Antiquities of Warwickshire* (1656) is one of the great pioneering county histories, and also a constant pleasure to read and refer to. The first edition has illustrations by the emigré Czech artist Wenceslas Hollar, and the second edition of 1730, by the Rev. William Thomas, Rector of Exhall, has views of several of the more important country houses by Henry Beighton, showing them before the mania for landscape gardening set in.

Several attempts were later made to revise, update and illustrate Dugdale's work. In the 1790s Henry Jeayes, a Coventry drawing-master, was commissioned to illustrate all the main county seats, many of the manor houses, and all the parish churches. The drawings were collected by Thomas Sharp, a Coventry hatter with antiquarian interests, and presented in 1821 to the 5th Earl of Aylesford, who kept them at Packington Hall. They were bought by the Birmingham City Library in 1885, and are preserved there now under the name of the Aylesford Collection.[19] More drawings of Warwickshire country houses can be found, along with copious — though not always accurate — documentation, among the collections of the Rev. Thomas Ward, vicar of Weston-under-Wetherley. The drawings, most of which are kept, together with Ward's manuscript notes, in two large bound volumes in the British Library, were done in a deliberately naive and old-fashioned style in which the rules of perspective play little part. But they are nevertheless an invaluable record, especially of vanished or altered houses.[20] They are supplemented by the often miniscule drawings of houses in the Stratford area by Captain Saunders, now kept in the record office of the Shakespeare Birthplace Trust at Stratford.[21]

Among 19th-century printed books, the most useful are the 15th volume of J.N. Brewer, *The Beauties of England and Wales* (1814), with the text by the antiquarian John Britton; William Field, *An Historical and Descriptive Account ... of Warwick* (1815), which covers much of the county as well as the county town; J.P. Neale, *Views of the Seats of Noblemen and Gentlemen*, 1st series, Vol. 4 (1821), with descriptions as well as views of several houses; and William Smith, *A New and Compendious History of the County of Warwick* (1830), illustrated with artistically rather less accomplished engravings by W. Radcliffe. There are some excellent engravings, by David Cox and others, in the *Graphic Illustrations of Warwickshire* (1829). The county directories by William West and Francis White also contain useful information, as does William Hannett, *The Forest of Arden* (1863, 2nd ed. 1894), the latter albeit restricted to the centre and west of the county. Several houses are briefly described, and a few illustrated, in the four volumes of J. Burke, *Visitation of Seats and Arms* (1852-8). The best late 19th-century views of Warwickshire houses can be found in the Everitt collection in the City Museum and Art Gallery at Birmingham;[22] W. Niven, *Illustrations of Old Warwickshire Houses* (1878); and in the photographs by Sir Benjamin Stone and other photographers for the Warwickshire Photographic Survey in the Birmingham City Library.

Genealogical and biographical information can be found in *The Complete Peerage*, Burke's *Complete Baronetage*, and various editions of Burke's *Landed Gentry*. Much can also be gleaned from the *Dictionary of National Biography* and F.L. Colvile, *The Worthies of Warwickshire* (1869). Potted information about the size of estates in the 19th century, from the 1872-3 Parliamentary Return of Owners of Land (or 'New Domesday'), is in John Bateman, *The Great Landowners of Great Britain and Ireland* (1883).

The most important published contributions to Warwickshire local history in the 20th century have been the six topographical volumes of the *Victoria County History* (1945-69). These invaluable volumes contain not only summaries of the history of each of the major estates in the county, but also descriptions, often quite lengthy, of several of the older houses, often accompanied by plans. Many Warwickshire houses have been the subject of meticulously researched and beautifully illustrated articles in *Country Life*, and most of the surviving houses of any size or antiquity are briefly and perceptively described in Nikolaus Pevsner, *The Buildings of England: Warwickshire* (1966), and in Douglas Hickman's imaginatively illustrated *Warwickshire, a Shell Guide* (1979). The second volume of *Burke's and Savile's Guide to Country Houses* by Peter Reid (1980), contains brief histories of all the major houses and many of the smaller ones, including demolished houses, with a good selection of photographs. H.M. Colvin's magisterial *Biographical Dictionary of British Architects 1600-1840* (1978) has references to many Warwickshire houses.

Historians of Warwickshire are fortunate to have no fewer than three first-class record offices at their disposal: the County Record Office at Warwick, the Shakespeare Birthplace Trust record office at Stratford, and the archives department of the Birmingham City Library. Collections of family papers, on which much of this book is based, are mostly to be found at Warwick, but some important collections (e.g. the Leigh and Willoughby de Broke papers) are deposited at Stratford, and a few are kept in the houses themselves. The Hearth Tax returns of 1663 are at Warwick (those for 1666 are in the Public Record Office). All three record offices also have good collections of photographs, prints and drawings, and printed ephemera like auction catalogues. Other important sources of visual material are the Royal Institute of British Architects drawings collection and the photographic collections of the National Buildings Record, currently kept at the headquarters of the Royal Commission on the Historical Monuments of England at Fortress House, Savile Row, London. Sources relating to the history of each house are listed at the end of each section.

Footnotes

1 *English Hours* (1905), p.187.
2 See A. Clifton-Taylor, *The Pattern of English Building* (1972), *passim*.
3 *Itinerary through England and Wales*, ed. Toulmin-Smith, ii (1907), p.47.
4 Discussed in more detail in G.C. Tyack, *The Making of the Warwickshire Country House* (Warwickshire Local History Society Occasional Paper, 1982).
5 WRO QS 11/5.
6 For the effects of the Civil War on south Warwickshire, see P. Tennant, *Edgehill and Beyond* (1992).
7 The following paragraphs are a distillation of G.C. Tyack, *Warwickshire Country Houses in the Age of Classicism* (Warwickshire Local History Society Occasional Paper, 1980).
8 See H.M. Colvin, 'Francis Smith of Warwick, 1672-1738', *Warwickshire History* ii (2) 1972-3. Professor Andor Gomme has also generously supplied information from his forthcoming book on the Smith brothers.
9 Joan Lane, 'Emerging from the Shadows, Robert Moore of Warwick 1711-83', *Country Life* 28 Jan 1984, pp.1912-4.
10 D. Wright, 'Notes on John Wright, a Worcestershire Plasterer working in Warwickshire', *Warwickshire History* v (2), pp. 59-64.
11 A. Gomme, 'William and David Hiorn' in R. Brown (ed.), *The Architectural Outsiders* (1985).
12 D. Stroud, *Capability Brown* (1975).
13 A. Wood and W. Hawkes, 'Sanderson Miller of Radway', *Cake and Cockhorse* iv (1969).
14 For Lightoler, see J. Lane, 'The Craftsman Architect: Timothy Lightoler of Warwick 1727-71?', *Country Life* 19 March 1987, pp.108-9.
15 R. Blome, *Britannia* (1673), pp. 436-8; J.N. Brewer, *The Beauties of England and Wales* (1814), p.28.
16 BL, Add MS 29264, f.4.
17 See G.C. Tyack, *The Country Houses of Warwickshire 1800-1939* (Warwickshire Local History Society Occasional Paper, 1989).
18 A. Stevens, *The Woodcarvers of Warwick* (Warwickshire Museums, 1980).
19 B. Ronchetti, 'The Aylesford Collection', *TBAS* lxxi (1953), pp.76-9.
20 G.C. Tyack, 'Thomas Ward and the Warwickshire Country House', *Architectural History* xxvii (1984), pp.534-41.
21 R. Bearman, *Captain James Saunders of Stratford-upon-Avon* (Dugdale Society Occasional Paper, 1990).
22 S. Price, *Town and Country in the Victorian West Midlands* (Birmingham Museums & Art Gallery 1986).

of Wootton Wawen; the work was carried out in a Neo-Tudor style, and the *pièce de résistance* was a splendid sideboard supplied by the Warwick carver William Cookes.

But the most important changes of the mid-19th century took place in the grounds and on the estate, which was enlarged by the purchase of land in the neighbouring parishes of Alderminster and Clifford Chambers. New lodges and gates were built on the Stratford road, probably by Clark, and balustrades were constructed on either side of the causeway which takes the drive between the two pools in the grounds. Terraces and parterres were also laid out beside the Stour to the west of the house in the 1850s, probably to the designs of William Davidson of Great Russell Street in London. Meanwhile a new bridge carrying the road to Preston over the Stour was built by George Clark in 1856, and at about the same time the estate villages of Preston and Alderminster were transformed by the building of new brick estate cottages in the Tudor-Gothic style; the local historian J. Harvey Bloom later remarked that, as a result of these improvements, Preston became 'a place of natural beauty, cleanliness and order'. James Roberts West was succeeded in 1882 by his son, who married the daughter and heiress of William Charles Alston of Elmdon Hall (q.v.), near Birmingham. Since then the house and estate have remained in the hands of the West family, and both are still beautifully maintained. Alscot was transferred from Gloucestershire to Warwickshire in 1931.

West papers at Alscot Park; *CL*, 15/22 May 1958; *History of Parliament, 1715-54*; J. Harvey Bloom, *History of Preston-upon-Stour* (1896); *VCH Gloucestershire* viii, pp.83-5.

ANSLEY HALL

Ansley Hall has the melancholy appeal of a little-known country house which fell into neglect and has now all but vanished. It originated as an L-shaped timber-framed house built or rebuilt in the late 16th century, probably by a member of the Ludford family, who had leased land in the parish since the 15th century. Their main residence was at Witherley, on the other side of Watling Street in Leicestershire, but George Ludford (d.1627) bought the manor of Ansley in 1611 and settled at the Hall, which had 12 hearths in 1666. The house probably consisted then of a gabled hall range and a cross-wing, and the hall range remained relatively unaltered through subsequent enlargements.

The direct male line of the Ludfords died out in 1699, and the estate was then inherited by a nephew, Thomas Bracebridge, a member of an old north Warwickshire family, who took the name Ludford. The house and estate were both enlarged by his nephew John Bracebridge Ludford, a lawyer who inherited in 1727 and married a daughter of Sir Richard Newdigate of Arbury Hall (q.v.). He bought the neighbouring manor of Bretts Hall from Francis Stratford of Merevale (q.v.) in 1732, and

4.   Ansley Hall from the south west. The view, first published in 1791, shows the gabled hall range of the original house with the east range to its right. To the left is the 18th-century Orangery and on the extreme left the stable block.

5.   The north front of Ansley Hall. This part of the house was remodelled in 1733 and the roof of the east range, heightened between 1800 and 1810, can be seen on the left. The house is now in ruins.

subsequently incorporated the land into a deer park. In about 1750 he demolished the remains of the old moated manor house, which stood to the south-east of Ansley Hall, in about 1750 and re-erecting some of the stone as a hermitage, complete with a hermit's parlour. Here in 1758 the poet laureate, Thomas Warton, extolled the merits of the simple life in rhyming couplets beginning:

> Beneath this stony roof reclin'd
> I sooth to peace my pensive mind:
> And while, to shade my lowly cave,
> Embow'ring elms their umbrage wave;
> ... I scorn the gay licentious crowd,
> Nor heed the toys that deck the proud.

A Chinese temple, taken from a plate in Sir William Chambers' *Designs for Chinese Buildings*, was also built within the island formed by the moat of Brett's Hall in 1767. It has sadly vanished, along with the temple, summer house and pavilion mentioned in the diaries of John Ludford's son, John Newdigate Ludford. But an Orangery next to Ansley Hall survived until quite recently, with a peculiar frontispiece made up of Ionic capitals and other fragments of carved stonework, possibly taken from Bretts Hall.

John Bracebridge Ludford also remodelled the interior of the parish church, some distance away to the west, and greatly enlarged Ansley Hall. In 1733, according to the Leicestershire historian John Nichols, he 'underbuilt' the existing house and added — or, more probably, remodelled — an extension on the north side alongside the former moat or canal. This refers to the brick entrance range by the present B4114 road, with its naive but charming juxtaposition of a classical porch, a cupola, and two crenellated projections, one of them containing a 'justice room', lit by a Venetian window. The north range faced the 16th-century hall range across a small courtyard closed on the west by outbuildings and on the east by the kitchen and reception rooms, with an early 18th-century staircase at the south-east corner.

There were further alterations after 1741, when a new library for 3,000 books was created after a fire had destroyed the room over the old parlour at the 'upper' end of the hall range. The east range was also rebuilt in brick at some time in the mid-18th century, with a canted bay window on the south side, and there are references in the diaries of John Newdigate Ludford, who succeeded his father at Ansley in 1775, to a Gothic Hall, perhaps similar in character to the rooms created by Sir Roger Newdigate at Arbury. The final alterations to the house took place between 1800 and 1810, when John Newdigate Ludford added a third storey onto the east range, with a new roof of slate and a crenellated tower rising up from the centre. He was described on his monument in the parish church as 'a most indulgent landlord ... [who] eminently sustained the character of an old English gentleman for integrity, hospitality and charity'.

Ansley Hall was described in 1814 as 'an irregular but very respectable family mansion', and so it remained for another 65 years. When John Newdigate Ludford died in 1825 it passed to his daughter, the wife of Sir John Chetwode, but the encroachments of the north Warwickshire coalfield made the house less attractive as a place of residence, and in 1879 it was sold to the Ansley Hall Coal and Iron Company, founded in 1874 by a Lancashire man, William Garrick Phillips, great-grandfather of Captain Mark Phillips, former husband of Princess Anne. He turned the house into a club for the staff of the colliery, which was only a short distance away from the house, and laid out a bowling green and tennis court in the gardens. After the coal mines were nationalised the building was used by the miners and their families, but the colliery closed in 1959 and the house then fell into disrepair; when I first visited it in 1968 I was allowed to take away the wooden clock face from the cupola. The house became a complete ruin in the 1970s, and it now appears to be beyond saving.

VCH iv, pp.5-7; J. Nichols, *History of Leicestershire* (1811) iv(2), pp.1018-9, 1044; E.B. Bramwell, *The Ludford Journals of Ansley Hall* (1988); Brewer, pp.310-1; J. Bland and others, *Ansley Remembered* (1988); NMR photos.

ARBURY HALL

Arbury Hall is the most impressive 18th-century Gothic house in England, Horace Walpole's Strawberry Hill not excepted. It stands on the site of an Augustinian priory which was granted to Charles Brandon, Duke of Suffolk, after the Dissolution of the Monasteries, but was sold in 1567 to a lawyer, Edmund Anderson, Reader at the Inner Temple and later Lord Chief Justice of Common Pleas and a scourge of the Puritans. According to Dugdale, Anderson totally demolished 'the old fabrick of the House, and Church, and built out of their ruins a very fair structure, in a quadrangular form'. His house was built around the old cloister-garth, using stone from the monastic buildings, and Henry Beighton's drawing of 1708 shows that it was an orthodox building for its date, with a gabled south façade and a porch rather like that at Charlecote (q.v.) leading into the Hall. According to an inventory of 1666, there was a Great Parlour and Little Parlour in the East range, with a Dining Chamber upstairs, and a Gallery on the first floor of the north range which was 'furnished with pictures'. The panelling of the Gallery was installed in 1606, and the stone chimneypiece with a painted heraldic overmantel of that date still survives, along with some of the original furnishings.

In 1586 Anderson exchanged the house and estate for property at Harefield (Middlesex). The new owner was another lawyer, John Newdigate, who married Anne Fitton of Gawsworth (Cheshire), sister of Mary Fitton, one of Queen Elizabeth's maids of honour and a possible candidate for the 'Dark Lady' of Shakespeare's sonnets; Mary's portrait, possibly by George Gower, still hangs in the present Dining Room, along with a portrait of the Queen herself by John Bettes. John Newdigate's son Richard also

6.   Arbury Hall from the south, drawing by Henry Beighton, 1708. The 16th-century house is in the centre, and in the top left corner is the stable block, built in 1675-7.

7.   The Chapel of Arbury Hall in 1909. The plasterwork is by Edward Martin (1678) and the woodwork is of the same date.

became a lawyer, rising to the position of Chief Justice of the Upper Bench in 1660. He resigned at the Restoration, but he subsequently developed a lucrative private practice, and in 1677 he was made a baronet. His income was further augmented by a fortune brought him by his wife, Juliana Leigh of King's Newnham, and he invested some of the money in purchases of land, buying back the Harefield estate, and also acquiring the manor of Astley (q.v.), a mile or so away to the west.

Sir Richard's son, the 2nd Baronet, made important alterations to Arbury, starting with the building of a handsome new stable block to the north-west of the house. Work began in 1675, and finished in 1677, the year of his father's death. The second Sir Richard was a keen horseman and horse-breeder, and the stables provided a suitably dignified home for some at least of the 67 horses he is known to have owned in 1697. They were built of red brick, probably to the designs of the Leicester statuary and architect, William Wilson, whose name appears in a fragmentary sheet of accounts for the porch. The three large Dutch gables over the porch and wings seem to be a trademark of Wilson's rather conservative style (c.f. Four Oaks Hall), but the stone-framed main doorway is an accomplished piece of classical design, with paired Ionic columns supporting an open pediment enclosing the Newdigate coat of arms. It is possible that it was designed by no less an architect than Sir Christopher Wren, who provided two designs in 1674, one of which — though not the same as the present doorway — survives among the family papers. He was given two silver candlesticks as payment.

Sir Richard Newdigate also remodelled the Chapel, which stands in the north-east corner of the house. The elaborate plaster ceiling of 1678, like that in Lady Newdigate's closet, was by Edward Martin, who worked at St Nicholas Cole Abbey, one of Wren's City of London churches, and also at Burghley

House (Northants). And the white-painted panelling, with carved festoons of fruit and flowers between the panels, may be the work of a better-known craftsman, Grinling Gibbons, whose name appears in an account for the chapel wainscot and who later designed monuments to members of the Newdigate family in Harefield church. Sir Richard Newdigate also seems to have laid out the formal garden shown in Beighton's engraving, with gazebos at the corners of the walled enclosure in front of the house, a greenhouse for which there were payments in 1694, and extensive tree-planting, including yews and silver firs supplied from the nursery of London and Wise at Brompton in 1703.

Apart from the provision of iron gates and altar-rails in the chapel, to the design of Francis Foljamb of Nottingham in 1719, no further alterations were made to the house until after Sir Roger Newdigate inherited the estate at the age of 15 in 1734. Like his contemporary James West of Alscot (q.v.) he was a man of pronounced scholarly and antiquarian interests which are reflected in the present appearance of the house. These interests first developed at Oxford, where he matriculated in 1736, and he maintained a connection with the University for the rest of his life, serving as one of its M.Ps from 1750 to 1780 and endowing the Newdigate Prize for poetry. After leaving Oxford he made a Grand Tour, returning to England in 1742 with drawings of classical buildings and also the nucleus of a collection of antique sculptures, including two marble candelabra which are now in the Ashmolean Museum, Oxford. When he inherited Arbury he was already one of the richest landowners in north Warwickshire, but his income rose rapidly in subsequent years, reaching over £15,000 a year in the 1780s, partly because of his exploitation of the coal-mines on the estate. He recognised the necessity for improved communications to market the coal, and helped promote the Coventry and Oxford and Grand Union Canals; his portrait by Romney, which now hangs in the Drawing Room at Arbury, shows him standing by a desk on which the plans of the canal are laid out. Yet despite these entrepreneurial activities, he had a reputation as a representative of traditional squirearchical values — Horace Walpole called him a 'half-converted Jacobite' — and not long after his death. Thomas Ward called him 'a true English Gentleman of Polished Manners & of the OLD SCHOOL'. George Eliot, whose father was the agent to the estate, emphasised this aspect of his character in her portrait of him as Sir Christopher Cheverel in her novella 'Mr. Gilfil's Love Story', one of the *Scenes of Clerical Life* (1857). There seems little doubt that his rebuilding of the house was intended to conjure up its monastic origins, with all the connotations of 'ancient hospitality' and respect for the past which they implied.

As so often in the 18th century, the rebuilding of the house went hand in hand with a transformation of an older, formal garden. The Warwick mason-contractor David Hiorn was paid for building several new ornamental garden structures in 1748, including an orangery, a tea house and a rotunda, and in September 1745 there were payments for laying out a flower garden and setting down gravel walks. A lawn in front of the south front was mentioned for the first time in 1750, and a new cascade for the lake in front of the house was under construction in the following year, when the formal canal in the park was also

1. CARRIAGE PORCH.
2. ENTRANCE HALL.
3. CHAPEL (1678).
4. CHAPLAIN's BEDROOM, now SCHOOL ROOM (bedchamber & closet pre-1750).
5. LITTLE SITTING ROOM (bedchamber pre-1750).
6. SALOON (bedchambers and staircase pre-1750).
7. PARLOUR, now DRAWING ROOM.
8. DINING ROOM (hall pre-1750).
9. LIBRARY (little parlour and study pre-1750).
10. KITCHENS and OFFICES (not shown in detail).
11. CLOISTERS (added 1783-5).

Plan of Arbury Hall, as rebuilt 1750-1803.

filled in. There are also surviving drawings by Sir Roger for sham ruins which may or may not have been built. The gardens still largely retain their 18th-century form, with a series of irregularly sided pools to the south of the house linked by a cut to the Coventry Canal system; the arcadian character is particularly marked to the east of the house, where a semi-circle of classical 'terms' broods over a lawn.

The remodelling of the house began in 1750, and continued intermittently for the next 50 years until just before Sir Roger's death in 1806. It involved reconstructing the exterior, using grey sandstone from quarries at Attleborough, only two miles away, and from Wilnecote, near Tamworth, and creating a series of new reception rooms suitable for entertaining guests and displaying Sir Roger's works of art. The work was financed out of current income, and the design evolved gradually, as in the medieval houses and churches on which the house was based. Work started in the south-west corner — the service end of the old house — where Lady Newdigate's dressing-room was 'fitted up Gothic' by David Hiorn in 1750 to a design provided by Sanderson Miller, who had visited Arbury for a week in 1749, when he had taught Sir Roger the rudiments of architectural design. Miller must also have designed the canted bay windows lighting the rooms on either of the Hall on the south front; these are very similar to windows at his own house, Radway Grange (q.v.), and his mason William Hitchcox was employed to build the western bay window, lighting the Library. But by the time the Library was finished in 1756, with plasterwork by Robert Moore and woodwork by Benjamin King, William Hiorn had supplanted Hitchcox as mason, and Sir Roger had fallen out with Miller over politics. A perspective drawing by Sir Roger shows that he designed the Gothic ogee-arched bookcases himself, and they are clearly shown in Arthur Devis's famous portrait showing him sitting at his desk in the newly-completed room.

Attention now shifted to the Drawing Room — formerly the Parlour — at the easternmost end of the south front. By now Sir Roger was to some extent acting as his own architect. But he continued to draw on outside sources for advice, and in 1761 he recorded in his diary that the architect Henry

8.   The south front of Arbury Hall in 1909. This part of the house was rebuilt by Sir Roger Newdigate in 1750-73. The Library is on the left, the Drawing Room on the right and the Dining Room in the centre.

9. The Dining Room of Arbury Hall in 1909. The fan-vaulted ceiling (1769-73) is of plaster, and the niches contain casts of antique statues commissioned by Sir Roger Newdigate.

Keene, Surveyor to Westminster Abbey, was 'measuring the parlour, hall and front of the house'. Keene supplied Sir Roger with detailed drawings of monuments in the Abbey, and also had plaster casts made; he was an accomplished exponent of Gothic, and later redecorated the hall at University College, Oxford (since, alas, remodelled) at Sir Roger's expense. His influence can be seen in the extraordinarily rich decoration of the Parlour, the walls and ceiling of which are encrusted with net-like designs in plaster, based on the decoration of the vestibule of Henry VII's chapel in Westminster Abbey; the chimneypiece of 1764, by the Warwickshire-born sculptor Richard Hayward, is copied from Aymer de Vallance's superb early 14th-century tomb in the Abbey, and old portraits of Sir Roger's ancestors are inserted into the plasterwork.

The rebuilding of the south front ended with the remodelling of the Hall (now the Dining Room) in 1769-73. The Elizabethan hall was recessed between the two projecting wings, but in the rebuilt house the old south wall was pierced with three Gothic arches, and a one-storied extension built in the space between the Library and Parlour. In contrast to the rest of the exterior, this extension is very elaborately decorated with Gothic carving of late Perpendicular character — probably also betraying the influence of Keene — and the roof is adorned with battlements and pinnacles. The soaring interior, perhaps the finest 18th-century Gothic room to survive anywhere, is roofed with a plaster fan-vault reminiscent of that in the cloister of Gloucester Cathedral. Its bare walls are now hung with Elizabethan portraits interspersed with intricate Gothic niches containing copies of classical statues — a juxtaposition that seemed more natural to the taste of the 18th century than it might to ours. The effect was well described by George Eliot, in 'Mr. Gilfil's Love Story':

> A piece of matting stretched from door to door, a bit of worn carpet under the dining-table, and a sideboard in a deep recess, did not detain the eye for a moment from the lofty groined ceiling ... On one side, this lofty ceiling was supported by pillars and arches, beyond which a lower ceiling, a miniature copy of the higher one, covered the square projection which, with its three large pointed windows, formed the central feature of the building. The room looked less like a place to dine in than a piece of space enclosed simply for the sake of beautiful outline; and the small, dining-table...seemed an odd and insignificant accident, rather than anything connected with the original purpose of the apartment.

Another break in building now ensued, while Sir Roger went abroad for two years after his wife's death in 1774. Work on the house was resumed in 1776, but little seems to have been done until 1781-3, when a cloister was built along the northern and eastern sides of the courtyard; the courtyard itself was not as extensively rebuilt as the external fronts, and the old gables and much of the original 16th-century stonework can still be seen there. Keene died in 1776, and his place as Sir Roger's architectural right-hand man was taken by Henry Couchman, who had been clerk of the works at Packington Hall (q.v.); he remained at Arbury until 1789, when he was dismissed for being 'very unreasonable' over pay. He was responsible for building the rooms on the eastern side of the house to Sir Roger's own design. They had originally been bedrooms, but they were now turned into a large Saloon and two smaller rooms now called the School Room and the Little Sitting Room. The Saloon, begun in 1786, is the most elaborate room in the house. The phenomenally rich fan-vaulted ceiling, with plasterwork by the otherwise unknown W. Hanwell, was inspired by the roof of Henry VII's Chapel in Westminster Abbey — where Couchman was sent to make sketches in 1785 — and reminded George Eliot of 'petrified lace-work picked out with delicate and varied colouring'; the 'fans' rest on delicate scagliola columns. The ceiling was completed in 1794, and the large bow window projecting out of the east front was glazed in 1795. The other rooms in the east range, which were also redecorated at this time, were also given fan-vaults and marble chimneypieces of classic design.

The gaunt exterior of the east front, with its crenellated projections masking the chimney-stacks, presents quite a contrast to the lightness and delicacy of the house as seen from the south. The north or entrance front is equally severe. Work did not begin until 1792, and was still in progress in 1796 when a Coventry mason, John Alcott, was paid £121 for carving. The rooms in the north range are less important than those to the south and east, and they were less extensively redecorated. A new Entrance Hall was created, and the Jacobean Gallery on the first floor, reached by a new Staircase, was given a Gothic plaster vault in 1787, but otherwise remained largely as it was; photographs taken in the late 19th century show it filled with classical statuary and casts 'after the antique'. Work also proceeded intermittently on the west, or kitchen, block; payments began in 1789, and Alcott was still being paid for work on the west front in 1801. But by 1803 the rebuilding of the house was complete, and a drawing in the Aylesford Collection shows it in a landscape setting which was already mature. The last undertaking was probably the building of new lodges, including the formidable Round Towers lodge on the outskirts of Nuneaton, through which the house is approached today.

Sir Roger died childless in 1806, and the house and estate then passed to a cousin, Francis Parker, who took the name Newdigate. He was followed at Arbury by a great-nephew, Charles Newdegate Newdigate, a bachelor who represented North Warwickshire in Parliament from 1843 to 1885, and then by his cousin, Lt-Gen Sir Edward Newdigate Newdegate, Governor of Bermuda from 1888-92. His successor was his nephew, Sir Francis Newdigate Newdegate, Governor of Western Australia from 1920-4, whose daughter, the Hon. Mrs FitzRoy Newdegate, inherited on his death in 1936. She made the house over to her son, now Viscount Daventry, the current owner. Few alterations were made in the 19th and 20th centuries, and today, despite the proximity of both the former north Warwickshire coalfield and the suburban sprawl of Nuneaton, the house and grounds remains much as Sir Roger Newdigate left them, a monument to his remarkable creative passion for Gothic architecture.

Newdigate papers in WRO (CR 136, CR 764); *CL* 8/15/29 Oct 1953; *Wren Society* xii; E. Gooder, *The Squire of Arbury* (1990); A. Wood, 'The Diaries of Sir Roger Newdigate', *TBAS* lxxviii (1960), pp.40-54; C. Hussey, *English Country Houses: Mid Georgian* (1956); M. McCarthy, *The Origins of the Gothic Revival* (1987); Aylesford Collection, ff. 16-24; Arbury Hall guidebook (1985).

ASTLEY CASTLE

Astley Castle originated as a moated, semi-fortified house belonging to the Astley family, who held the manor from the Earls of Warwick. Its early history is obscure. Warin de Bassingburn, who was lord for a brief period in the mid-13th century, was granted permission in 1266 make a ditch and a crenellated wall, but it is not at all clear whether any of the masonry survives in the present curtain wall, which has been much reduced in height. The Astleys subsequently recovered possession of the manor, and in 1343 Sir Thomas Astley founded a collegiate church next to the castle, the chancel of which still survives as the parish church, one of the finest in Warwickshire.

On the death of Sir William Astley in 1420 the estate passed by marriage to Reginald, Lord Grey de Ruthin, whose son married the heiress of Lord Ferrers of Groby. Astley thus became part of a large concentration of land belonging to the Greys, one of the leading families in the Midlands in the late Middle Ages, and it remained in their hands until 1554, when Henry, Duke of Suffolk, the father of Lady Jane Grey, made the fatal decision to take part in the Wyatt rebellion against Mary Tudor. After the defeat of the rebels he fled to Astley and took refuge in a hollow oak tree near what was later known as Duke's Farm (a sandstone memorial marks the spot), before being captured and executed. This event marked the end of Astley as a seriously fortified house. Suffolk's widow married his steward, Adrian Stokes, and in 1601 the estate was purchased by Sir Edmund Chamberlain of Shirburn Castle (Oxfordshire), whose son Richard demolished the nave of the church after the tower (the 'lantern of Arden') had fallen down. He restored the chancel in 1607, and fitted up part of the old buildings of the castle as a residence, the date 1627 appearing on the parapet of the east front.

No illustrations of Astley Castle exist from before the late 18th century, and by then the house looked, at least from the outside, much as it did until it was gutted by fire a few years ago. It stands

10.   Astley Castle in 1829. The residential block stands on one side of the courtyard, which is entered through the romantically overgrown mock-ruined arch.

16

of an earlier picture in the Aylesford Collection shows a façade articulated by Ionic pilasters on the first floor and low gabled wings on either side; there is also a bird's-eye-view, now at Capesthorne (Cheshire), the home of the Bromley-Davenport family, showing a large three-storied structure with a 13-bay façade, formal gardens and an attractive hipped-roofed stable block. These paintings seem to show two distinct stages in the rebuilding of a house which was clearly one of the most impressive in the county by the end of the 17th century.

The stables shown in the Capesthorne picture survived to be photographed at the end of the 19th century, but the house was burnt down in 1706, and a new one built in 1714-23, on a site to the south of the church. The builder was Sir William Bromley, a Tory politician, 'of grave deportment and good morals', who was one of the M.P.s for the county from 1690-8 and subsequently sat as M.P. for Oxford University, becoming Speaker of the House of Commons in 1710 and Secretary of State in 1713-14. The architect was Francis Smith of Warwick, and the elevation bore all the hallmarks of his solid but pleasing style. The main block was three stories high, with a high roofline and elongated pilaster-strips like those at Newbold Revel (q.v.) to articulate the walls. As at Umberslade Hall (q.v.), there were two large rooms at the centre, with the staircases and parlours on either side; there were also one-storied extensions, one for the Chapel and one for Sir William's Library. The Frenchman Guillaume Beaumont, who worked for the Jacobite Col. Grahame at Levens Hall (Westmorland), was consulted over the gardens in 1709, and alterations to the house were made in 1732-5 by Sir William Bromley's son William, who married the heiress of the Throckmortons of Haseley (q.v.). According to John Loveday, who visited the house in 1742: 'the house stands high, has large Gardens but no water in them or considerable View except upon the city of Coventry; 'tis built of fine white stone, with a Parapet all round at top'.

The direct male line of the Bromleys came to an end with the death of William Davenport Bromley in 1810. The house then went to his sister, Lucy Price, and in 1814 was praised as being 'suited to a country gentleman of the first order; capacious, but devoid of ostentation, and adapted to all the purposes of hospitality except the parade'. In 1822 the estate was inherited by a cousin, the Rev. Walter Davenport, a younger son of the Davenports of Capesthorne. The house was leased out for most of the 19th century, and in 1889 it was gutted by fire. It was not rebuilt, and the site was sold in 1918, but the ruins were still standing in 1926, when four families were living in the basement and wings. The ruins have since been demolished, and the house and gardens have now totally disappeared.

VCH vi, pp.22-3; *Gentleman's Magazine* new series xxxi (1849), pp.25-9; Aylesford Collection, f. 50; George Clarke drawings, Worcester College, Oxford B3/194 (sketch plan); *Garden History* iii(4), (1975); *Loveday*, pp.342-3, 481; Brewer, p.47; Burke, ii(1), p.130; NMR photographs; newspaper cuttings, Coventry City Library; information from Professor Andor Gomme.

BARRELLS HALL

Barrells started life as a farmhouse in the parish of Ullenhall, to the west of Henley-in-Arden. A branch of the Knight family, from Beoley (Worcestershire), were living here as yeomen in the mid-16th century, and in 1681 John Knight was the possessor of what was described as a manor house, surrounded by a 400-acre estate. In 1730 Raleigh Knight sold the property to his second cousin Robert, whose father had made a fortune as cashier to the South Sea Company and had built a substantial house at Luxborough, near Chigwell in Essex in 1716-20; he later fled to Paris when the Bubble burst, and did not return to England until 1742. Robert Knight went into politics, becoming M.P. for Grimsby in 1734, and being raised to the Irish peerage as Lord Luxborough in 1745 and Earl of Catherlough in 1763. He was described by a contemporary as 'a man of letters, a man of sense, and a man of probity, but not a monster of perfection'. He spent little, if any, time at Barrells, and in 1736 he made the house over to his wife Henrietta, daughter of Henry, Viscount St. John, and half-sister of the Tory politician Lord Bolingbroke, from whom he became estranged after finding her in bed with her doctor. He meanwhile found solace in the arms of a local farmer's daughter, and the son who resulted from this union eventually inherited the estate.

Lady Luxborough was described by Horace Walpole as 'a high coloured, lusty, black woman'. Under the terms of her separation she was not supposed to travel outside England or within 20 miles of London. Instead, she took up the literary life, playing hostess at Barrells to a circle of minor provincial poets and writers, including Richard Graves, William Somerville, Richard Jago — vicar of Snitterfield and author of the poem *Edge Hill* — and William Shenstone. Both Shenstone and Lady Luxborough were enthusiastic gardeners, and Shenstone's *ferme ornée* at the Leasowes, near Halesowen in Worcestershire, was one of the landmarks in the history of English gardening. They corresponded often, and their letters give an engaging picture of Barrells in the mid-18th century.

Despite her husband's threats to reduce her allowance on the grounds of extravagance, Lady Luxborough carried out several improvements to both house and grounds. The house, possibly timber-framed, and of no great size, was externally remodelled in brick, and there was some internal redecoration in 1736. In 1748 Lady Luxborough told Shenstone:

> Your advice about my chimney pleased me greatly; but forced oeconomy forbids my following it: besides that good carving is too fine for my humble roof. The room, consider it, is only hung with sixpenny paper, and is so low that I have but five inches between Pope's Head [the poet Alexander Pope] and the Motto over it: so that I can neither have a compartment for that, nor an architrave, as is at Houghton [Sir Robert Walpole's magnificent house in Norfolk]. The contrast between that place and Barrells is so great, that it is ludicrous to name them together.

A new bedroom and dressing room were being created in 1752, and there was talk of using papier-mâché ornament, as James West was later to do at Alscot (q.v.); the plasterer Robert Moore was also employed on minor work in the house.

But most of Lady Luxborough's energies were devoted to her garden, which on one occasion she called her *ferme negligée*. Under her supervision, and with Shenstone's advice, the existing formal garden was transformed into a pastoral idyll, allowing views over the surrounding landscape with its 'amphitheatre of wooded hills'. The former farmyard became a small kitchen garden, and elsewhere there were serpentine walks, a shrubbery, and a coppice with mossy seats and a root seat, all encompassed by a ha-ha, which was being dug in 1749. Flowers and flowering shrubs played an important part in the overall effect, as Lady Luxborough told Shenstone in June 1749: 'In the Shrubbery, I think, the finest ornament is the large bushes of Whitsun roses, which are still in blow, and give us an idea of snow balls this cold weather. The lilac is already over, and has given place to the Syringa; of which I have enough to perfume the place

25.   The Library of Bilton Grange looking towards the Great Drawing Room (1861 sale catalogue).

down of chimneys. The ground-floor Gallery, however draughty and inconvenient it may once have been, is a useful asset to a school, and the collegiate-looking Dining Hall could not be more appropriate for its present use.

T. Deacon, *History of Willoughby* (1828), p.83; Burke i (2), p.157; RIBA Crace MSS/PUG 3; A. Wedgwood, *A.W.N. Pugin and the Pugin Family* (1985); Pugin drawings in V & A; *Illustrated London News*, 27 Jan 1855; WRO, EAC 411/4 (sale partics, 1861); P. Stanton, *Pugin* (1971).

CASTLE BROMWICH HALL

Castle Bromwich is now a suburb of Birmingham, but the nucleus of the village is still intact, and at its heart is the red-brick Hall, with its walled gardens, approached from the south by an avenue of old horse chestnut trees. The original motte-and-bailey castle after which the village is named stood just to the north of the present Hall and church — originally a chapelry of Aston — overlooking the present M6 motorway. Dugdale called it a 'little Pile, or Castle ... situate upon the brow of the Hill, on the southern bank of Tame, as by the vestigia thereof yet remaining may appear', and in Henry Beighton's engraving of the Hall (1726) a modest farmhouse is shown on top of the motte, which is called the 'old castle hill'.

The castle and manor belonged in the late 13th century to a Henry of Bromwich, and from his descendants it passed through the female line, first to the Roche family and then to Sir Edmund Ferrers of Chartley (Staffordshire), who also had extensive holdings of land in Wales and Ireland. When his son, Lord Ferrers of Chartley, died in 1450 the estate passed to his daughter, who married Walter Devereux, and it remained in the Devereux family for the next two centuries. In the 16th century they were raised

26.   Castle Bromwich Hall, watercolour by A.E. Everitt, c.1860. The south and west fronts are shown, with the 17th-century porch and the top of Thomas Rickman's tower of 1825.

in the peerage, acquiring the titles of Viscount Hereford and subsequently Earl of Essex, but Castle Bromwich was not their main place of residence, and the present house was not built until after the manor had been acquired in 1572 by Sir Edward Devereux, younger son of the first Viscount Hereford; the rest of the family estates remained with his nephew, the 1st Earl of Essex, whose son led the rebellion which cast a shadow over Queen Elizabeth's declining years. Sir Edward Devereux married Katherine Arden of Park Hall, the other important estate in the parish (the house has since gone), and when his mother Lady Hereford died in 1599 he set about replacing the old manor house at Castle Bromwich with the present brick-built Hall. It is still essentially his house which we see today.

The new Hall was built on a square plan, with four gabled ranges arranged around a small internal courtyard — a plan found in several important country houses built at the turn of the 16th and 17th centuries, like Chastleton (Oxfordshire) and Burton Agnes Hall (Yorkshire). The elevations are very plain, with walls of red brick and blue criss-cross patterning, straight-sided gables, large mullioned and transomed windows, and tall chimneys rising up from within the courtyard. The entrance range faces south, with the Hall placed in the traditional fashion to one side, and entered through a porch and screens passage. It still retains some of its original plain wooden panelling, but the only other important room to retain any of its Elizabethan workmanship is the Gallery on the first floor, which has been subdivided. To the east of the house were detached outbuildings, one of which, an L-shaped structure containing the bakehouse, brewery and laundry, still survives.

Sir Edward Devereux died in 1622 (there is a monument to him in Aston church), by which time we can assume that the house had been finished. He left the estate to his second son, Leicester Devereux,

and in 1657 it was sold to John Bridgeman, the eldest son of one of the country's leading lawyers, Sir Orlando Bridgeman (d.1674), a staunch Royalist who later presided over the trial of the regicides and became Lord Chief Justice of Common Pleas and Lord Keeper of the Great Seal. Sir Orlando was made a Baronet by Charles II, and in 1685 his son Sir John Bridgeman, now the 2nd Baronet, began remodelling the house.

Work started on the interior, where the Elizabethan embellishments must have seemed barbarous to the classically-trained sensibility of the late 17th century. The work was placed under the supervision of William Winde, one of the leading country-house architects of the late 17th century (c.f. Combe Abbey), and the husband of Sir John Bridgeman's cousin Magdalen. A set of letters from Winde to Lady Bridgeman survives, allowing us to reconstruct its somewhat leisurely progress in some detail and to identify the people responsible for the outstandingly fine craftsmanship. This includes superb plaster ceilings by Edward Gouge — who Winde said in 1690 was 'looked on as the best master in England' — marble chimneypieces by Edward Pierce, one of the stone carvers who assisted Wren at St Paul's Cathedral, woodwork by Jonathan Wilcox, and ceiling paintings by Louis Laguerre, now alas no longer in the house. In one of his letters Winde told Lady Bridgeman that 'according to the rule of Building, the upper Rooms (and specially the Dining

27. Castle Bromwich Hall, the foot of the main staircase, drawing by A.E. Everitt, *c.*1860. The interior was remodelled in 1685-1702 under the direction of William Winde, with woodwork by Jonathan Wilcox.

28.	The Drawing Room (originally the upstairs Dining Room) at Castle Bromwich Hall in 1891. The plasterwork is by Edward Gouge.

Rooms) are always the most ornamented', and the finest rooms are indeed on the first floor, as they had probably been in Sir Edward Devereux's time. They are reached by a wooden staircase in the west range with twisted balusters and a splendid ceiling by Gouge, made up of exuberant wreaths of fruit and flowers. The Dining Room (the former great chamber) has an even more opulent plaster ceiling with a coved central section, and Gouge also carried out the plasterwork in the ground-floor room known as the Boudoir. The furniture in these rooms included items by Gerrit Jensen and clocks by Thomas Tompion.

The main change to the exterior took the form of heightening the third storey on the south or entrance front and remodelling the two-storied porch. Some of the work seems to have been carried out by the Yardley brickmaker William Lattimer, who was employed by Sir Orlando Bridgeman in 1666, but further alterations were made in 1697-9, and there are rainwater-heads dated 1719. The top floor is surmounted by a balustrade punctuated by urns, and at the centre there is a pedimented centrepiece framing a doorway leading out onto a balcony on top of the porch, which is surrounded by an elaborate wrought-iron balcony. The porch itself is a striking composition, with the doorway framed by pairs of Corinthian columns supporting a broken pediment containing the Bridgeman coat of arms, and statues of Peace and Plenty (by the Leicester-born statuary William Wilson, 1697) in niches on either side of the first-floor window. The striking use of twisted columns on either side of the entrance harks back to the 1630s, when the same motif was used in the porch of the church of St Mary the Virgin, Oxford, but the overall design bears a striking similarity to one published in Francini's *Livre d'Architecture*, translated into English in 1669.

It is not certain how far Winde was responsible for the exterior of the house, but he certainly conceived the layout of the formal gardens, which escaped later landscaping and still retain the original arrangement of a series of 'outdoor rooms' demarcated by walls, clipped hedges and straight paths. He supplied designs for parterres to the north and west of the house in about 1698, and he later sought advice from two of the leading gardeners of the time, George London and Charles Hatton, brother of Christopher Hatton of Kirby Hall (Northamptonshire) and 'a very great virtuoso in gardening'. In the event Winde's elaborate designs were somewhat modified, but Beighton's view of the house shows that there were intricate parterres to the north and west in the 1720s. By this time Sir John Bridgeman had died, and his son, the 3rd Baronet, extended the garden down the hill slope to the west, surrounding it by a brick wall punctuated by ornamental buildings to the north and south (the Orangery and Music Room), with gates at the western end. Sir John Bridgeman also built the impressive stable block to the south-east of the house and the pigeon-house of 1725, possibly to the designs of the Worcester architect John White, who rebuilt the parish church to the north in 1726-31. Like the gardens, the church remains a largely intact specimen of early Georgian taste, with much of its original woodwork still *in situ*.

Castle Bromwich ceased to be the main country seat of the Bridgeman family in 1762, when they moved to Weston Park (Staffordshire), a 17th-century house inherited through the marriage of the 3rd Baronet's son Orlando to the daughter, and eventually the heiress, of Richard Newport, 2nd Earl of Bradford. But in 1765 Sir Henry Bridgeman, the 5th Baronet, was living at Castle Bromwich, and the Long Gallery and other rooms still contained many of the portraits and tapestries which can now be seen at Weston. The Bradford title was revived for Sir Henry in 1794, and in 1825 his grandson the 2nd Earl of Bradford employed Thomas Rickman, who had opened an office in Birmingham five years earlier, to add a kitchen and service wing with an ogee-topped neo-Jacobean tower onto the north-east corner of the house, thus introducing that element of picturesque irregularity and variety which the early 19th century craved. By this time the 'Old English' style of the original house was back in vogue, and in 1837-8 the Hall was also given a neo-Jacobean face-lift by Rickman, with new panelling, a richly carved screen and a reasonably authentic-looking chimneypiece. Rickman also made some alterations to the late 17th-century Dining Room upstairs.

Little more happened to the house during the rest of the 19th century, but at the end of the century the old formal gardens, which had escaped landscaping and were now recognised as a valuable example of 'Old English' gardening, were reinstated — though not 'authentically' restored — by Lady Ida, wife of the 4th Earl of Bradford. She lived at the Hall with interruptions from 1870 until her death at an advanced age in 1936; early photographs show an elaborate formal arrangement of flower-beds on the south side of the house. She was the last of the family to live at Castle Bromwich, and the house was subsequently let out as a training establishment to General Electric Company, and finally sold in 1969. Since 1972 it has been the headquarters of Bovis Homes (Midland Region), and has been extensively refurbished. In 1987 the lower part of the garden was conveyed by the current Earl of Bradford to a Trust which has recognised its value as one of the finest surviving early 18th-century country house gardens, and is currently in the process of restoring it, along with their ancillary buildings. This part of the garden is now open to the public on certain days during the summer.

VCH iv, pp.43-5; *CL* 4 Aug 1900, 17 Aug 1912, 9 May 1952; Dugdale, p.887; Bradford papers at Stafford Record Office; G. Jackson-Stops, 'French Ideas for English Houses', *CL* 29 Jan 1970; M. Locock, 'The 18th-century Brickmaking Industry in the Forest of Arden', *Warwickshire History* viii (1990-1); *Loveday* pp.444-5, 490; BL, Add. MS 37796 (Rickman's notebooks); N. Stockton, *Castle Bromwich Hall Gardens* (1988); M. Batey & D. Lambert, *The English Garden Tour* (1990).

CHARLECOTE

The Lucys have lived at Charlecote, on the banks of the River Avon, since the 12th century, though the family name was only adopted in the 13th century. But the history of the present house, one of the largest and most famous in the county, does not begin until the time of Thomas Lucy, who inherited in 1551. He married an heiress, Joyce Acton of Sutton (Worcestershire), and enlarged his Warwickshire estate to include the lands of the suppressed friary of Thelsford, a mile away, founded by his ancestor Sir William de Lucy in the early 13th century. He later became Sheriff of Warwickshire and one of the M.P.s for the county, was knighted by Queen Elizabeth, and lived to a great age as a respected local worthy.

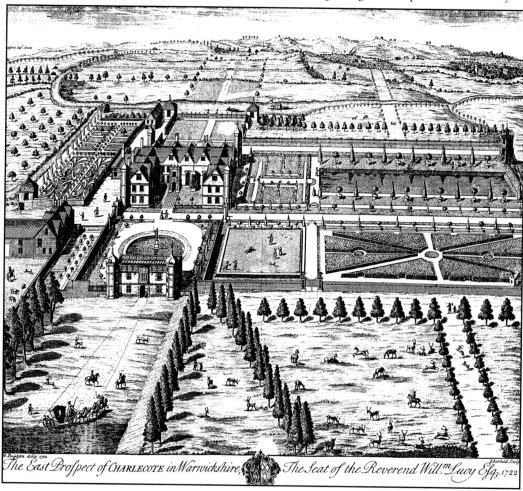

The East Prospect of CHARLECOTE in Warwickshire, The Seat of the Reverend Will.ᵐ Lucy Esq. 1722

29. Charlecote from the east, drawing by Henry Beighton, 1722. The detached gatehouse leads into a walled forecourt, with the stables and brewhouse to the left and the house in front. The formal garden to the right was laid out towards the end of the 17th century.

According to Dugdale, the house was built in the first year of Queen Elizabeth's reign (1559-60), but this date may refer to its completion. It was built of brick, and was given a regular and near-symmetrical façade, with the roofline punctuated by gables, chimneys and turrets. The house was originally made up of a main block one room deep, with two long projecting wings: a plan found in several country houses of the mid-16th century (e.g. Barrington Court, Somerset; Melford Hall, Suffolk). The main block contains the hall, two stories high, as in medieval houses, but with an attic above. It was originally entered through a screen which presumably supported the 'spacious music gallery' mentioned by an early 19th-century writer, and was lit at the high table end by a tall oriel window, replaced in the 19th century; much of the original heraldic stained glass still survives. The Hall is approached through a porch, far more classical in feeling than the rest of the house, and similar in character to the porches at Deene Park and Kirby Hall (Northamptonshire), both of them dating from the early 1570s; it was probably added after the rest of the building was finished, perhaps at the time of Queen Elizabeth's visit to the house *en route* for Kenilworth in 1572. The round-headed archway is flanked

30. The porch at Charlecote, with Queen Elizabeth's coat of arms over the doorway. The sophisticated classical detailing is reminiscent of contemporary work at Kenilworth Castle.

by paired Ionic pilasters, while above, on the first floor, there are pairs of Corinthian columns on either side of a mullioned and transomed window of traditional form, with a balustrade at roof level. In the south range, to the left of the Hall, were the service rooms and kitchen, and the parlours were in the north range. The upstairs rooms were reached by spiral staircases in turrets at the corners of the house; they are surrounded by ogee-shaped domes, echoing the early Tudor royal palaces.

To the south of the house there were outbuildings, including a stable block and brewhouse which survives largely intact, and at the entrance to the forecourt to the east there is a free-standing brick gatehouse with a large upstairs room, surmounted by a carved parapet: an up-to-date version of the detached gatehouses commonly found in late-medieval houses. The round archways, and the carvings on the parapet, are of Renaissance inspiration, but there are more ogee-shaped domes on the staircase turrets, and the passageway has a Gothic ribbed vault — a characteristically Elizabethan synthesis of styles. Unlike the main house, the gatehouse escaped 18th- and 19th-century 'improvements', and it is now the least altered part of the whole complex of buildings.

Little appears to have been done to the house in the early 17th century, but towards the end of the century an ambitious formal garden was laid out, probably by Thomas Lucy, who inherited in 1677, or by his cousin Davenport Lucy, who succeeded him after his premature death in 1684. An oil painting of *c.*1696, which now hangs in the Hall, shows avenues (still traceable) aligned on the house on both sides of the Avon, with a formal parterre on the west front, stretching to the River Avon, and two straight parallel canals of Dutch inspiration to the north, not unlike those still to be seen at Westbury

Court (Gloucestershire). It also shows sash windows in the west front facing the river. Davenport Lucy was succeeded by his brother George, who began remodelling the interior of the house, a process which was continued by his younger brother William in 1715-23. The wood carver Joel Lobb was paid £15 in 1717 for 'two Corinthian round Capitalls and two pilaster Capitalls and fifty foot of Modillion Cornish', but the only work of this period to survive is the main staircase, an impressive wooden construction with delicately carved balusters.

More sweeping changes to both house and grounds occurred in the time of George Lucy's nephew, another George Lucy, who came into possession in 1744. Trees were being planted in the park in 1747, and the Hall was 'varnished and beautified' in 1750. Five years later, in 1755, the Warwick road was moved further to the south of the house, beyond the River Dene, and a new bridge built to the designs of David Hiorn of Warwick. Lucy spent much of the 1750s in Portugal and Italy — his portrait by Pompeo Batoni still hangs in the house — but in 1760, two years after returning, he called in 'Capability' Brown to landscape the grounds. His improvements involved widening the Avon, giving 'a natural and easy level' to the banks, making a cascade or waterfall, and creating lawns in place of the 17th-century formal gardens with a ha-ha near the house. There were also changes to the interior, but these seem to have been of a modest nature. George Lucy explained in a letter to his housekeeper in 1765 that he was 'happy to have a good old house', and hoped that she would 'be of my opinion that fitting it up in a neat manner which I shall spare no reasonable expense in doing, will be better approved than attempting a Grandeur which I'm not able to support'. Sash windows were introduced where they did not already exist, and new panelling and plasterwork commissioned, some of the latter by Robert Moore of Warwick. The work was placed in the hands of William Hiorn, who redecorated the Great Parlour in 1763, but was transferred two years later to the more obscure John Standbridge, who was responsible for the Drawing Room and George Lucy's bedroom.

George Lucy never married, and in 1786 he was succeeded by a cousin, the Rev. John Hammond, Rector of Hampton Lucy and Charlecote. It was his son, George Hammond Lucy who, together with his wife Mary Elizabeth, gave the house and its immediate surroundings their present character. The house was already becoming a place to be visited on the 'Shakespeare circuit', due largely to the fact that the future dramatist was supposed to have been caught as a young man poaching deer in the nearby park at Fulbrook by Sir Thomas Lucy, who was later parodied as Justice Shallow in *The Merry Wives of Windsor*. When Sir Walter Scott visited the house in 1828 he commented that the building 'really brought Justice Shallow freshly before my eyes', and Mary Elizabeth Lucy later remarked that when she first saw Charlecote after her marriage in 1822 it

> was very different to what it is now and the Great Hall did indeed look as it might have done in Shakespeare's time, with its old worn paved floor, its small panes of glass in its large oriel window, and every window frame creaking and rattling with every gust of wnd, and so cold — oh the cold! No hot air then as now, no beautiful garden in the court — only a few large beds with shrubs and old-fashioned flowers. I soon caused my husband to let me root them all up and I planned the present one.

George Lucy's main aim was to restore the Elizabethan character of the house, enhancing its Romantic associations and at the same time making it more comfortable. As his father-in-law said in a letter to his daughter when the improvements were first being contemplated in 1824: 'The first thing is to preserve the old House as much as possible and to adapt the improvements to its external appearance ... any man with money can build a new house but money will not build an old respectable mansion like Charlecote'. The work, which was carried out in 1829-37, involved replacing much of the brickwork and nearly all the stone dressings in the hall range of the main house, reinstating mullioned and transomed windows, and adding a new range built of a rather harsh blue brick onto the west of the hall range, overlooking the Avon; this contained a Dining Room and Library, both of them essential for the spacious country-house entertaining at which the 19th century excelled. A kitchen wing was also built to the south, a hot air heating system installed, and the entrance forecourt laid out with an

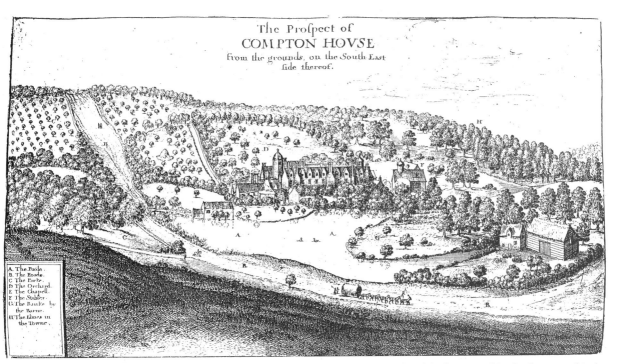

The Prospect of
COMPTON HOVSE
from the grounds, on the South East
side thereof.

A. The Poole.
B. The Roade.
C. The Parke.
D. The Orchard.
E. The Chapell.
F. The Stables.
G. The Banke by
the Barne.
H The Elmes in
the Towne.

47.   Compton Verney, drawing by Wenceslas Hollar, *c.*1656. The chapel is to the right of the house, and in the foreground is the mill pool which now forms part of the lake.

48.   The west front of Compton Verney. It was built in 1714, and originally looked out onto a formal garden and sheet of water.

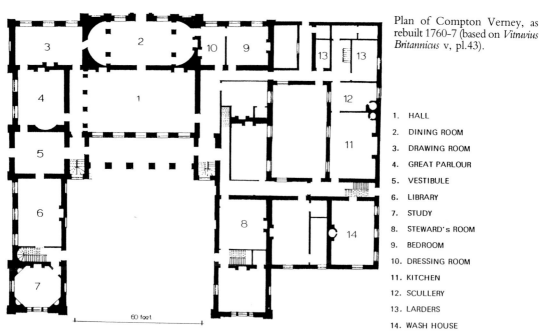

Plan of Compton Verney, as rebuilt 1760-7 (based on *Vitruvius Britannicus* v, pl.43).

1. HALL
2. DINING ROOM
3. DRAWING ROOM
4. GREAT PARLOUR
5. VESTIBULE
6. LIBRARY
7. STUDY
8. STEWARD's ROOM
9. BEDROOM
10. DRESSING ROOM
11. KITCHEN
12. SCULLERY
13. LARDERS
14. WASH HOUSE

The 12th Lord Willoughby died in 1728, and the house was then occupied by his younger son the Hon. John Verney, who became Master of the Rolls in 1738. He may may have been responsible for completing the west range — Loveday said that only part of it was built by the 12th Lord — and he certainly, according to the same authority, 'built the Stables which are very handsome and which above Stairs contain Lodging-Rooms, and Rooms for other uses'. They stand on the hillside to the north-east of the house, and were built in 1736-43 by Francis and William Smith to the designs of James Gibbs, who had worked extensively for the family of Verney's nephew, the 2nd Earl of Oxford. The stables are arranged around a courtyard, and the architraves to the doors and windows are heavily emphasised with large blocks of masonry, a mannerism which the Italian-trained Gibbs borrowed from the Italian Renaissance, and employed frequently in his own buildings.

The 12th Lord Willoughby not only rebuilt the house; he also, in the words of Dugdale's editor Dr. Thomas, 'made the Gardens and Plantations, intirely as they now are'. The 1656 engraving of the house shows it surrounded by orchards and unadorned parkland, but by 1736, when James Fish prepared his plan of the estate (now in the Shakespeare Birthplace Trust record office at Stratford) there was a geometrically planned layout to the north of the house, a 'Great Walk' leading to the entrance from the east, and a parterre with an ornamental canal facing the new west front. To the south was the 'Old Mill Pool' and there were two more pools — the Middle and Upper Long Pools — further east, no doubt dug to provide an extra head of water for the mill; there is also a New Pool to the west of the road from Kineton to Stratford. John Loveday thought that the gardens were 'well-contrived for Use and Convenience', and particularly commended the views from the house down to the pools.

The house and its setting were again transformed by John Peyto Verney, who succeeded as the 14th Lord Willoughby in 1752. He was a Lord of the Bedchamber, and in 1761, soon after commissioning the first plans for the house, he married a sister of Lord North, the future Prime Minister, whose house, Wroxton Abbey, is only a few miles away to the south over the Oxfordshire border. He also inherited the Chesterton estate (q.v.) from the Peyto family, and during the 1760s his landed income rose fourfold; by the 1880s the family had the second largest estate in the county (after the Leighs of Stoneleigh), and were among the half-dozen richest landowners.

His architect was the young Robert Adam, recently returned from his epoch-making tour of the Continent. Compton Verney was one of his first commissions, and he may have owed it to his fellow-Scot, Lord Bute, Prime Minister at the beginning of George III's reign, who would undoubtedly have known Lord Willoughby. Adam's task was to extend and modernise the existing building so as to make it suitable for large-scale entertaining. His first plans, produced in 1760, envisaged retaining the interior of the 1714 house intact, but rebuilding the north and south wings to the same height as the main block, extending the service quarters, opening up the entrance courtyard, and adding a giant Corinthian colonnade reminiscent of that proposed by Palladio for the Palazzo Iseppo Porti in Vicenza: a master-stroke, which gave the house a new character of Roman magnificence and pomp. When work finally started in 1762, under the supervision of William Hiorn of Warwick, a more ambitious scheme was adopted, in which the Entrance Hall was also enlarged and given a coved and coffered ceiling, with a screen of Ionic columns at the southern end and walls decorated with large paintings of classical ruins by the Italian Andrea Zucchi, one of Adam's regular collaborators. At the same time a new Saloon or dining room was created at the centre of the west front, with apsidal ends screened off from the rest of the room by pairs of columns — a favourite Adam device. To the south, there was now a sequence of spacious, high-ceilinged reception rooms, starting with the Drawing Room, and proceeding through the Parlour, Vestibule, Library to an octagonal Study at the end of the south wing, with a Venetian window on the eastern side.

Though grand in concept, the interior, except for the Hall, had few of the decorative felicities usually associated with Adam, and the formation of the new Dining Room meant that the house lost its only impressive staircase. These omissions must represent a deliberate decision to keep costs down; the total cost of the alterations (excluding furniture, of which there are no surviving records) was £2,500, less than an average year's landed income for Lord Willoughby in the late 1760s or 1770s. The same motives must have led to the employment of local craftsmen; a Mr. Rose, presumably a member of the Rose family who worked at many of Adam's houses, was paid £100 for plasterwork in 1765, but by 1767, when work came to an end, he had been replaced as plasterer by Robert Moore

49.   Compton Verney from the south east in the mid-19th century. The house is set among Capability Brown's lawns, with the lake in the foreground. To the right is James Gibbs' stable block (1736-43).

50. The Entrance Hall of Compton Verney in 1913. The room was created by Robert Adam in 1762-7, and the paintings of classical subjects were by Antonio Zucchi. They have now gone, as has most of the interior decoration.

of Warwick. There were also payments to the Birmingham locksmith Thomas Blockley and to two carpenters, William Wilkins and John Maunton, who may have made the Rococo-style chimneypieces which still survive in several of the rooms.

The remodelled house is the focus of what is still, despite depredations, one of 'Capability' Brown's most beautiful landscapes. Brown first prepared plans for transforming the formal gardens into a 'natural' arcadian landscape in 1768, and the work began in 1770. The early 18th-century gardens to the west and north of the house were swept away, and the two upper mill pools were joined together to form a single serpentine sheet of water. A new drive was also created, sweeping through woodland and dramatically revealing the house from the point where the lake was crossed by a new stone bridge. The landscaping was largely finished by 1774, by which time £3,830 had been spent.

The making of the new landscape involved the destruction of the medieval chapel, which stood between the house and the lake. This was demolished in 1772 in order to improve the view of the lake from the rooms on the south side of the house — cedar trees now stand near the site — and a new Chapel was begun, probably to Brown's designs, in 1776 on the rising ground to the north, with Samuel Eglington as master mason and William Hiatt as plasterer; the cost was £981. This plain though well-proportioned building still retains its original Adam-esque plasterwork, along with some of the monuments from the old chapel; the 16th-century armorial glass was also removed from the old building, but this was unfortunately sold by a later owner, and much of the original woodwork has also gone. So too has the handsome Doric-pilastered Greenhouse near the Chapel, built in 1769-70 and decorated with plasterwork of 1774-5 by Robert Moore.

The enlarged Compton Verney, with its improved grounds, attracted the admiration of contemporaries. Richard Jago, in *Edge Hill* (1767), was swift to salute the 'noble master ... studious of elegance', and to point out how:

> At his command,
> New Pillars grace the House with Grecian pomp
> Of Corinth's gay design. At his command,
> On hill, or plain, new culture clothes the scene
> With verdant grass, or variegated grove;
> And bubbling rills in sweeter notes discharge
> Their liquid stores.

In 1785 John Byng thought the house 'as an habitation worth twenty Warwick Castles', while in 1802 George Lipscomb, in his *Journey into South Wales*, observed that 'the exterior of the house is rather neat than splendid, and the rooms should rather be called commodious than magnificent; but the pleasure grounds are varied with great elegance, and the water and plantations are delightful' — a judgement with which few would wish to quarrel. Further improvements were instigated by the Birmingham engineer, William Whitmore, in 1814-5, including the enlargement of the Lower Lake which was subsequently extended westward to the estate village of Combrooke. Much of Brown's tree-planting has since been removed, especially around the upper part of the lake, but the essential components of his scheme still remain.

The 14th Lord Willoughby lived until 1816, acquiring a local reputation for hospitality and liberality which caused him to be remembered as 'the good Lord Willoughby'. Henry Hakewill was called in to carry out some internal alterations in 1824, including the removal of the curved ends from the dining room on the west front, and in about 1863 John Gibson, who had also worked at Charlecote (q.v.) for Mary Elizabeth Lucy, the sister-in-law of the 16th Lord, remodelled some of the rooms in the south wing; he also added the carved stone frieze over the entrance to the Hall and made some minor alterations to the Hall, probably including the addition of a relief carving of a hunting scene over the screen. In 1866 he was employed once more to enlarge the church at Combrook, this time in the Gothic style. The church has remained virtually untouched, and the village, with its contemporary school and houses, is now one of the best-preserved Victorian estate villages in the county.

In his autobiography *The Passing Years* (1924) the 19th Lord Willoughby de Broke left an evocative account of life at Compton Verney in the second half of the 19th century. Born in 1869, he remembered how the house still brewed its own beer: '... no one ever came to the house with a message, or for any other purpose, without drinking a glass (or two) of the famous Compton beer. In the same frank style did they burn a ton of coal in the kitchen every day.' Life revolved around the hunting field, and a paternalistic neo-feudalism flourished on the estate. Lord Willoughby inherited the estate and title in 1902, having sat as Conservative M.P. for Rugby in the 1895 Parliament, and after his elevation to the Lords he played a leading part in the 'last ditch' resistance to the Liberal government's Parliament Bill of 1911, which emasculated the Upper House. He died in 1923, having been forced by rising taxation and death duties to sell the house two years earlier. The family subsequently moved to Woodley House, Kineton, but for many years they retained the core of their Warwickshire estate, which amounted in the 1950s to some 4,000 acres.

The recent history of the house has been a sad one. The purchaser in 1921 was Joseph Watson, a soap manufacturer and racehorse owner, who was raised to the peerage as Lord Manton in 1922 and carried out some internal improvements. His son sold the house in 1929, and since the Second World War it has been uninhabited. It was sold in 1958 to Harry Elland, a millionaire industrialist from Birmingham, but he did not live there, and the empty building was let out for filming, its interiors falling into ever greater decrepitude. In 1984 it was sold to Christopher Buxton, who has specialised in converting decaying country houses into flats. He created several flats in the stable block, but the house itself was not tackled, and its future became entangled with grandiose proposals to create a new opera house — the 'Glyndebourne of the Midlands' — alongside the lake in the grounds. At the time of writing the opera house project was still under discussion, but late in 1993 the house and 40 acres of land were bought on behalf of the Peter Moores Foundation, a charity whose resources derive from the Littlewoods Football Pools. It is intended to turn the building into an art gallery, thus rescuing one of Warwickshire's finest 18th-century houses after nearly 50 years of neglect.

Dugdale, p.565; *Walpole Society,* xxiv (1936) & xxx (1955) (Vertue Notebooks); Willoughby de Broke papers at SBT (DR 98); *Loveday,* pp.190, 332, 496-7; Adam drawings in V & A and Sir John Soane's Museum; D.Stroud, *Capability Brown*; *Vitruvius Britannicus* v, pl 43; *Torrington Diaries,* p.103; Richard Greville Verney, *The Passing Years* (1924); *CL* 18 Oct 1913; R. Chaplin in *Warwickshire History,* i (1970); G.Tyack in *Warwickshire History,* iii (1975); D. King, *The Complete Works of Robert and James Adam* (1991); S. Brindle, 'Compton Verney, Warwickshire' (typescript, English Heritage, 1993).

COMPTON WYNYATES

For many people Compton Wynyates is the *beau ideal* of the English country house. It stands on an ancient site, hidden away in a hollow near the site of a deserted village in the remote southern uplands of the county, and the walls of deep red brick with blue diapered patterning, the roofs of local stone slates, and the skyline bristling with chimneys and turrets combine to create an ensemble rarely matched in England

51. Compton Wynyates from the south west. The entrance is through the gateway in the west range (to the left), and to the right is the tower at the western end of the south range.

for picturesque variety. This effect came about not so much by design as by gradual accretion. The Compton family were lords of the manor sometimes known as Compton in the Hole ('Wynyates' refers to a long-vanished vineyard) from at least the 13th century, but the present house — the oldest surviving brick-built country house in Warwickshire — cannot have been started before the end of the 15th century or the beginning of the 16th. The work may have been instigated by Sir Edmund Compton, who increased the family fortunes by marrying an heiress and died in 1493. But it is more likely that it was begun by his son Sir William Compton, who was made a ward of Henry VII at the age of eleven. He held a series of important Court appointments under Henry VIII, rising from being Groom of the Bedchamber to become Keeper of the Privy Purse in 1524, and he was made steward of several royal manors and custodian of seven castles, including Maxstoke (q.v.). During his lifetime (he died in 1528), Compton Wynyates became one of the most impressive gentleman's houses in Warwickshire.

The house is surrounded by parkland — the village disappeared at a very early date — and consists of four ranges around a courtyard, with the Hall in the east range facing the entrance, lit by two tiers of windows (possibly a later alteration). There was originally also an outer service courtyard containing stables, a barn and a brewhouse; remnants of these buildings, most of them timber-framed, survived into the 19th century, by which time the moat had been drained except to the north of the house. It is clear from looking closely at the main house that several additions were made to the original structure at an early date, and it has usually been assumed that they date from after Sir William's return from campaigning with the King in France in 1513. They were carried out piecemeal, possibly at different dates, and the lack of any obvious predetermined plan accounts for the haphazard appearance of the exterior, especially as seen from the south and west. The additions included the gatehouse, battlemented and

52.   The Hall at Compton Wynyates, drawing by W. Niven, 1878. The bay window lights what was once the high-table end, and the wooden screen can be seen on the extreme right.

53. Interior of the courtyard at Compton Wynyates. The Hall is on the left, and the south range, containing the parlour and great chamber, on the right.

entered through a large archway with a flattened Gothic arch embellished with royal emblems and surmounted by Henry VIII's coat of arms, probably in recognition of a royal visit. A tall tower (Plate III) was also built onto the southern flank of the south range of the house, possibly as an adjunct to Sir William's private apartment; it imparts an air of quasi-military grandeur which the houses of the ordinary Warwickshire gentry lacked. Next to this is the Chapel, apparently another afterthought, and there is another, lower, tower next to the Kitchen at the north-east corner. The additions are crowned by elaborate chimneystacks, similar in character to those of the early Tudor royal palaces.

Sir William Compton also carried out alterations to the interior, notably to the Hall, the finest of its date to survive in Warwickshire. It is entered from the courtyard through a screens passage, and the screen still survives, with its delicate linenfold panelling and a relief carving thought to represent the Battle of Tournai (1512), in which Sir William participated. The high-table end is lit by a tall bay window of stone, externally more elaborate in style than the rest of the buildings round the courtyard, and quite possibly brought by Sir William from the 15th-century Fulbrook Castle, 10 miles to the north, of which he was keeper. John Leland, writing in the 1530s, said that Sir William 'seeing [the castle] going to ruine helped it forward, taking part of it, as some say, for the buyldeinges of his house at Compton'. The spoils may well have included not only the oriel window of the hall but also the impressive timber roof, whose principal braces do not correspond with the window openings below.

The most important rooms were placed in the south range; the north and west ranges were largely given over to lodgings for members of Sir William's household. A doorway at the 'upper' end of the

Hall led into the parlour (now the Dining Room), furnished, according to an inventory of 1522, with two long tables covered with carpets of 'course verdure', with five 'hangings of tapestry imagery' on the walls. The room upstairs (the Chamber over the Parlour — now the Drawing Room) had more tapestry hangings and led into the Chapel Chamber (now the Chapel Drawing Room), from which it was, and is, possible to look down into the Chapel below. In Dugdale's time the Chapel itself contained 'a costly window of rare workmanship, the passion of our Saviour being therein very lively represented'; this has since disappeared, along with the rest of the original glass, but some panels of 1530 are now in the chapel of Balliol College, Oxford. Beyond the Chapel Chamber were two bedrooms, with tapestry-hung walls and elaborate hangings to the beds. The Chamber over the Nursery, probably the room now known as Henry VIII's Room, contained six 'verdure' tapestries with roses and fountains and an oak bedstead with a canopy of cloth of gold 'trailed with yellow and violet sarcenet', a counterpane of tapestry, and a red blanket. This room adjoins the tower, which has a room on each floor, reached by a complicated arrangement of spiral staircases. Here presumably Sir William could retire in privacy from the noise and bustle of his household.

Compton Wynyates has remained relatively untouched because from the early 17th century until very recently it was used only as a secondary residence, and was left uninhabited for long periods. Sir William Compton's grandson Henry was made Lord Compton in 1572, and two years later he began building Castle Ashby (Northamptonshire). This became the main family seat in the time of his son, who succeeded him in 1589, married the daughter of the prodigiously wealthy Sir John Spencer, Lord Mayor of London, and became Earl of Northampton in 1618. The 1st Earl carried out some internal remodelling at Compton Wynyates in the early 17th century, notably in the Dining Room (the former Parlour), where the present wood panelling replaced the tapestry hangings of Sir William Compton's time and a plaster ceiling was introduced; similar ceilings in other rooms date from the same time.

The 2nd and 3rd Earls were leading Royalists, and in 1644 the house was seized and plundered by Parliamentary troops, who turned it into a garrison. The Royalists counter-attacked by moonlight in January 1645, and threw 100 'hand Granadoes' into the building, but failed to dislodge the enemy. It is not clear how much damage was done to the house, but the nearby parish church was destroyed; it was rebuilt after the Restoration, in 1665, and survives largely intact, along with its early 18th-century fittings. There was probably also some remodelling of the house, but in general it seems to have remained largely untouched until the time of the 5th Earl, who inherited in 1727 and spent much of his time at Compton. There are dated rainwater heads ranging from 1723 to 1732, referring to the provision of a parapet and new gutters in the courtyard, and in 1738 a new block of rooms was added on the east side, doubling the width of the hall range; sash windows were probably also introduced at this time, and up-to-date panelling introduced into some of the rooms.

The house narrowly escaped complete destruction after the ruinously expensive Northampton election campaign of 1768, when the 8th Earl ordered it to be abandoned. The contents, including the gilt bed in which Henry VIII was believed to have slept, were sold in 1774, and the building was only saved by the by the agent's decision to brick up the windows in order to avoid payment of window tax. Thereafter the house was inhabited by a tenant farmer, and when William Howitt visited it in 1839 he noticed that the outer courtyard was in a state of extreme dilapidation (it was subsequently removed and replaced by lawns) and the rooms in the main house empty, except for one or two kept furnished in case the Marquess should visit the house in the shooting season: 'Except in these few rooms, the walls are all naked ... or the paper is of the most ordinary or course kind ... the place has a most forlorn air; yet it is by no means a ruin'.

Rescue came from the 3rd Marquess of Northampton, an amateur artist and collector who had lived in Rome from 1846-8 before inheriting the estate in 1851. He used the rising income from his north London estate in Canonbury and Islington to carry out a thorough restoration in 1859-60 under the direction of Matthew Digby Wyatt (who also worked at Castle Ashby), with woodwork by Theodore Phyffers. This involved the restoration of the lost mullioned and transomed windows, the repair of the 17th-century plaster ceilings, and the building of a new main staircase of wood leading from the upper

54. Compton Wynyates from the north west in the late 1850s. The east range, to the right, still has its sash windows of 1738. The large Perpendicular Gothic window next to the tower on the left lights the Chapel.

end of the Hall to the Drawing Room (the 'Chamber over the Parlour' in Sir William Compton's time). This room was transformed at the same time by the introduction of splendid early 17th-century wood-work from Canonbury House at Islington in London, the family's former suburban residence; more grandiose redecoration schemes were halted by Lady Northampton's death in 1864. Meanwhile appro-priate 'period' furniture and Old Master paintings were introduced into the rooms. The 3rd Marquess also began a remodelling of the gardens with formal terraces and yew hedges of the kind thought appropriate for old houses in the later 19th century. The romantic appeal of the house to the late Victorians was well expressed by Henry James, who visited it in 1877, the year of the 3rd Marquess's death:

> But of Compton Wyniates ... I despair of giving any coherent or adequate account. It belongs to the Marquis of Northampton, and it stands empty all the year round ... When I came out in front of the house from a short and steep but stately avenue I said to myself that here surely we had arrived at the limits of what ivy-smothered brick-work and weather-beaten gables, conscious old windows and clustered mossy roofs can accomplish for the eye. It is impossible to imagine a more finished picture. And its air of solitude and delicate decay — of having been dropped into its grassy hollow as an ancient jewel is deposited on a cushion, and being shut in from the world and back into the past by its encircling woods — all this drives the impression well home.

The 5th Marquess, a prominent Liberal politician and founder-member of the London County Council, made extensive use of the house in the summer, and laid out a splendid topiary garden on the slope rising up from the south range in 1895 and a water garden to the north; he also removed the ivy from the walls of the house. Most of the family's remaining Warwickshire estates were sold after the First World War (much had been sold already in the late 18th century), but they still continued to occupy the house, mainly as a hunting seat in the winter, and the 6th Marquess installed central heating and electric lighting in 1919-20. In the summer the house was opened to the public, and it continued to be accessible to visitors until fairly recently, when the present Marquess decided to turn Castle Ashby into a conference centre and to live permanently at Compton. Today the casual visitor is afforded only a tantalising glance of house, sheltered in its hollow, from the main gates on the hillside above.

VCH v, pp.60-5; *CL* 30 Oct/6 Nov 1915; William Compton, 5th Marquess of Northampton, *Compton Wynyates* (1904); William Compton, 6th Marquess of Northampton, *History of the Comptons of Compton Wynyates* (1930); Leland ii, pp.47-8; P. Tennant, *Edgehill and Beyond* (1992), pp.161-6, 205-6; *Archaeological Journal* cxxviii (1971); Brewer, pp.177-9; W. Howitt, *Visits to Remarkable Places* i (1840), pp.303-26; *Building News*, 21 June 1861, p.516; WRO, PH 631/1 (album of mid-19th-century photographs); Henry James, *English Hours* (1905), pp.208-9; guidebooks to Compton Wynyates (n.d.).

I   Baddesley Clinton from the north west. The grey sandstone masonry and some of the windows date from the 15th century, but there were alterations by the antiquary Henry Ferrers in the early 17th century and by Edward Heneage Dering in 1891.

II The Dining Room at Charlecote. The guiding spirits behind this sumptuous room were George Lucy, the stained glass designer Thomas Willement and the wood carver James Willcox. The work was completed in the 1830s.

III Compton Wynyates from the south west. The brick tower built by Sir William Compton is in the foreground, and the window of his private chapel to the right. To the left is the site of the outer courtyard, the last remains of which was demolished in the 19th century.

IV The gatehouse at Coughton Court from the west. Built by Sir George Throckmorton in the early 16th century, the stone-built gatehouse is one of the finest surviving examples of early Tudor domestic architecture. Sir Robert Throckmorton turned the ground floor into an entrance hall and the room above it into a drawing room in the 1780s, and also built the extensions on either side.

V Ettington Park from the south. The walls are built of four kinds of stone, making the house a striking example of Victorian 'constructional polychromy'.

VI   Honington Hall, view of the garden by Thomas Robbins, 1759, showing the Chinese temple, the cascade and the grotto.

VII   Leicester's Gatehouse at Kenilworth Castle. This massive red sandstone structure formed an important part of the alterations to the castle carried out by Queen Elizabeth's favourite Robert Dudley, Earl of Leicester. It was turned into a residence by Colonel Hawkesworth, the Parliamentarian soldier who resided over the 'slighting' of the castle in 1649.

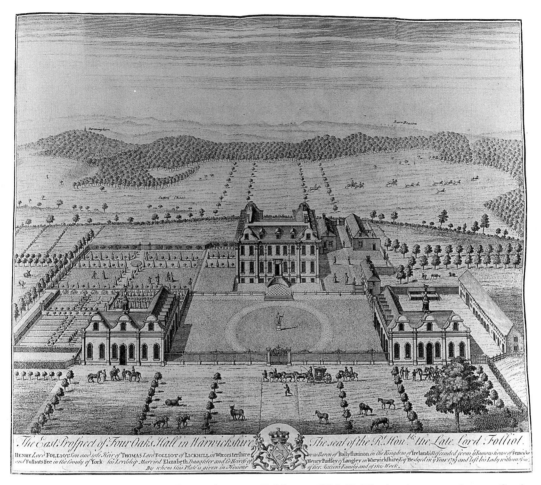

The East Prospect of Four Oaks Hall in Warwickshire. The seat of the R.! Honble the Late Lord Folliot.

67. Four Oaks Hall from the east, drawing by Henry Beighton, *c.*1720-30. The drawing was made soon after the death of Lord Folliott, the builder of the house.

of the rottenest of them all. By making himself useful to the Court interest he was given an Irish peerage, as Lord Irnham, in 1768, later becoming Viscount Carhampton and, in 1785, Earl of Carhampton. And with the purchase of the Four Oaks estate he had a landed base to match his political pretensions.

Some time after purchasing the estate, Luttrell made a series of drastic alterations to the house and grounds. First, in 1757, he 'privatised' the surroundings by inclosing 48 acres of Sutton Park and incorporating them into his own park, a process which required an Act of Parliament. The entrance courtyard, with its outbuildings and iron gates was swept away some time after 1763, when the house was shown in its pristine form in John Snape's survey drawing. The ground was then put down to lawns, and the outside of the house turned into an imitation of the influential Hagley Hall (Worcester-shire), by raising the four corners into low pyramid-roofed towers (replacing the Dutch gables), hiding the attics behind a balustrade, and adding an engaged temple-front to the entrance, approached by a broad flight of steps. These changes may have increased the dignity of the house, but they removed much of its charm. The interiors — or those whose appearance has been recorded — were lavishly decorated with the Rococo plasterwork of which the Warwickshire gentry and nobility of the time were so enamoured. There is no indication of the architect or craftsmen involved, although the work

68.   Four Oaks Hall as rebuilt by Simon Luttrell, Lord Irnham, drawing by J.P. Neale, *c.*1821.

would fit very well within the *oeuvres* of local men like William Hiorn and the plasterer Robert Moore.

Luttrell's ambitions outran his purse, and in 1778 he sold the Four Oaks estate to the Rev. Thomas Gresley of Drakelow (Derbyshire), who sold it a few years later to Hugh Bateman. In 1792 it was sold again to Edmund Cradock-Hartopp of Freathley (Leicestershire), who married the heiress of one of the Directors of the East India Company, and was made a Baronet in 1796. He further enlarged the park, but neither he nor his successors made much of a mark on the house. The estate was put up for sale in 1868 as 'a safe and sound investment, situated as it is ... in an improving District, where building operations are being extensively carried on'. In 1880, with Birmingham encroaching from the south, it was finally sold by Sir John Cradock-Hartopp, 4th Baronet, to a company which planned to develop a racecourse in the park. This project languished and, as the demand for 'desirable residences' near Sutton Coldfield was proving increasingly insatiable, the land was divided up for the building of substantial villas. The house was finally demolished in 1899, but there was some compensation for its loss in the quality of the houses built within the former park, some of them by architects of the calibre of W.R. Lethaby, W.H. Bidlake and C.E. Bateman. These ensure that Four Oaks is still a place of interest for the architectural historian.

Bracken, *History of the Forest and Chase of Sutton Coldfield* (1860); *Wren Society* xi (1934) (1763 survey drawing); BRL, archives WSO 204-6; Colvile, p.830; *History of Parliament 1754-90*; W.K.R. Bedford, *The Luttrells of Four Oaks* (pamphlet at WRO); Neale; BRL photos (WK/F2/1-19); WRO, EAC 412 (sale partics 1868).

HONINGTON HALL

Honington Hall is an unusually attractive late 17th-century house of red brick, with a fine interior dating largely from the mid-18th century. The manor belonged to Coventry Priory in the Middle Ages, and after the Dissolution of the Monasteries it was acquired by the Gibbs family. Nothing survives of their house, but the stone-built stable block, with its central arch framed by giant Ionic columns, was presumably built, along with a nearby dovecote, by a member of the family in the mid-17th century. In about 1670 the estate was sold to Henry Parker, the son of a successful London merchant whose family had migrated from Devon, and soon afterwards he began building the present house, which carries the date 1682 on rainwater heads. He was trained as a lawyer, and in 1665 he married the daughter of Alexander Hyde, Bishop of Salisbury, and first cousin of Charles II's minister the Earl of Clarendon. His father died in 1670, and in 1679 he was elected M.P. for Evesham, which he represented in six Parliaments, becoming Recorder of the town in 1684. He built up a substantial estate in south Warwickshire, and in 1697 he inherited a baronetcy granted by Charles II to his uncle, Sir Hugh Parker of Shoreditch. He died in 1713, and is commemorated by an ostentatious monument in the parish church, which stands next to the house and was rebuilt at about the same time in a style which recalls that of the Wren City churches.

The house originally stood among elaborate formal gardens which were depicted by Samuel and Nathaniel Buck in an engraving of 1731. Stylistically, it represented a complete break with local building traditions. It is a neat, well-proportioned two-storied building of red brick with sandstone dressings, a white-painted wooden cornice, a hipped roof, and tall chimneys punctuating the skyline. The three central bays of the entrance front are slightly recessed, and there are busts of Roman personages in niches over the ground-floor windows, something also found at Ham House, near Richmond (Surrey). The front door is framed by a wooden doorcase with a broken pediment, and there is another elaborate doorway on the north or service side of the house, surmounted by a carved shell-hood of a kind popular in the London area. Apart from the introduction of sash windows in place of casements, the entrance front has changed very little since it was first built, but there is no indication of who designed either the house or the church, or of the craftsmen involved.

Internally, the layout was of a kind common enough in the smaller country houses or larger town houses of the late 17th century. It was, said Roger North, '... elegant for the decorations on all sides ... and no less curiosity on the inside, by wainscot of forein oak, marble &c ... the front being an hall or room of *entrata* in the middle large enough; and at one end a great parlor, and at the other a lesser parlor. The great parlor and its withdrawing room, makes the end to the garden, and the litle parlor, with a passage to the back yard, and a litle back stair, with the kitchen, makes the other end; and against the hall backwards is the great staires ... In short all together speaks no height of spirit, tho pride enough'. In one of these rooms Sir Henry Parker housed his collection of 'rarities', over which the Oxford antiquary Anthony Wood enthused when he visited the house in 1678: '... after dinner was shewed to me a cabinet of rarities collected mostly at Constantinople and other Eastern parts of the world — such rarities that my eyes never beheld the like — all sorts of shells, divers sorts of natural stones — medals, gold and silver — coins, gold and silver — Turkish pictures and others of England, in miniature — all sorts of lookish [sic] glasses — a piece of Dido's tomb — and many other things that my eyes never before beheld. They were valued at 500 li[£], besides the cabinet'. Little of the original interior decoration of Sir Henry Parker's time survives, apart from the panelling of some of the downstairs rooms and a small upstairs bedroom with painted pine panelling, an ornamental plaster ceiling and Chinoiserie paintings on leather in imitation of lacquer: an early, though not unprecedented, use of Oriental motifs in a country house.

When Sir Henry Parker died, the house went to his grandson, who sold it in 1737 to Joseph Townsend, the son of a London brewer. He was a minor politician who represented a succession of rotten boroughs in Parliament, and in 1744 he married the heiress of John Gore, M.P. for Grimsby. This seems to have been the signal for him to carry out a series of major alterations to both house and grounds. The main changes to the house were internal, starting with the redecoration of the Entrance Hall, probably in the mid-1740s, and culminating in 1751 in the creation of a new octagonal Saloon, lit by a canted bay window, on the site of the old staircase, in 1751. An open five-sided loggia was built onto the south front, and quadrant walls were also added to enclose the entrance forecourt, only one of which now survives; they were articulated by Doric pilasters, with an unusual form of bell-like *guttae* in the frieze which can also be found in a number of buildings associated with the Woodward brothers of Chipping Campden, including Foxcote (q.v.) and Radbrook Manor (q.v.).

80. The Hall at Honington Hall looking south in 1946. The plaster picture over the fireplace, by an unknown craftsman, is of Hector bidding farewell to Andromache.

The Hall, Saloon and Staircase Hall contain plasterwork of outstanding quality, comparable to that introduced by William Holbech at Farnborough Hall (q.v.) and by Lord Hertford at Ragley (q.v.) at about the same time. The Hall has a fairly coherent scheme of Classical iconography, with representations of the four Elements and a sunburst on the ceiling, figures of the Arts on panels over the doors, and pictures of 'Venus appearing to Aeneas' and 'Hector bidding farewell to Andromache' on the walls at each end, set within a swirling borders of Baroque richness. The plaster pictures have been attributed to the Danish craftsman Charles Stanley, who carried out similar work at Langley Park (Norfolk). But there is no documentary proof, and even if he did work at Honington other plasterers were almost certainly involved too; they may have included Thomas Roberts of Oxford, who worked with Stanley and others on the decoration of the Radcliffe Camera in the early 1740s. More plaster ceilings of the same date can be found in the former great parlour (now the the Oak Room), which was also fitted up with a massive Palladian doorcase complete with cherubs sprawling over the pediment, and in the withdrawing room (now the Boudoir).

The Saloon and the new staircase were designed by a talented amateur architect, John Freeman of Fawley Court (Buckinghamshire), who was distantly related to Townsend. The Saloon is essentially Palladian in character, with a handsome coffered dome, 'tabernacle frames' — as Robert Adam later called them — around the doorcases, and a chimneypiece in the style of Inigo Jones. But a letter from Freeman to Townsend makes it clear that the original design was altered by the builder, William Jones, surveyor to the East India Company and architect of Edgcote (Northamptonshire), another house with good decorative plasterwork. Freeman disliked the newly fashionable Rococo motifs ('dolphins, rocks & bits of glass I don't well understand') which Jones introduced in the plasterwork around the mirrors in the Saloon and in the festoons tumbling down the walls in the corners. And he was exasperated that 'the man whom I had recommended endeavoured by various schemes to demolish every thing that I had designed ... I believe he is the first man that we ever recommended that ever made alterations without showing them first to his patron'. Despite these vexations, the spacious and airy Saloon is one

81. The Saloon at Honington Hall, built by William Jones to the designs of John Freeman in 1751. The doorcase and coved ceiling are in the Palladian taste, but the mirror and plaster festoons are Rococo in character.

of the most handsome rooms of its date in England, and the shadowy Staircase Hall between it and the Entrance Hall presents a dramatic and highly effective contrast. It is lit only by openings in the west wall of the Entrance Hall, and the stairs are screened off from the central passageway by arches on Tuscan columns. The staircase has a delicate wrought-iron balustrade, and there is more good plasterwork there, possibly carried out, like that in the Saloon, by William Perritt of York; he had worked for William Jones in the long-demolished Rotunda in the Ranelagh pleasure gardens at Chelsea, and had also been active at Farnborough Hall, only a few miles away.

Joseph Townsend was also responsible for sweeping away the formal gardens and creating a new landscape setting which still, despite some modifications, survives today. Like most of his Warwickshire contemporaries, he consulted Sanderson Miller, who seems to have designed the grotto and cascade mentioned in a letter of 1749, and may also have given advice on the alterations to the house. The gardens are shown in a pair of drawings by Thomas Robbins dated 1759, one of them depicting the house set among lawns and groves of trees, and the other (Plate VI) the River Stour broadened to form a lake surrounded by ornamental buildings, including the grotto and an absurdly flimsy Chinese summer-house — the very epitome of Rococo garden design. Most of the buildings have disappeared, but the grotto and cascade with its 'two quaint recumbent figures' were still discernible in the early years of this century, when Dickins and Stanton brought out their edition of Miller's letters. A small temple with a Tuscan portico also survives, hidden away in a glade not far from the house, close to a sundial, and on the banks of the river, next to the house, there is a much larger Doric portico not shown in the 1759 drawings. On the other side of the river a belt of trees was planted to screen off the garden from the Oxford-Stratford road.

When Joseph Townsend died in 1763, Honington passed to his son Gore Townsend. He and his son the Rev. Henry Townsend were successively lords of the manor for the next 110 years, but they did nothing of significance to the house. Henry Townsend was succeeded in 1873 by his nephew Frederick, M.P. for South Warwickshire from 1886-92, and he built a new service wing on to the north-west corner, tactfully echoing the style of the rest of the building. In 1905 the house and estate passed to a distant cousin, Sir Grey Skipwith, who introduced furniture formerly housed at Newbold Revel (q.v.), but they were sold in 1924 to Sir Charles Wiggin. In 1978 his son carried out a thorough and successful restoration of the main house, demolishing the now-redundant service wing in the following year. Honington is still the home of the Wiggin family, and is open to the public once a week during the summer.

CL 13/20/27 Nov. 1920, 21/28 Sept 1978; C. Hussey, *English Country Houses: Early Georgian*; Roger North, *On Architecture* (ed. H.M. Colvin), p.73; *Life and Times of Anthony à Wood* (ed L. Powys, 1961), p.229; Bodleian Library, Gough Maps 32, f.29; H.M.Colvin, 'Bell-Guttae and the Woodwards of Chipping Campden', *Georgian Group Journal* (1993), pp.75-7; Strickland-Freeman papers at Gloucester Record Office (D1245/FF38); L. Dickins & M. Stanton, *An Eighteenth Century Correspondence* (1910), pp.266-7.

KENILWORTH CASTLE

Until it was made uninhabitable by Parliament after the Civil War, Kenilworth Castle was the grandest and most impressive house in Warwickshire. It was founded by Henry I's Chamberlain, Geoffrey de Clinton, in the 1120s, but the oldest surviving portion is the massive Keep of local red sandstone, built *c*.1175-85 by Henry II, who took over the castle from Geoffrey de Clinton's grandson, recompensing him with a smaller castle in Buckinghamshire. The Keep was almost certainly built over and around the earthen mound or motte of Geoffrey de Clinton's castle. It had four crenellated turrets, one at each corner, and was entered by a staircase in a 'forebuilding' to the west; this gave access to two floors, one used for storage, and the other for a hall. To the south of the Keep was the roughly circular inner ward or courtyard, surrounded by a wall enclosing a collection of timber buildings; outside this was the outer ward or base court.

In 1206-13 King John built a stone curtain wall around the outer ward, punctuated by towers, one of which, Mortimer's Tower, served as the main gatehouse; these all contained lodging rooms for members of the King's household. The King also greatly enlarged the artificial lake or mere which

82.   The Hall of Kenilworth Castle, drawing by J. B. Barber, 1821—the year of Sir Walter Scott's famous novel. The Hall was built in the 1390s as part of John of Gaunt's remodelling of the castle, but lost its roof when the building was 'slighted' in 1649.

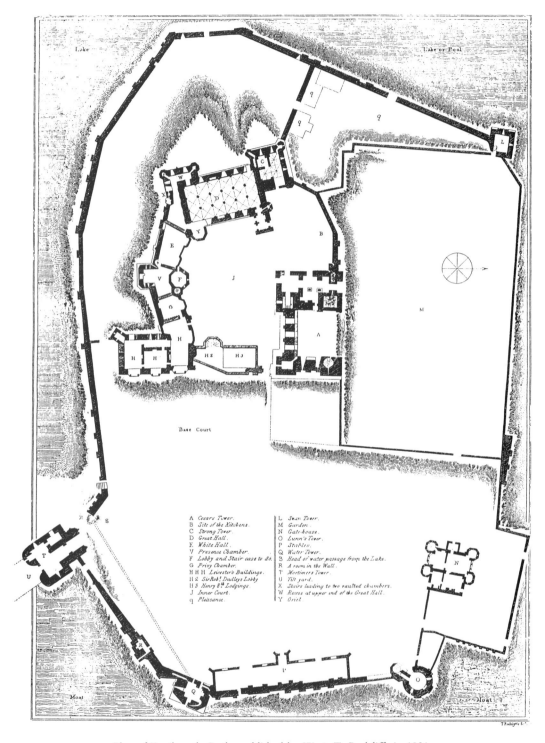

A Cesars Tower.
B Site of the Kitchens.
C Strong Tower.
D Great Hall.
E White Hall.
V Presence Chamber.
F Lobby and Stair case to do.
G Privy Chamber.
H H H Leicester's Buildings.
H 2 SrRobt Dudleys Lobby
H 3 Henry 8th Lodgings
J Inner Court.
q Pleasance.

L Swan Tower.
M Garden.
N Gate-house.
O Lunn's Tower.
P Stables.
Q Water Tower.
S Head of water passage from the Lake.
R A room in the Wall.
T Mortimers Tower.
U Tilt yard.
X Stairs leading to two vaulted chambers.
W Recess at upper end of the Great Hall.
Y Oriel.

Plan of Kenilworth Castle, published by W. & T. Radcliffe in 1821.

Geoffrey de Clinton had created outside the castle for defensive reasons, thus giving Kenilworth an improbably spectacular setting which survived until the mid-17th century. Later in the 13th century an earthwork known as the Brayes — the site of the present car park — was created as an outer defence to the south-east, joined to Mortimer's Tower by a raised causeway, which also served as a dam for the lake. A tiltyard was laid out on the causeway, and in 1279 jousting took place there before 100 ladies.

In 1238 Henry III granted the castle for life to his brother-in-law Simon de Montfort, Earl of Leicester, and it played a crucial part in the de Montfort rebellion of the 1260s. Henry III recaptured it in 1266 and gave it to his younger son Edmund, Earl of Lancaster, whose descendant Blanche married Edward III's younger son John of Gaunt, 'time-honoured Lancaster', in 1361. As Duke of Lancaster John of Gaunt was one the most powerful men in the kingdom, and he rebuilt the domestic quarters in a palatial manner early in the 1390s, with a new hall, kitchen, chambers and towers of red sandstone arranged around three sides of the inner ward; the master mason was Robert de Skyllington. Even in its ruined state, this is one of the finest pieces of domestic architecture of its date in England, and in its heyday, before the destruction of the timber roofs and the internal decorations, it must have been even more so. The Hall was placed on the first floor, over a vaulted undercroft, as at the nearly contemporary New College, Oxford. It was lit by tall windows with Perpendicular tracery and covered by a single-span roof — one of the widest in England at the time of construction — and was flanked by two towers. The kitchen was on the north side of the courtyard, next to the keep, and the Great Chamber and a presence chamber lay to the south. There were also chambers in the towers, some of them commanding views over the Mere, with large windows 'very commodiously [placed] to see the the deer coursed and to see the fish taken', as a surveyor put it in the 1540s.

John of Gaunt's son became Henry IV in 1399, and in about 1417 his son Henry V built a lodge or pleasure-house — 'the pleasance in the marsh' — with its own hall, parlour, kitchen and six chambers, some distance away from the castle on the other side of the lake to the west. Here he could, in the words of a survey of c.1563, 'go in a Bote owte of the Castell to bankete [banquet]' — an appealingly romantic vision. For the rest of the 15th century, and the first part of the 16th, the castle remained in royal hands. Henry VIII spent 'great cost', in Leland's words, in modernising it and providing adequate accommodation for his sizeable entourage. According to a survey of c.1545 there were 'houses for 200 people to lodge in' around the base court, including Henry V's 'pleasance' — described by Leland as a 'praty banketynge howse of tymbre' — which was re-erected near the Swan Tower in the outer ward; there was also a 'large great house newly builded of timber and tiled' on the eastern side of the inner ward.

In 1553 Edward VI granted the castle to John Dudley, Duke of Northumberland, who had already acquired the site of the dissolved Kenilworth Abbey, another of Geoffrey de Clinton's foundations. Northumberland was executed in the first year of Mary's reign, but in 1563 Queen Elizabeth restored the castle to his son Robert, who became Earl of Leicester in the following year. Leicester was the most favoured of all the Queen's favourites, and until his death in 1588 he was the greatest potentate in Warwickshire. During his tenure there were three royal visits to Kenilworth, the third of which, in 1575, lasted for 19 days and was of legendary splendour.

When Leicester acquired the castle it was, apart from the addition of the timber-framed buildings by Henry VIII, much as John of Gaunt had left it at the end of the 14th century. Surprisingly perhaps, he paid attention to the defensive role of the castle. The Queen allowed him to keep a hundred retainers there, and in 1570 he had, in the words of a contemporary, 'many workmen at his seat called Killingworth Castle to make it strong; and furnished it with armour, munition, and other necessaries for defense'. But the main emphasis was on show and lavish display. A new and much larger gatehouse of stone was constructed on the north side of the outer ward, and a stable block ('Leicester's Barn') built of stone and timber inside the eastern curtain wall. The Keep was remodelled with larger windows, and the 12th-century forebuilding reconstructed internally to give access to a new formal garden in the northern part of the outer ward. This was laid out in the fashion of the Italian Renaissance, with a terrace

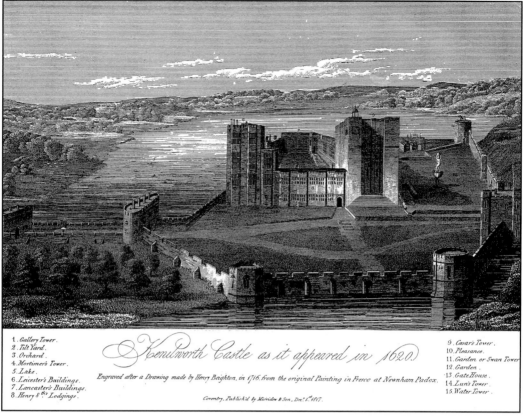

1. Gallery Tower.
2. Tilt Yard.
3. Orchard.
4. Mortimer's Tower.
5. Lake.
6. Leicester's Buildings.
7. Lancaster's Buildings.
8. Henry 8:th Lodgings.

Kenilworth Castle as it appeared in 1620.

Engraved after a Drawing made by Henry Beighton, in 1716, from the original Painting in Fresco at Newnham Padox.

Coventry. Publish'd by Merridew & Son. Dec:r 1:st 1817.

9. Cæsar's Tower.
10. Pleasance.
11. Garden. or Swan Tower.
12. Garden.
13. GateHouse.
14. Lun's Tower.
15. Water Tower.

83. Kenilworth Castle looking west in 1620, drawing by Henry Beighton from a lost painting at Newnham Paddox. The Keep is on the right of the central complex of building, 'Leicester's Building' on the left, Henry VIII's lodgings block in between, and the Hall in the distance. Leicester's Gatehouse and garden is on the extreme right, and Mortimer's Tower and the Brayes to the left. Beyond is the lake, drained after 1649.

84. Kenilworth Castle from the south. The area in the foreground formed part of the lake until 1649. Beyond is the curtain wall, and behind it the ruined buildings around the Inner Ward.

to the north of the Keep facing an aviary, fountains, obelisks, and four pillars 15 feet high, each surmounted by an orb of porphyry. A new block of stone-built lodgings for the Queen was constructed on the southern side of the inner ward, next to Henry VIII's lodgings range, lit by large mullioned and transomed bay windows. John Laneham, an official in Leicester's household, who wrote a description of the festivities mounted for the Queen in 1575, was most impressed by the copious use of glass. Every room, he said, was

> so spacious, so well belighted, and so hy roofed within: so seemly to sight by [due] proportion without: [at] day tyme, on every syde so glittering with glass by day; [at] nights, by continuall brightnesse of candel, fyre, and torch-light, transparent thro the lyghtsome windows, as it [were] the Egiptian Pharos relucent untoo all the Alexandrian coast.

Leicester's additions were designed to complement the mighty medieval buildings. The new lodgings range was intended to match the architecture of the Keep, and the gatehouse (Plate VII) can also be seen as a piece of self-conscious medievalism, with its four corner turrets and crenellated roof-line, like the 14th-century gatehouse at Maxstoke Castle (q.v.); there is, however, a classical porch in the form of a triumphal arch on the garden side, probably brought from 'Leicester's Building' when the gatehouse was turned into a house after the Civil War. The building work, which was finished by the time of the Queen's third and last visit in 1575, was supervised, and probably also planned, by William Spicer, a master mason from Somerset who had earlier worked at Longleat (Wiltshire), and who later became Surveyor of the Queen's Works.

The interiors vied with any of their date in England, judging from an inventory compiled in 1583. There were no fewer than 155 tapestries, and among many splendid beds there was one 'of walnut, all painted over with crimson and silvered with roses, four bears and ragged staffs, all silvered, standing in the corners'. There were also 16 'pieces of gilt leather hangings' and 'an instrument of Organs, regals and virginals covered with crimson velvet and garnished with gold lace'. A fine fireplace with a carved overmantel still survives in the

85. The porch to Leicester's Gatehouse at Kenilworth Castle. The porch, which bears Leicester's initials, may originally have been in the lodgings block known as Leicester's Building. It is a good example of the classicism of the 1570s.

gatehouse, to give some some idea of the quality of the workmanship; Leicester's initials and motto are carved there, and the overmantel is decorated with arabesque designs of Renaissance (and ultimately ancient Roman) origin, and flanked by classical columns and obelisks. Lieutenant Hammond's description of the castle in 1634, after it had come into the hands of the Crown, makes it clear that Leicester's alterations also encompassed some of the medieval rooms at the 'upper' end of the Hall:

> ... we next view'd the Great Chamber for the Guard, the Chamber of Presence, the Privy Chamber, fretted [plastered] above richly with Coats of Armes, and all adorn'd with fayre, and rich Chimney Peeces of Alabaster, blacke Marble, and of Joyners worke in curious carv'd wood; and all those fayre, and rich Roomes and Lodgings in that spacious Tower not long since built, and repayr'd at a great Cost by that great Favourite of late dayes; the private, plaine, retiring Chamber wherein our renowned

Queene ... always made choise to repose her Selfe. Also the famous, strong, old Tower, called <u>Julius Caesar's</u> [the Keep], on the top whereof, wee view'd the pleasant, large Poole ... the Parke, and the Forrest contiguous thereunto.

All this magnificence vanished after the Civil War. When Leicester died the castle went first to his brother Ambrose, Earl of Warwick, and then to his son Sir Robert Dudley, but doubts about the latter's legitimacy gave James I an excuse to recover possession in 1611. Charles I granted a lease to Lord Carey in 1624, but the castle was occupied by Parliamentary troops after the Battle of Edge Hill, and in 1649 it was 'slighted', the north wall of the keep blown up, and the lake drained, apparently to pre-empt the possibility of a Royalist come-back. Colonel Hawkesworth, who presided over these acts of vandalism, took up residence in Leicester's Gatehouse in the following year, blocked up the ground-floor passage and added a two-gabled extension on the eastern side. Having been recovered by the Crown after the Restoration, the ruined castle was granted in 1665 to Lawrence Hyde, Earl of Rochester, and subsequently to Thomas Villers, Earl of Clarendon. It remained in the hands of his descendants until the 20th century, but it was too large and too damaged to restore as a country house. Yet the ruins survived, to be visited, sketched, and enthused over by countless searchers after the romantic and the picturesque down to our own day. The publication of Sir Walter Scott's *Kenilworth* in 1821 ensured the castle's continuing celebrity, but damage still continued to occur, and in 1842 Thomas Ward remarked that the tracery of two of the Hall windows had been destroyed 'by the order of the Rev, Mr. Villiers ... who said the Castle looked much better as a Ruin'. In 1937 the ruins were purchased from the 6th Earl of Clarendon by Sir John Davenport Siddeley, 1st Viscount Kenilworth, and conveyed them into the management of the Ministry of Works. They are now maintained by English Heritage.

Dugdale, p.242-52; *VCH* vi, pp.134-8; J. Harvey, 'Sidelights on Kenilworth Castle', *Archaeological Journal* ci (1944), pp.92-106; *History of the King's Works*, ii (1963), pp.682-5, iii (1975), pp.258-60; J. Nichols, *Progresses of Queen Elizabeth* i (1823); Hist MSS Comm, *De Lisle & Dudley* i, pp.278-298 (1583 inventory); G. Wickham Legg (ed), *Short Survey of Several Counties, 1634*; Kenilworth Castle guidebooks (1973 and 1991).

KNOWLE HALL

In the later Middle Ages the manor of Knowle belonged to Westminster Abbey, and in 1404 there was a moated manor house with a hall, pantry, Lord's chamber, chapel and stable, presumably standing near the site of the present Knowle Hall, some distance away to the east of the village. The manor was retained by the Crown after the Dissolution of the Monasteries, but the house and much of the land were granted to the Bishopric of London in the 1550s, and in 1556 a lease was granted to John Cope of Canons Ashby (Northamptonshire). In 1622 the manor and park were granted by James I to the poet and courtier Fulke Greville, 1st Lord Brooke. He had recently made Warwick Castle (q.v.) habitable after long years of disuse, but he does not appear to have spent much time at Knowle, and the Grevilles did not gain full possession of the manor house and land until 1659, in the time of the 4th Lord Brooke. Lord Brooke's younger brother Fulke married a daughter of the wealthy London merchant Francis Dashwood in 1664, and they settled at Knowle Hall, which remained in the possession of the family until 1743.

The earliest drawings of the house show an impressive brick building of mid-17th-century appearance, probably representing the rebuilding and enlargement of the earlier manor house at about the time of Fulke Greville's marriage in the 1660s. It was a rather old-fashioned house for that date, with a hall block entered centrally and wings projecting forward, as at Aston Hall (q.v.). The walls were articulated

86.   Knowle Hall, drawing by Thomas Ward, *c.*1820–30. The core of the house seems to have been built in the late 16th century and to have been remodelled and extended by Fulke Greville, later 5th Lord Brooke, in the 1660s.

87.   The interior of the hall at Knowle Hall, drawing by Thomas Ward, showing the elaborate Elizabethan or Jacobean panelling.

with giant Ionic pilasters, the windows were of the upright type with single mullions and transoms which were becoming increasingly fashionable in the 1620s, and there was a hipped roof — all features widely employed by London and provincial builders in the middle of the 17th century. The panelled and plastered interiors, now known only from Thomas Ward's rather eccentric drawings, were richly embellished in the Elizabethan manner, perhaps in the time of the Cope's tenancy. Ward also mentioned a bowling green, an avenue, a lake and remnants of 'canals', suggesting that an elaborate formal garden was formed by the Grevilles in the latter part of the 17th century.

Fulke Greville succeeded his brother as 5th Lord Brooke in 1677, and when he died in 1710 the Knowle estate passed to his younger son Algernon, whose son Fulke sold it in 1743 to the builder and architect William Smith, son of the better-known Francis Smith of Warwick. Smith's widow sold it in 1754 to Benjamin Palmer of Olton, near Solihull, a cousin of the Greswoldes of Malvern Hall (q.v.), and the estate later passed by inheritance to the Rev. William Wilson, during whose tenure the park was turned over to agriculture. The house was leased out after 1720, and William Smith had some of the panelling removed; it later became a farmhouse, and it was still serving that purpose when John Constable drew it in 1820 on one of his visits to Henry Greswolde Lewis at Malvern Hall.

William Wilson died in 1831, and his son, William 'Gumley' Wilson, a member of the fast-living Melton Mowbray hunting set, made plans to demolish the old house and take up residence in a new one. They were set aside, having drawn forth protests from Thomas Ward, who had a particular affection for the building, and in 1834 Wilson commissioned Edward Blore to prepare designs for a thorough rebuilding instead. A drawing by Blore in the British Library shows a new wing and conservatories, and a second irate letter from Thomas Ward (now in the Warwick Record Office) shows that the architect intended to remove most of the old features from the interior, including the floors and ceilings. In the event Blore's plans were also abandoned, and the house was mostly demolished in about 1840, 'Gumley' Wilson having by then been persuaded that it was structurally unsound, although, as Ward recorded, 'so far from the Walls being unsafe, it was with the greatest Labor pulled down'. A surviving wing continued to be used by Wilson on sporting visits until 1849, but even this was finally demolished in the 1870s. Some of the panelling from the house was removed to Olton Hall, which has since been demolished.

The estate, of 1,660 acres, was sold in 1849 to Robert Wilson, apparently no relation of 'Gumley', who emigrated to America. Robert Wilson then set about building a new house — the present Knowle Hall — to the designs of an unknown architect. It is a restrained building in the Italian Renaissance style, of rendered brick comprising a main block of five bays and three stories (one of which was later removed), with a service wing on one side and a one-storied projection on the other. The main feature of the interior, which until recently retained its attractive Victorian furnishings largely intact, is a two-storied galleried Hall. In 1865 the house was sold again to G.A. Everitt, and it remained in the hands of his descendants until 1982.

BL, Add MS 29265, f.225; Tate Gallery, London, catalogue of Constable exhibition (1991); Add. MS 42028, f.11 (Blore drawing); Kelly, *Directory of Warwickshire* (1940); WRO, CR 71/41, /47, /107 (Ward letters); WRO, EAC 320 (sale partics 1982); G. Fleetwood Wilson (ed.), *Green Peas at Christmas* (1924); information from Jean Powrie.

MALVERN HALL

The Greswolde family was associated with Solihull from at least the 15th century. But it did not have a substantial country seat in the parish until 1702, when Humphrey Greswolde, a younger son from a branch of the family which had settled at Greet, in the parish of Yardley, to the south of Birmingham, built a handsome, though plain, brick house in a newly-created park to the south-east of the parish church. It stood on the site of Malvern Farm, bought in 1680 by the Rev. Henry Greswolde, Rector of Solihull, and Humphrey Greswolde's memorandum book makes it clear that work on the interior was still in progress in 1704, when he served as Sheriff of Warwickshire. The stables were being built in 1706, with the otherwise unknown Henry Lynall acting as bricklayer and George Field as carpenter, but there is no record of who designed the house, which was of a standard kind, seven bays wide and three stories high, with a pediment over the centre, and stone quoins and window architraves. An estate plan of 1726 shows an avenue leading to the Warwick-Solihull road, but otherwise the gardens were only of the most rudimentary kind.

On the death of Humphrey Greswolde's great-nephew Marshall Greswolde in 1749, the estate passed by marriage to David Lewis. His son Henry Greswolde Lewis married a daughter of Lord Bradford (c.f. Castle Bromwich Hall), and in 1783 he called in the as yet relatively inexperienced John Soane to extend and modernise the house. Soane had returned from Italy three years before, and was in the process of building up a country-house practice; his introduction to Lewis may have come from the Hon. Wilbraham Tollemache (later the 5th Earl of Dysart), who had married Lewis's sister and had employed Soane to carry out alterations at Coombe House, near Kingston (Surrey). The work was mostly carried out in 1784, and involved remodelling the existing house and adding lower wings of five bays on either side, at an estimated cost of £3,083. Externally, the most important change was the

88.   The entrance front of Malvern Hall from John Soane's *Plans ... of Buildings* (1788). The central block was built by Humphrey Greswolde in 1702-4, and the wings were added by Henry Greswolde Lewis to Soane's design in 1783-4. Soane also remodelled the central block.

89.   Malvern Hall, the Warwick Road lodge, or 'Barn à la Paestum', built to John Soane's designs in 1798.

addition of a curved porch of Ionic columns at the entrance, its frieze enriched with carvings of wreaths between rams' heads symbolising hospitality. The house was also coated in stucco, and the original balustrade replaced by a plain parapet or blocking course, in accordance with the prevailing taste for neo-classical simplicity. Inside, the Entrance Hall was opened up to allow a vista through round arches to the main staircase, which was altered and given 'a new moulded handrail with enriched ironwork', and the Drawing Room to the left of the entrance hall was given a curved end — a favourite Soane device. One of the main reasons for the alterations was to supply more and larger reception rooms, one of which was placed in each wing: a Dining Room in the north wing, and a second Drawing Room (later turned into a conservatory) to the south, adjoining a suite made up of bedroom, dressing room and back staircase. These rooms do not seem to have boasted any of the elaborate spatial effects for which Soane later became famous, but they presumably satisfied Lewis's need for a house suited to the entertainment of large numbers of guests.

Soane's final involvement with Malvern Hall occurred in 1798, when he was asked to design a new lodge and coach-house on the Warwick road. The lodge also served as a grain store or 'barn à la Paestum', alluding to the Grecian temples at Paestum in southern Italy which the architect had visited in 1779. It is an uncompromising essay in the austere and 'primitive' neo-classicism which was sweeping Europe at the time. Built of brick, with stumpy Doric columns supporting a wooden triglyph cornice, it served, when used for its original purpose, as a formidable entrance to the estate, and it still retains the power to impress.

The 'barn' was conceived in connection with a series of improvements to the surrounding land-scape. They were celebrated in a group of paintings and drawings by John Constable, who went to Malvern Hall to paint Lewis's 13-year-old ward Mary Freer in 1809 (Lewis's sister, by now the Countess of Dysart, was one of the artist's early patrons); one of the pictures, which now hangs in the Tate Gallery in London, shows the house in a 'natural' setting overlooking the lake to the east, formed by damming the River Blythe. Constable paid a second visit to Malvern in 1820 after painting a picture of Lewis's ancestor Humphrey de Greswolde, supposedly a follower of William the Conqueror, dressed in Norman costume. By this time Lewis had turned against Soane, and was trying to reverse some of his alterations to the exterior of the house. He was also planning to introduce more 'intricacy' and 'variety' in the park, as he told Constable in 1819: 'I shall have great pleasure in ... taking your opinion, in forming the Landscape of the park by cutting glades .. so as to give a forest scenery. I have brought the house to nearly what it was 60 years ago — before that <u>modern Goth</u>, Mr. Soane, spoilt a handsome house by shaving clean every ornament, architraves, coins [*sic*], keystones, string courses & ballustrade, the latter I could not replace, all the rest I have accomplished'. The remodelled house, with its gate-piers 'from an old design of Inigo Jones' and its new shrubberies and flower-beds (Plate VIII), is shown in paintings now in New Haven (U.S.A.) and Le Mans.

Lewis died childless in 1829, and the house then passed to a cousin, Edward Wigley, from whom it went to an uncle and then by marriage in 1849 to F.E. Williams, whose family came from Worcester and had land in Ireland. In 1896 F.W.G. Williams sold it to David Troman, who found it in a very dilapidated state and employed a local firm of builders to lop off the top storey, reduce the size of the wings, and form a terrace around the building. The truncated house was sold again in 1915 to a local benefactor, Horace Brueton. He lived there until 1926, when some of the land was bought by the local authority as a park, most of the rest of the estate having been sold off for building. The house has been a school since 1931, and is now St Martin's Independent Day School for Girls.

R. Pemberton, *Solihull and its Church* (1905), pp.42-5; WRO, CR 299/577-8 (memo book); Sir John Soane's Museum, London, v.3(13); Soane, *Plans, Elevations ... of Buildings* (1788); Tate Gallery, London, catalogue of Constable exhibition (1991); R.B. Beckett (ed.), *John Constable's Correspondence* iv (1966), pp.57-63; H.L. Greenhalgh & E. Edmondson, *Malvern Hall* (1974).

NEW HALL

New Hall is a moated house of medieval origins, situated about a mile to the south-east of Sutton Coldfield and still hidden away in semi-rural seclusion despite the proximity of the Birmingham conurbation. The manor of Sutton belonged to the Earls of Warwick from the early 12th century, and one of their sub-tenants, possibly Sir John Lizours, built the core of the present building; he was in possession in 1341, when the name New Hall was first recorded. The lack of details makes it impossible to attempt a precise dating, but enough of the grey sandstone rubble masonry survives to show that the house was a relatively modest L-shaped building in the south-east corner of the moated enclosure, comprising a hall range with a chamber wing bounded on two sides by the waters of the moat.

The house as we see it today is the result of several remodellings and enlargements, the first of which occurred in the 16th century, when the estate came into the hands of William Gibbons (d.1542), brother-in-law of Sutton's most famous inhabitant and greatest patron Bishop Veysey (c.f. Moor Hall). Gibbons's son Thomas, who was Warden of Sutton, seems to have remodelled the medieval chamber wing, and also to have built a second wing of red sandstone at the northern end of the Hall. The house thus acquired the 'half H' plan commonly found in the second half of the 16th century, with triangular gables at the end of each wing; the Hall was also divided into two stories at about the same time.

Soon after the death of Thomas Gibbons in 1586 the house was sold to Henry Sacheverell of Morley and Callow (Derbyshire), and in 1590 he added a one-storied bay, lit by large mullioned and transomed windows, onto the south-west corner of the Hall, which was panelled in wood at about the same time; the extension looks out onto a garden, with the western side of the moat beyond. Sacheverell

104.   New Hall from the east, drawing by T. Radcliffe, c.1830. The wing projecting forward to the left of the hall range forms part of the medieval core of the house. The gabled wing to the right was added in the 16th century, and the towers form part of the alterations carried out by Charles Chadwick in and around 1796.

105. The Hall at New Hall, watercolour by A.E. Everitt, c.1870. The medieval Hall was remodelled and extended in 1590 by Henry Sacheverell. The billiard table stands in the extension, and the furniture and armaments were no doubt brought in to enhance the 'Old English' atmosphere, probably by John Chadwick, the owner in 1870.

also created a spacious Great Chamber on the first floor of the north wing, lit by bay windows which still retain their original glazing. With its carved wood panelling, heraldic glass, plaster frieze of goats (the Sacheverell crest) and elaborate ribbed ceiling displaying bunches of grapes and the Sacheverell coat of arms, this is the most impressive room in New Hall, and one of the finest of its date in the county. It is reached by a wooden staircase of c.1600, with carved newel posts surmounted by heraldic beasts, and a balustrade with strapwork ornament. In 1666 the house had 17 hearths, and it may have been about this time that a cupola was added to the hall block, and rooms with dormer windows created in the roof space; these have now disappeared, but they are shown in the earliest photographs of the house, taken in the 1860s. The terraces of the formal garden to the south of the moat must also date from the 17th century, along perhaps with the yew walk on the western side.

The last of the Sacheverells to live at New Hall was George (d.1715). He was suspected of being an alchemist, and he certainly sheltered his namesake, the notorious clergyman Dr. Henry Sacheverell, in the house after being suspended in 1709 for preaching inflammatory pro-Jacobite sermons. George Sacheverell scratched some cryptic inscriptions onto the windows of the Great Chamber in 1689, and he may also have introduced the panelling into the present Dining Room (the ground floor of the medieval chamber wing), and created the present approach to the house from the east, where pairs of early 18th-century gate piers still survive. With his death the direct male line of the Sacheverells came to an end, and the estate passed by inheritance to Charles Chadwick, who took the name Sacheverell, and later inherited the estate of Mavesyn Ridware (Staffordshire) from his father. New Hall became the home of his sister and then of a cousin, but in 1793 it came into the hands of his younger brother John, whose son Charles took up residence there just before his father's death in 1797, when the Staffordshire house was abandoned.

By now the taste for the picturesque was well established, and New Hall, with its medieval origins and its wooded ambience, was a good candidate for 'improvement'. This took the form of raising three crenellated brick towers with Gothic windows (the Rookery Tower, the High Tower and the Water Tower), one of them on the base of what may have been a garderobe turret on the south side of the medieval chamber wing, one (the tallest) to the west of the hall and the third at the northern end of a new service wing; two of the towers carry the date 1796, but no architect is recorded. These changes transformed the character of the house, especially as seen from the gardens to the south and west. There were also some internal alterations, notably the insertion of large quantities of painted Flemish glass to impart a suitably venerable appearance.

106. New Hall from the north west. The bridge over the moat was built by John Chadwick in 1868-70, and he also enlarged the block in the centre of the picture to provide more bedrooms. The tower is one of those built by John Chadwick, and to its right is the 1590 extension to the Hall.

Charles Chadwick died in 1829, and the house was then leased out to a farmer by his son Hugh. Hugh Chadwick returned in 1850, and his son John, who inherited in 1854, embarked on another set of repairs and alterations. The gardens were laid out in a formal manner, the roof of the hall block raised, an extra storey added to the highest of the late 18th-century towers, and a new wing of red sandstone, containing service quarters and guest bedrooms, built to the north of the 16th-century Great Chamber wing. The house now extended to the northern side of the moat, and a covered bridge over the moat was built from the north of the service wing. These alterations were carried out between 1868 and 1870, but once again the name of the architect is not known.

Gambling debts and the agricultural depression wreaked havoc with John Chadwick's finances, and in 1883 he went bankrupt, having sold many of the contents of the house two years before. The estate was sold off, and the house, with only 20 acres of land, was bought as a school, which lasted until 1903. It was then sold to William Wilkinson, the owner of a millinery business, and he turned it once more into a family home. In 1923 it was sold to Alfred Owen, engineer and co-founder of the Rubery Owen engineering company, who died six years later. When his son, Sir Alfred Owen, died in 1975 the house was left empty for six years, but in 1982 it was purchased by a local businessman, Michael Blakemore, who renovated it and sold it in 1985 to Thistle Hotels. After further major restoration, and the addition of a luxury courtyard extension on the north side of the moat, it was opened as a country house hotel in 1988, and it is now maintained in an exemplary manner by Ian and Caroline Parkes.

VCH iv, pp.231-3; P.B. Chatwin & E.G. Harcourt in *TBAS* lxiv (1941-2), pp.1-19; Bracken, *Forest and Chase of Sutton Coldfield* (1850); Aylesford Collection, f.546; S. Shaw, *History of Staffordshire*, i, pp.184-5; BRL photogaphs; NMR photographs; E. Marvin, *New Hall: the First 800 Years* (pamphlet, n.d. — copy in Sutton Coldfield library).

NEWBOLD REVEL

Originally known as Fenny Newbold, Newbold Revel now perpetuates the name of the family which supplied a succession of lords of the manor during the 14th and 15th centuries. The estate, along with lands in Easenhall, Pailton and Stretton-under-Fosse, passed by marriage into the hands of the Mallory family in the 15th century, the most famous member of which was Sir Thomas (d.1470), author of the *Morte d'Arthur*. After a complicated series of sales it came in the early 17th century into the hands of the antiquary Sir Simon Clarke of Broom Court (q.v.), in the extreme south-west of the county. He died in 1651, leaving the house at Newbold to his widow, and then after her death in 1659 to her niece, who had married Fulwar Skipwith.

The Skipwiths originally came from Yorkshire and Lincolnshire, but Fulwar was born at Shacklewell, a hamlet in the parish of Hackney (Middlesex), the son of a leading Royalist who was killed at Edge Hill. On inheriting the Newbold estate he fixed his main residence in the manor house, which had 15 hearths in 1666, and bought up more land in the area, both in Warwickshire and over the Leicestershire border. He was made a Baronet by Charles II in 1670 but died seven years later, leaving the property to an infant grandson, also called Fulwar, who later 'visited most parts of England' and 'travelled through Holland, Flanders, France, Italy and Germany'. He subsequently married a daughter of the first Sir Francis Dashwood of West Wycombe (Buckinghamshire), served as one of the M.P.s for Coventry in 1713-14, and in about 1716 he built the large red-brick house which we see today.

Though there is no documentary proof of its authorship, the house is so similar to houses by Francis Smith of Warwick as to make it almost certain that he was the architect. A plate in the second volume of *Vitruvius Britannicus* (1717) shows a building with all the Smith characteristics: a tall, rectangular elevation with the roof hidden behind a balustrade punctuated by urns and gesticulating figures, bold architraves around the windows with large keystones at the top and 'aprons' underneath, quoins 'rusticated in the French manner' at the corners of the wings which project from the main body of the house, and volutes on either side of the window over the main entrance — a feature which first appeared at William Talman's long-demolished Thoresby Hall (Nottinghamshire) and which can also be seen in the west wing of Stoneleigh Abbey (q.v.), definitely by Smith and almost contemporary with Newbold. There were also tall Ionic pilasters like those at Stoneleigh on the sides of the wings, and there was a pediment on the roofline at the centre of the garden front. But the most unusual thing about Newbold is its internally asymmetrical plan, with a narrow entrance passage next to the main staircase, leading through to a large rectangular two-storied Saloon; and 'large and convenient apartments' in the wings. An estate plan of 1708 makes it clear that the new house reflected the arrangement of the previous house on the site, with the Saloon on the site of the original hall, and there seems to have been some re-use of the original materials, including even a rainwater head dated 1673.

The structure and plan of Sir Fulwar Skipwith's house survive largely intact, but there have been many alterations to the interior, and to some extent to the exterior too. The main staircase still survives, with its turned balusters typical of houses of this type and date, but otherwise most of the original decoration has gone. There are also some late 18th-century chimneypieces, possibly introduced by Sir Fulwar Skipwith's son, the 3rd Baronet in or around 1763, a date which appears on rainwater heads. They include a particularly monumental one in the Saloon. The drawing of the house in the Aylesford Collection shows the exterior stuccoed over and the grounds landscaped in the conventional manner, with lawns coming right up to the house, an ornamental lake to the south-east of the garden and a handsome red-brick stable block of about the same date as the house.

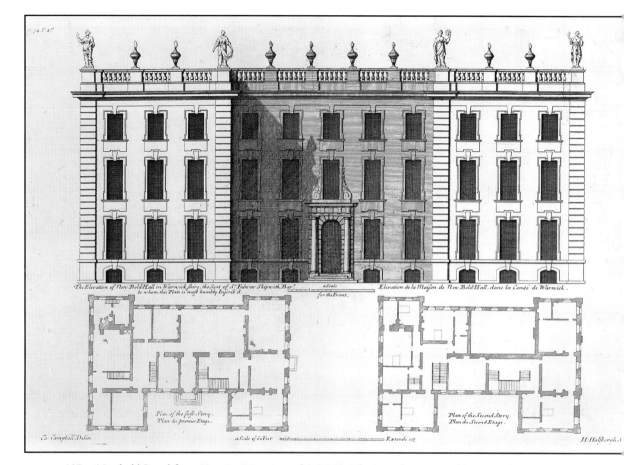

107. Newbold Revel from *Vitruvius Britannicus* vol.2 (1717). The irregular nature of the internal planning makes it clear that Sir Fulwar Skipwith's new house was a remodelling of an older one on the site. There is no reason to doubt the traditional attribution to Francis Smith of Warwick.

Much of the present appearance of Newbold Revel is the result of drastic work undertaken by new owners in the late 19th century. When Sir Fulwar Skipwith's grandson, the 4th Baronet, died in 1790 the house went to his widow and then on her death in 1832 to a cousin, Sir Grey Skipwith of Alveston, near Stratford, a descendant of a branch of the family which had emigrated to Virginia in the 17th century, and M.P. for South Warwickshire from 1832-5. He died in 1852, and his son subsequently sold much of the estate, which by now was heavily encumbered with debt, before finally selling the house to Charles Ramsden (some of the furniture ended up at Honington Hall, q.v.).

In 1862 the house was sold again to Edward Wood, a financier and railway promoter, who had already acquired 17,551 acres of land in Scotland, with a house on Raasay, one of the Western Isles. The purchase of Newbold Revel gave him a place among the English landed gentry, with an estate of 1,739 acres in Warwickshire, along with smaller holdings in Staffordshire and Cheshire. He put some of his considerable wealth (£11,440 a year in land alone) towards the renovation and modernisation of the house and grounds, a process which was continued by his grandson Arthur, who succeeded him. This involved adding a new hall between the two projecting wings of the entrance front and a one-storied conservatory-like addition to the garden front, divided from the existing rooms by round-headed arches and ornamented externally by paired Doric columns. The stucco was also stripped from the outside walls and plate-glass windows were installed. Arthur Wood was keen on physical exercise and field sports, and among his additions to the house were a wing added to the garden front for the accommodation of visiting cricket teams, a gymnasium, a squash court and a set of hunting stables. Meanwhile the gardens were expensively laid out in a formal style, with a copious provision of urns, balustrades and flower-beds. Thus a run-down early 18th-century house became a luxurious late-Victorian country seat.

Arthur Wood sold the house in 1898 to Arthur Heath, an iron manufacturer from Madeley (Staffordshire), and he carried out more alterations to the interior, including the introduction of mahogany doors and marble chimneypieces of a characteristically opulent Edwardian kind; these can still be seen in some of the rooms. In 1911 his son sold the house again, to Leopold Bonn, whose son, Major Walter Bonn, was the last private occupier. From 1931 to 1946 the house belonged to British Advent Missions of Watford, who used it as a centre for training missionaries, but it was taken over by the Royal Air Force during the Second World War and in 1946 it was sold to the Sisters of Charity of St Paul, who used it as a teacher training college. This involved alterations to the interior and the addition of not very sympathetically designed extensions. In 1978 it was sold to the Post Office as a management centre, but was later put up for sale again, and in 1985 the house became the H.M. Prison Service College.

S.M. Stanislaus, *Newbold Revel* (1949 — pamphlet at WRO); Colen Campbell, *Vitruvius Britannicus* ii (1717); Aylesford Collection, f. 538; *CL*, 7 March 1903; sales partics 1980 at NMR; Nichols, *History of Leicestershire* (1811), iii (1), pp.368-71; *H.M. Prison Service College, Newbold Revel* (pamphlet at WRO); information from Professor Andor Gomme.

NEWNHAM PADDOX

Newnham Paddox is one of the greatest losses among the country houses of Warwickshire. The estate, near the Leicestershire border, has belonged since 1433 to the Feilding family, who subsequently (and erroneously) claimed descent from the Hapsburgs, and in the late 16th or early 17th century they built, or rebuilt, a large, sprawling house, probably of timber, which had 34 hearths in 1666. The building, or expansion, of this house coincided with a rise in the family's fortunes, culminating in the elevation to the peerage of Sir William Feilding, who became Baron Feilding in 1620 and Earl of Denbigh in 1622. He married a sister of James I's and Charles I's favourite the Duke of Buckingham, became Master of the Great Wardrobe to James I in 1622, took part in the abortive expedition to marry Charles to the Spanish Infanta in the following year, and commanded the fleet intended to relieve La Rochelle in

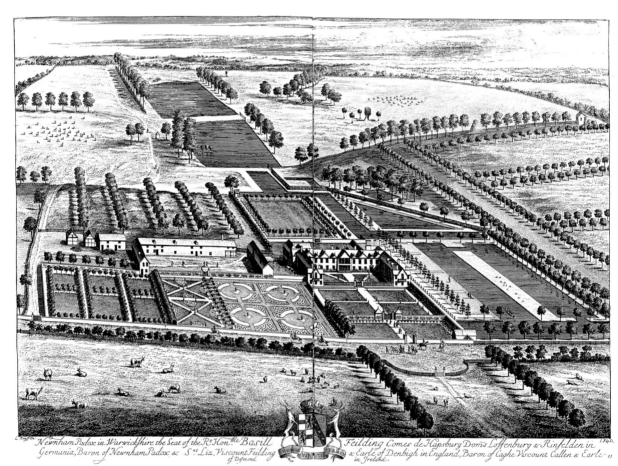

Newnham Paddox in Warwickshire the Seat of the R.t Hon.ble Basill Feilding Comes de Hapsburg Dom's Loffenburg & Rinfelden in Germania, Baron of Newnham Padox & S.t Liz, Viscount Feilding of Defmond & Earle of Denbigh in England, Baron of Caghe Viscount Callen & Earle in Jreland.

108.   Newnham Paddox, from Kip's *Britannia Illustrata* (1707). The gardens were probably created at the end of the 17th century. They were swept away by 'Capability' Brown, starting *c.*1741, and the pools were joined together to form the present lake.

1628. In 1631 he made a voyage to India, immortalised in Van Dyck's famous portrait (now in the National Gallery in London) showing him striding through the jungle, but he was killed near Birmingham during the Civil War, when he fought on the Royalist side (his son fought for Parliament).

Though both the 1st and 2nd Earls of Denbigh played an important part in national life, their house was a relatively modest one from an architectural point of view. Kip's illustration of *c.*1700 shows a long, low structure of indeterminate date, not unlike the original Coleshill Hall (q.v.), with a long gabled hall block two stories high and one room deep, and two wings projecting forward to enclose an entrance courtyard closed by gates; a visitor in 1743 remarked on the stained glass, which she thought was 'prodigious old'. In 1668 the 2nd Earl built a chapel adjoining the house — perhaps in one of the wings — and he subsequently entertained the Bishop of Lichfield and 'several persons of worth' to a magnificent dinner. The gardens were expanded at the end of the century, probably by the 4th Earl, who inherited in 1685. Their main feature was a complicated arrangement of geometrically-shaped pools to the east of the house; there were also two large rectangular pools on the main axis of the house to the north, and a parterre was laid out in front of the outbuildings.

The rather homely-looking house, with its old-fashioned gardens, was not grand or dignified enough for the 5th Earl, who returned to England in 1741 after a long period living abroad, and immediately embarked on a process of modernisation. According to a 'building book' which charts the gradual progress of the work, operations began in the gardens, starting with the transformation of the 'lower waters', which were 'altered from their old state' in 1741. Denbigh was a friend of Lord Cobham, the creator of the garden at Stowe (Bucks), and in 1746 he began work on 'the alteration of the great canal, and carrying it on to the head of the pond in the park, by a plan and the direction of Mr. Brown, Gardener to Lord Cobham'. This marks the creation of a serpentine lake to the north and east of the house, and there was also a good deal of tree planting, including 'hanging slopes' along the lake side. 'Mr. Brown' was 'Capability' Brown, the most famous of all English landscape gardeners, and Newnham Paddox was one of his first independent commissions. The work was subject to interruptions, but when Lord Denbigh died in 1755 his son the 6th Earl, whom Horace Walpole called 'the lowliest and most officious of the Court tools', employed Brown to finish 'the large piece of water and bridge, which were absolutely necessary for the place', using a bequest of £2,000 from an aunt.

Work on the house began two years before the 5th Earl's death. The nursery wing of the old house was repaired in 1753, but in the following year the greater part of the old building was demolished to make way for what was in essence a new house, described by Horace Walpole in 1768 as a 'plain good brick front built ... before the old house'. 'Capability' Brown produced the design, which was in the strictest Palladian taste, with low pyramid-topped towers on either side of a pedimented nine-bay front, its dimensions probably determined by those of the older house; the layout echoes that of Lydiard Park (Wiltshire) — another rebuilding of an older house — and the corner towers, ultimately of Italian inspiration, may have been directly influenced by those at Hagley Hall (Worcestershire). Wings stretched back from the towers, one of them containing the chapel; these seem to have corresponded to the wings of the old house.

The construction of the new wing was supervised by the London carpenter John Hobcraft, who worked with Brown on several occasions and also did some of the wood carving; there were also payments to the wood-carver Benjamin King of Warwick, to James Lovell (who also worked at Hagley and Stowe) for marble chimneypieces (e.g. in the Library), to the well-known London cabinet-maker John Cobb for chairs and tables in the new 'Eating Room', and to Joseph Duffour of Soho, who specialised in papier-mâché ornament, for mirror. The lower floor contained the Entrance Hall, reached by a flight of steps, the Library, a Dining Room, a Study and two bedrooms, one of them with Chinese wallpaper which, according to Winefride Elwes, one of the daughters of the 8th Earl, 'had a great fascination for us — the design was so beautiful and delicate yet *never repetitive*'. The upper floor was treated as a *piano nobile*, with a gallery or passage leading to a suite of state rooms: a somewhat old-fashioned arrangement for the 1750s, and one condemned by the Earl of Warwick, who said that he did not like 'an apartment above and one below to serve the same purposes'. Work was largely complete

109.   Newnham Paddox from the south east, drawing by Henry Jeayes, *c.*1790-1800. The house is shown after its rebuilding by 'Capability' Brown. The southern end of Brown's lake is in the foreground.

110.   The south front of Newnham Paddox in the early 20th century. The gates were brought from Berwick (Shropshire) by the 8th Earl of Denbigh, who commissioned the rebuilding of the house by T.H. Wyatt in 1876-9.

by 1768, by which time £6,220 had been spent, and another £1,309 was spent before 1781 on creating and decorating the 'Cove Room'. Judging from the accounts, and from later photographs, there was no especially elaborate interior decoration, but some of the chimneypieces were in the Rococo taste so popular in Warwickshire in the 1750s, and some Adam-esque neo-classical chimneypieces were introduced later.

The 7th Earl employed John Webb (c.f. Ettington Park) to carry out landscaping in 1818-21. The Earl also made more alterations to the house during the 1820s, probably including the addition of a third floor for bedrooms, and coating the exterior in stucco. This work had cost £2,503 by 1830. Meanwhile the Countess, according to Sharp, introduced 'a splendid collection of ancient carving, adapted with great taste and skill to the conveniences and decorations of the Chapel'.

More drastic changes occurred in the time of the 8th Earl, who succeeded his father in 1865, having married the heiress to the Downing estate, near Holywell (Flintshire). He inherited an estate at Berwick (Shropshire) from an uncle, but sold it off in order to pay off the mortgages on Newnham, and brought a splendid set of 18th-century wrought-iron gates to Newnham, where they were placed in front of the main entrance to the house. At the same time the southern end of 'Capability' Brown's lake was drained, and a sunken formal garden laid out on the site, overlooked by the east wing of the house. The sale of Berwick realised more than expected, and Lord Denbigh therefore decided to embark on what began as 'repairs and alterations' to the house, but developed into a much larger remodelling, partly occasioned by the discovery that the foundations of the east wing were inadequate and had to be reinforced with concrete. The work was carried out in 1876-9 to the designs of T.H. Wyatt, who had already designed the church at Pantasaph (Flintshire) for Lord Denbigh and his first wife. Under his supervision the entrance front took on a striking French Renaissance appearance, with red-brick walls, a projecting porch, and steep pavilion roofs over the centre and the corner towers; towers were also built at the ends of the wings, new kitchens constructed, and a new Gothic Chapel built (in 1888) to the west.

The 8th Earl was a Roman Catholic convert, and he took both his religion and his responsibilities to his dependents seriously; in the words of his daughter Winefride Elwes:

> There were thirteen farms on my father's estate, and he ... made a habit of visiting one or other of his tenant farmers every Sunday afternoon ... [He] was a guardian of the workhouse, the inmates of which he invited each summer to spend a day at Newnham ... Those who needed help and advice came to the back door, while those seeking food and clothing sat in a little room across the courtyard where benches were installed. In cold winters there were fires lit in this little waiting-room; and once, during a great snow, my father himself, wearing a Roman cloak, took the bowls of soup across to the needy.

The house remained the home of the Earls of Denbigh until the Second World War, but it fell victim to the fear of taxation which led to the loss of so many country houses in the post-war years, and was demolished in 1952, leaving the gates in magnificent isolation. But the family continued to own the core of the estate, and the 18th-century stables still survive.

Building book, in possession of the Earl of Denbigh; Hist MS Comm *Denbigh*, v., p.243; D. Stroud, *Capability Brown*; Bodleian Library, Gough Maps 28, f.28 (Brown's design for the façade); Sharp, p.119; J.M. Robinson, *The Wyatts*; W. Elwes, *The Feilding Album* (1950); A. Wood in *Warwickshire History* (1969), pp.3-17.

PACKINGTON HALL

Packington Hall is an impressive late 18th-century classical house standing at the heart of a still flourishing estate a few miles to the east of Birmingham. The manor belonged to Kenilworth Priory in the Middle Ages, and after the Dissolution of the Monasteries it was bought by the tenant, John Fisher, a Gentleman Pensioner of Henry VIII and Steward to Ambrose Dudley, later Earl of Warwick. According to Dugdale, he 'built the whole body of the present Fabrick here at Packinton, as may be seen by the Armes carved on the timber work, and set up in Glass through sundry parts thereof'. An inventory of 1651 shows that the house had a 'matted gallery' as well as the hall, parlours, great chamber and other chambers like those found in any country house of the period. Dugdale made it clear that it stood to the west of the lake known as the Great Pool, probably on or near the site of the present house, a mile or so south-west of the vanished village of Great Packington.

John Fisher died in 1571, and his son Clement, who was knighted by James I, enclosed a park, which still exists. Further improvements were made by Sir Clement's son Robert, who inherited in 1619 and was made a baronet in 1622. Dugdale wrote that he 'raised that large Pool [the Great Pool] Eastwards from the House, built the Lodge in the Park, and much adorn'd this Seat with other places of delight'. These 'places of delight' may have included a mysterious 'newe house on the Hill', which, along with the rest of the estate, was 'rent, torne, and dyvers tymes plundered' by Parliamentary troops in 1642.

Sir Robert died in 1649, and was succeeded by his son Clement, the 2nd Baronet, who later married Jane Lane, the courageous woman who helped Charles II flee the country after the Battle of Worcester. In 1657-8 he employed two carpenters from Knowle, Richard Heath and Edward Assers, to build a new coach house and stable block, and in 1661 he was elected M.P. for Coventry. Not long afterwards he embarked on further improvements to the house and grounds. New gardens were being laid out in 1666, the park was expanded in 1674, and in 1669-71 there were payments to William Daniell for bricklaying at the 'new Hall'. Work was also carried out on the compact red-brick house now known as Packington Old Hall, which stands in the park on the edge of the former village of Great Packington. It is dated 1679 by rainwater heads, and has a striking façade in the 'artisan Mannerist' style, with a three-storied porch crowned by a segmental pediment; inside, there is some good, plain, late 17th-century woodwork. But, attractive though it is, it seems highly unlikely that this house, which is similar in character to many of the more prosperous Warwickshire farmhouses of the time, was ever intended as the main seat of the family.

Sir Clement Fisher was succeeded in 1683 by his nephew, another Sir Clement, who married the daughter of the wealthy Birmingham ironmaster Humphrey Jennens (c.f. Erdington Hall). He built a new house, possibly on the site of the one recorded by Dugdale, and the date 1693 was later inscribed on the roof. Though altered beyond recognition in the 18th century, this house survives as the core of the present building, and an unsigned and undated elevation of a handsome hipped-roofed house inserted into the Aylesford Collection of drawings of Warwickshire houses in the early 19th century may give an idea of its appearance. Dugdale's editor Dr. Thomas also informs us that Sir Clement beautified the grounds with 'delightful Gardens, Statues, Canals, Visto's and other suitable Ornaments', and that he rebuilt 'the House in the middle of the Great Pool' — a tantalising reference to a building which has now totally vanished. According to the traveller John Macky, the new Packington Hall was 'new, and very beautiful; in the Middle of a spacious Park, with fine gardens, Fish-ponds, and a Decoy for Ducks; and may all together vye with the best seats in England'.

Sir Clement Fisher had no male heirs, and when he died in 1729 his estates passed to his only daughter and heiress, who had married Heneage Finch, the 2nd Earl of Aylesford. He later made

I suppose this was for the East Front of Packington Hall

111.   Late 17th-century elevation of a house by an unknown architect in the Aylesford Collection of drawings. It bears the legend: 'I suppose this was for the east front of Packington Hall' and may relate to the building of a new house at Packington by Sir Clement Fisher in 1693.

Packington over to his eldest son, Lord Guernsey, and Guernsey set in motion a series of more far-reaching changes which eventually transformed both the house and the grounds. He was a member of the circle of Warwickshire *virtuosi* which included Sanderson Miller and Sir Roger Newdigate, and in 1746 he consulted Miller about a proposed Gothic building in the grounds. Four years later he married the youngest daughter of the Duke of Somerset, who brought with her a fortune of £50,000, and in 1751 he employed craftsmen including the Warwick plasterer Robert Moore and the carpenter Timothy Lightoler to decorate Lady Charlotte Finch's dressing room; there were also payments in 1759 to the carver Benjamin King for work in the parlour.

Meanwhile, work began on the transformation of the landscape. Guernsey was writing to Miller in 1748 about alterations to the Pool, presumably the Great Pool, and in 1750 he asked for the help of Miller and Sir Roger Newdigate in 'placing the Cascade here, as my plantations depend on it'. Guernsey placed the work in the hands of 'Capability' Brown, who, though still only at the threshold of his career, had already worked for Lord Denbigh at Newnham Paddox (q.v.) and Lord Brooke at Warwick Castle (q.v.). He created the present ornamental lakes out of the earlier Great Pool and the Hall Pool to the west, swept away a formal avenue, and laid out lawns, studded with the usual clumps of trees, with 'belts' of woodland around the circumference of the park. In his plan of the improvements

112.   The stable block at Packington Hall. It was built to the north of the house by David Hiorn in 1756-8.

he also included elevations of new entrance gates, a new Lodge with an open loggia on the first floor, and a grotto, but these remained unbuilt. But there was still enough for Richard Jago to praise, in characteristically enthusiastic couplets, in his poem *Edge Hill* (1767):

> ... In formal Bonds
> The long canal no more confines the stream
> Reluctant — Trees no more their tortur'd limbs
> Lament — no more the long-neglected fields
> Like outlaws banish'd for some vile offence,
> Are hid from sight — from its proud reservoir
> Of amplest size [the Great Pool], and fair indented form
> Along the channel'd lawn the copious stream [the Hall Pool]
> With winding grass the stately current lead.

Even John Byng thought in 1789 that the grounds were 'as well managed as possible' though lacking 'such charms as arise from hills of wood, and a velocity of water'.

  Brown may also have had a share in the design of the new stable block, which was being built under the supervision of David Hiorn of Warwick in 1756 and was finished by 1758. This is a noble building with a tangible air of Roman dignity and gravity which is a feature of all the subsequent buildings at Packington. The stables are arranged around a quadrangle, with a Tuscan portico at the entrance and low towers at the corners, topped with pyramid roofs like those Brown had introduced a year or two earlier at Newnham Paddox (q.v.). This neo-Palladian arrangement was clearly borrowed from Roger Morris's stables at Althorp (Northants), but was probably influenced more immediately by Croome Court (Worcestershire), built to Brown's designs in 1751 and mentioned in Lord Guernsey's letters to Sanderson Miller.

The 2nd Lord Aylesford died in 1757, and his son, with the whole of the resources of the family estates in Warwickshire and the Home Counties at his command, then turned his attention to the further rebuilding and enlargement of the house. His architect was Matthew Brettingham, who had recently published a book of engravings of Holkham Hall (Norfolk), another corner-towered building inspired by classical antiquity, where he had worked as executant architect under William Kent and the Earl of Leicester. Work began in 1763, under the supervision of William Hiorn, but in 1766 Hiorn was replaced by Henry Couchman, a builder recommended by Brettingham. According to Couchman, the project involved 'adding a Wing to each end of the House, filling up the Nich [sic] or half H which was in the West front, and making a Story under all the old House, and then building another Story all over the whole building — there being no atticks in the old House, leaving it the most complete Stone Building instead of Brick'. Couchman took over as architect after Brettingham's death in 1769, and the alterations continued until 1781, by which time £15,222 had been spent.

The rebuilt house was faced throughout with local sandstone, and its design reflects Brettingham's neo-Palladian training. The treatment of the façades is reticent and dignified, though less plain than originally envisaged, with a rusticated ground floor and pedimented centrepieces to the east and west fronts. The centre of the first floor of the west front, which looks out to the Hall Pool, was originally an open loggia or portico *in antis* — an arrangement derived from Inigo Jones's Queen's House at Greenwich which was thought by the traveller Thomas Pennant to be 'most admirably adapted for the encouragement of rheums and rheumatism'.

In contrast to earlier neo-Palladian practice, the main reception rooms were placed on the ground floor, with two top-lit staircases on either side of the central axis leading to the bedrooms upstairs. Work on decorating the interiors proceeded at a leisurely pace. Benjamin King was being paid for carving and Tristram Percival for painting in 1771, and in 1776 the plasterer Thomas Clark, a frequent associate of Brettingham, was finishing the decoration of the main Staircase Hall, an impressive space with cantilevered

113.   The west or garden front of Packington Hall, drawing by Matthew Brettingham. Brettingham enlarged the 1693 house for the 3rd Earl of Aylesford and gave it a new-Palladian exterior, the most striking feature of which was the open loggia on the first floor. The loggia was filled in in 1828.

stairs and an iron balustrade mounting to the top of the house. Next came the Entrance Hall, for which Couchman produced designs in a restrained neo-classical style in 1778; this is separated by a Doric colonnade from an Inner Hall in the centre of the house, through which both the staircase and the saloon or Music Room at the centre of the west front could be reached.

But the most interesting interiors at Packington Hall were carried out in the time of the 4th Earl of Aylesford, who succeeded his father in 1777. He was a skilled artist, who had been taught drawing as an undergraduate at Oxford by John Baptist Malchair, and later became a Fellow of the Society of Antiquaries, a member of the Society of Dilettanti and a trustee of the newly-founded British Museum. He amassed the finest collection of Rembrandt etchings in England, and his own drawings, several of which still survive at Packington, include not only views of Roman buildings, some of them reflecting the influence of Piranesi — whose work he had admired while on the Grand Tour in Italy — but also sensitive studies of the Warwickshire countryside which draw on the influence of the 17th-century Dutch School. In architecture, as some of his own drawings show, he favoured the most advanced neo-classical taste, and at Packington he had the opportunity of indulging that taste to the full.

His architect was the Italian-born Joseph Bonomi, who had worked for some years in the office of Robert Adam and subsequently taught Lord Aylesford architecture and perspective. In 1782, a year after Aylesford's marriage to the eldest daughter of Lord Weymouth, Bonomi made designs for the Gallery in the south wing, which the 3rd Earl had intended as a sculpture gallery. But his first executed room was the Music Room at the centre of the west front, so named after an organ (now in Great

114.   The Gallery at Packington Hall. This is the most impressive of the rooms created for the 4th Earl of Aylesford by Joseph Bonomi. The 'Pompeian' decorations on the walls and ceilings were inspired by a book published in 1786, and were carried out by Jean François Rigaud.

Packington church) which was inherited from the Jennens family and had been played by Handel. The room has a delicate, somewhat Adam-esque, plaster ceiling which may have been executed by the younger Joseph Rose, who received payments for work between 1784 and 1786. By this time work had started on the Gallery, redesigned by Bonomi for the display of Lord Aylesford's collection of Greek vases. This magnificent room is mainly notable for its Pompeian-style decoration, the first use in England of this quintessentially neo-classical mode of design. The walls and ceiling are adorned with delicate paintings on a black ground, taken from a book published in 1786 by the Frenchman Nicholas Ponce on the decoration of the Baths of Titus in Rome. Grecian-style chairs of the *klismos* pattern were placed around the walls, and there are splendid marble chimneypieces reflecting the influence of Piranesi. Domenico Bartoli received payment for the scagliola coating of the Corinthian columns dividing the room in 1785, and in the next three years there were payments to Joseph Rose, to Giovanni Borgnis, and to the French painter Jean François Rigaud, who had settled in England in 1772. Rigaud's son recorded that his father was responsible for the paintings on the Gallery ceiling 'alluding to the Mysteries of Bacchus', and he also carried out decorative painting elsewhere in the house, notably on the ceiling of the Dining Room and in a roundel in the ceiling of the Library.

The 4th Earl also carried out improvements to the grounds and the estate. He was a friend of Sir Uvedale Price, one of the apostles of the Picturesque, and in 1814 Britton commented on the way in which he had given the grounds 'an air of wildness, likely to convey general pleasure'. A new drive was laid out in 1787 and a flower garden formed in 1789. The same year also saw the laying out of a new road (the 'straight mile') across Meriden Heath, and the construction beside it of a model farm, Heath Farm, with austere buildings which may well have been designed by Bonomi. Bonomi was also responsible for designing the equally austere Forest Hall, near Meriden, the headquarters of the Woodmen of Arden, an archery club of which Lord Aylesford — 'perhaps the best gentleman archer in the Kingdom', as Byng called him — was a co-founder. But Bonomi's main contribution to Packington was the building in 1789 of a new parish church on an isolated site in the park. With its uncompromising exterior and tenebrous vaulted interior, this is one of the most powerful neo-classical buildings of its date in Europe, paying an even more compelling tribute than the Hall to the late 18th century's obsession with the Antique.

Lord Aylesford died in 1812, and in the same year his son, the 5th Earl, employed Henry Hakewill to build terraces on the south and west sides of the house, obscuring the basement. In 1828 Hakewill designed a top-lit Billiard Room on the first floor over the Inner Hall and filled in the adjacent open loggia for use as a subsidiary Library for the 5th Earl's extensive book collection. These rooms were plainly decorated, but drawings survive to show that more opulent schemes were considered. The house was then left untouched until 1862, when the 6th Earl employed William Burn, one of the most popular mid-Victorian country-house architects, to build a conservatory between the house and the stables, replacing an earlier one shown in Neale's *Views of Seats* (1821), and a carriage-porch on the east front. These additions, which have since been removed, were executed in a manner broadly agreeable to the rest of the building. The house still remains the home of the Earls of Aylesford, and has been expertly restored after fire damage in 1979.

Drawings and Aylesford papers at Packington Hall; *CL* 16/23 July 1970, 15/22 July 1971; Tennant, *Edgehill and Beyond* (1992), pp.47-8; John Macky, *Journey through England* (1732); D. Stroud, *Capability Brown*; WRO, Z14 (Henry Couchman's MS autobiography); T. Pennant, *The Journey from Chester to London* (1782); Torrington diaries, pp.206-7; Aylesford Collection, ff. 563-4; Brewer, p.321; *Print Collectors' Quarterly* xii Oct 1924, pp.263-292; *Walpole Society* l (1984) (Rigaud's biography); D. Fitzgerald, "A Gallery after the Antique", *Connoisseur* clxxxi Sept 1972, pp.2-13; D. Watkin, 'Bonomi at Packington', *Georgian Group Report and Journal* (1989); information from the Earl of Aylesford.

PACKWOOD HOUSE

The builder of this timber-framed house was probably William Fetherston (d.1601), a member of a family who established themselves as yeoman farmers at Packwood, a small parish in the heart of the Forest of Arden, in the 15th century, and gradually built up a small but productive estate there. With only nine hearths in 1663, it was not one of the great houses of Elizabethan Warwickshire, and it was not even, strictly speaking, a manor house. But since the lords of the manor (the Spencers of Claverdon) were non-resident the 'great mancient house', as it was called in 1599, became by default the most important house in the parish. It was built on a compact square plan, quite different from that of a typical medieval house, with four main rooms on each floor; there were two massive central chimneystacks of brick, two main stories of rooms, and gabled attics. Externally, as in many West Midlands houses of the late 16th century, the outer walls were originally adorned with an impressive display of decorative framing, with a criss-cross pattern on the first floor and quatrefoils in squares at gable level, and projecting bay windows let light into the main rooms. An inventory taken on the death of William Fetherston's son John in 1634 shows that the main rooms on the ground floor were the hall and parlour (probably the present Dining Room), neither of them very richly furnished. Upstairs there were bedrooms, including a 'painted chamber', and next to the house were the normal farm buildings, including a corn chamber, a cheese chamber and a servants' chamber.

115.   Packwood House from the south, drawing of c.1756. The late 16th-century timber house overlooks the walled garden created by John or Thomas Fetherston in the late 17th century, with John Fetherston's stable block to the right. The niches for beehives at the base of the wall in the foreground still survive.

116.   Packwood House from the east, showing the stable block built by Roger Hurlbut in the 1660s. The house has been covered in rendering since at least the early 19th century.

John Fetherston described himself as a yeoman, but his son, another John, was trained as a lawyer and married into one of the local gentry families, the Woodwards of Butlers Marston. He felt entitled to call himself 'esquire', and soon after the Restoration he built an attractive new L-shaped red-brick stable block for his horses — a sure mark of gentlemanly status — at right angles to the house, with a kitchen garden and a set of farm buildings on the other side of the road which runs in front of the house. There were also some relatively minor alterations to the house itself, including the addition of three unidentified rooms in 1670, possibly those in the projecting wing in front of the main entrance, containing the present Parlour. The builder was the local carpenter Roger Hurlbut.

The most important change in the late 17th century was the creation of a formal garden. Either John Fetherston or his son Thomas, who succeeded him in 1670, walled off the courtyard in front of the present main entrance to the east and created another walled garden to the south, with gazebos at the corners, a viewing mound, and niches for beehives at the bottom of the wall nearest the house. A Cold Bath on the western side of the house was also in existence by 1723. The southern part of the garden is now famous for its collection of clipped yew trees said, according to a tradition recorded by the architect Reginald Blomfield in 1892, to represent Jesus, the Apostles and the Multitude listening to the Sermon on the Mount. This is an attractive conceit which could well have appealed to the 17th-century mind, but it has been recently shown that most of the yews were only planted in the mid-19th century, when topiary gardens became highly fashionable. Whatever the actual age of the trees, the ensemble evokes the spirit of late 17th-century gardening, unaffected by the later mania for landscaping.

When Thomas Fetherston died in 1714 the estate, which had now grown to between 600 and 700 acres, went to his great-nephew, from whom it passed to his daughter, the wife of Thomas Leigh of Aldridge (Staffordshire). Their daughter Catherine Fetherston Leigh died unmarried in 1769, and the estate was then inherited by Thomas, the eight-year-old younger son of William Dilke of Maxstoke Castle (q.v.) and his wife, the half-sister of Catherine Fetherston Leigh. A drawing of 1756, now at Maxstoke, shows the house in its original form, with its timber framing still exposed, but by the middle of the 19th century

117.   The Long Gallery at Packwood House, built in 1925-32 as part of Graham Baron Ash's additions to the house. It still contains some of his collection of tapestries and furniture.

the walls had been covered with cement rendering, presumably to preserve the timbers. This had visually unfortunate results, which were not mitigated by the insertion of sash windows.

Thomas Fetherston Dilke died in 1814 and was succeeded by his younger brother Charles (d.1831). According to West, he kept up 'the true style of an English gentleman who seems to feel a patriotic pride in being clad in the produce of his own estate. His hat, coat and under apparel, stockings, &c, and even his shoes are the produce of his own lands ... and were manufactured within his own walls'. The family's conservatism must explain the survival of the house and, even more, the gardens, but in the mid-19th century the house was let, and the estate was finally sold to George Arton in 1869. The contents were then dispersed, but the gardens remained in a good state of preservation, and were even improved by the planting of some of the present topiary.

In its present form, Packwood is an excellent example of the way in which the profits of industry have been used to save and restore neglected old houses in the 20th century. In 1905 the house was sold to Alfred Ash, who had inherited a fortune in zinc and other metals built up by his father in Birmingham in the 19th century. He bought the house for his son Graham Baron Ash, who, like many men of his generation, turned his back on the grimy sources of his wealth and became a fastidious and obsessive collector, haunting salerooms and accumulating furniture, pictures and tapestries, mostly of the 16th and 17th centuries (some 18th-century purchases were sold after the Second World War). In order to accommodate these purchases, and to entertain guests in the style which Ash thought appropriate, the house underwent a drastic remodelling. Mullioned and transomed windows were reinstated, a new staircase added, the old galleried Hall transformed, an open-roofed room known as the Great Hall created out of a former barn, and a Long Gallery built to link it to the main house at ground-floor level. Some changes had been been made by 1914, but the house in its present form is the result of a second set of alterations carried out in 1925-32 by the Birmingham architect Edwin Reynolds, of the firm of Ward, Kendrick and Reynolds. A drawing in the house shows that Ash originally intended to reveal the exposed timber framing, but this was unfortunately not put into effect.

The main interest of the interior lies in the contents, which came from many different places but which blend together in a seemingly effortless way. Some of the most impressive objects, including the tapestries and refectory table in the Great Hall, came from Baddesley Clinton (q.v.), only a short distance away, and most of the chimneypieces, stained glass and even floorboards came from other houses which had fallen on hard times; the chimneypiece and plaster overmantel in the Great Hall came from a former inn in Stratford-upon-Avon. Baron Ash — as he was always, revealingly, known — gave an indication of his motives when he wrote: 'I do this as an antidote to the decay and demolition of so many old houses all over the country. I am rescuing whatever I can from other places and preserving it here. Of course, there are many glaring examples of "over" restoration, and I am proceeding with the utmost caution'. The result was a series of interiors which are as evocative of the antiquarian taste of the inter-war period as any others in England.

Ash also made improvements to the gardens, especially to the south-east of the house, where a sunken garden lined with herbaceous borders was created (Plate IX). He gave the property to the National Trust in 1941, but moved away six years later, devoting the rest of his life to the restoration of another old house, Wingfield Castle in Suffolk. Packwood has since remained virtually as he left it, a beguiling monument to the continuing appeal of the 'Old English' style to the 20th-century sensibility.

CL 4 Jan 1902, 9/16 Aug 1924, 19 Oct 1989; J.J. Belton, *The Story of Packwood* (1951); M.W. Farr, *The Fetherstons of Packwood in the 17th Century* (Dugdale Society Occasional Paper 1968); SBT, DR 12/27 (inventory 1634); West, *Directory of Warwickshire* (1830); W.H. Hutton, *Highways and Byways in Shakespeare's Country* (1914), 296-7; G.S. Thomas, *Gardens of the National Trust*, pp.192-3; Packwood House guidebook (1992).

RADWAY GRANGE

The main interest of this moderately-sized stone-built house lies in the fact that for more than 60 years it was the home of Sanderson Miller, one of the pioneers of the Gothic Revival in the mid-18th century. In the late Middle Ages there was a monastic grange or farm belonging to the monks of Stoneleigh on or near the site of the present house, at the foot of the Edge Hill escarpment. In 1554 the land was bought by Walter Lyght or Light (d.1597), and from him it passed, by the marriage of his daughter Elizabeth, to Robert Washington of Sulgrave (Northamptonshire), an ancestor of the first President of the U.S.A. The house was built at the end of the 16th or the beginning of the 17th century, either by Robert Washington's younger son Walter, who described himself as 'of Radway', or by his son John. It was a square two-storied building of brown Hornton stone, with gabled attics and two parallel roofs: an early example of the 'double pile' arrangement, also found at Packwood House (q.v.), with one large central chimneystack to heat the rooms. The house was not especially large (there were eight hearths in 1663), and, except for the rather innovative plan, there was little to distinguish it from the other small stone-built manor houses and substantial farmhouses which were being built in large numbers in south Warwickshire at the time.

In 1642 the Battle of Edge Hill, the first major encounter of the English Civil War, was fought over the fields of Radway, and not long afterwards John Washington sold the Grange to William Goodwin of Hornton, just over the Oxfordshire border; Goodwin also acquired Arlescote House (q.v.), not far away to the east, which he left to his eldest son. Radway went to his younger son Thomas, but he went bankrupt, and in 1715 the estate, consisting of 70 acres of enclosed land and 240 acres in the common fields, was sold by Act of Parliament to Sanderson Miller, the father of the architect. He was a merchant from Banbury, and served as Sheriff of Warwickshire in 1728. He died in 1737, leaving the property to his 20-year-old son, who had already developed a taste for books and antiquities which he nurtured as an undergraduate at Oxford in the years after 1734. A few years later he began to give tangible expression to these interests.

Sanderson Miller's buildings at Radway are interesting both as his own first efforts at architectural design and also as the first in a remarkable group of structures which make mid-18th-century Warwickshire one of the most important areas in England for the early Gothic Revival. Miller wanted to modernise his house, but he also wanted to express the historical associations of the estate. This involved giving the house a Gothic face-lift, improving the grounds, which stretched to the top of Edge Hill, planting trees, and erecting buildings in the small hamlet on the hill-top. He began the garden improvements soon after inheriting the estate by building a cascade and viewing platform at the top of the hill; they have long since vanished, but they were described by the poet and gardener William Shenstone in 1750: 'At the top is a Reservoir ... it falls over three rustick arches, runs down through broken stone work to a Bason in the midst of which is a Jetteau [*jet d'eau*] and on each side tumuli or little mounds of earth artificially cut up. But this is a juvenile performance, and only retained because it is there and has cost him money'.

The first building was a thatched cottage (since altered and spoilt) for estate workers at the top of the hill, built in 1743-4 of coursed rubble from the Hornton quarries and lit by pointed-arched windows: an interesting, and for its time probably unique, example of the self-conscious revival of vernacular architecture, looking forward to John Nash's Blaise Hamlet near Bristol and to countless *cottages ornées*. Next to this, on the spot where Charles I was reputed to have raised his standard at the beginning of the Battle of Edge Hill, Miller built a much more ambitious structure in the form of an octagonal tower modelled on Guy's Tower at Warwick Castle (q.v.), linked by a drawbridge to a lower,

118.   The Edge Hill tower in the 1930s. It was built by Sanderson Miller to his own designs in the 1740s, and his thatched cottage of 1743-4 can be seen in the background.

square tower of 1750, with a set of sham ruins (since demolished) on the opposite side of the road, dismissed by Shenstone as being 'too much of a solid lump'. The mason was William Hitchcox, who was later involved with Miller in the early stages of the rebuilding of Arbury Hall (q.v.). The main tower served both as a gate lodge, leading to a steep drive which descended to the house far below, and as an eye-catcher to be seen from the house rising above the trees which Miller planted. Like other 18th-century garden buildings, it was also used for occasional meals, a practice which did not fill Miller's friend George Lyttelton with enthusiasm: 'Mrs Lyttleton will like to dine at the house better then at the Castle, and my stomach prefers hot meat to cold ... so, if you please, we will dine at the foot of the hill and have the pleasure of looking up at your Castle Old and New'. Inside, the main feature was a large upstairs room with plaster embellishments by Robert Moore, painted glass windows, coats of arms on the ceiling, and ogee-arched niches, one of which contained (or was to contain, according to Pococke), a stone statue of Caractacus in chains 'modelled, under Mr. Miller's directions, by a country-man of great genius now settled in London'; he was James Lovell, who worked at Hagley Hall (Worcestershire), and subsequently at Newnham Paddox (q.v.).

In his poem *Edge Hill* (1767), William Jago was eloquent in his praise for Miller's improvements to the grounds, which continued after the completion of the tower, and included the construction of an urn (since vanished) to commemorate a visit by William Pitt the elder in 1754, during which he planted two Scotch firs and a mountain ash:

Thanks Miller to thy paths
That ease our winding steps! Thanks to the fount,
The trees, the flowers, imparting to the sense
Fragrant or dulcet sound of murm'ring rill,
And stilling every tumult in the breast!
And oft the stately towers, that overtop
The rising wood, and oft the broken arch,
Or mould'ring wall, well taught to counterfeit
The waste of time, to solemn thought excite,
And crown with graceful pomp the shaggy hill.

Miller's alterations to the house were less ambitious, largely because he decided to channel his relatively limited resources into the gardens and the estate, for which an Inclosure Act was passed in 1756. A drawing dating probably from the early 1740s shows the old square house embellished with pinnacles and canted bay windows with Gothic detailing on the south front, facing towards Edge Hill. These windows, which were later copied in the library and parlour at Arbury, were built in 1746, and by this time Miller had extended the house to the east and given it a new façade flanked by pinnacles (which have since lost their tops), with a somewhat incoherent feature surmounted by a pediment in the centre. A new doorway to the south front followed in 1752, and there was also some extensive internal remodelling, though Miller later bemoaned the fact that funds did not permit him to indulge his taste for Gothic decoration beyond a fairly rudimentary level:

119.   Radway Grange from the south east, early 19th-century drawing in an interleaved copy of A. Beesley, *History of Banbury*. The bay windows on the left were added to the late 16th- or early 17th-century house by Sanderson Miller in 1746, and the pedimented eastern extension was built at about the same time.

My House! 'tis true a small and old one,
Yet now 'tis warm tho' once a cold one.
My study holds 3,000 volumes
And yet I sigh for Gothick Columns
Such as Sir Roger [Newdigate], learned Knight of Taste,
At Arbury so well has placed.

But the remodelled house was comfortable enough to attract visitors from Miller's extensive circle of friends — who included the novelist Henry Fielding as well as members of the extensive Pitt/Lyttleton clan — and the staircase, as well as some Gothic chimneypieces and other details, still survive there now.

Miller had a mental breakdown in 1759, but subsequently recovered and lived until 1780. His descendants made relatively few alterations to either house or grounds, apart from the construction of a new porch on the west side of the house in the 19th century (date unknown) and an obelisk on the hill-top in 1854. The estate remained in the hands of the Miller family until 1916, when it was sold. It was sold again, to Henry Fenwick, in 1922, and he employed Percy Morley Horder, an architect with a good understanding of materials and texture, to make tactful alterations both to the interior and the exterior; the most important of the latter was the addition of a service wing to the north-east corner of the house, almost indistinguishable in style and detailing from the original Elizabethan or Jacobean building. The house was sold to Colonel Starkey in 1925, and he carried out improvements to the gardens. His family remained at Radway until 1975, and since then the house has been sold on at least two more occasions.

WRO, CR 125B (building accounts), CR 1382 (drawings); G. Miller, *Rambles round the Edge Hills* (1900), pp.18-31; L. Dickins & M. Stanton, *An Eighteenth Century Correspondence* (1910); *CL* 6/13 Sept 1946; W. Hawkes, 'Sanderson Miller' (thesis deposited in WRO); *The Letters of William Shenstone* (ed. M. Williams 1939), pp.252-4; A. Wood & W. Hawkes, 'Radway, Warwickshire: the Making of a Landscape', *Jnl. of Garden History* vii (2), (1987), pp.103-123; NMR photo and sales partics.

RAGLEY HALL

The first mention of a dwelling at Ragley occurs in 1370, when John Rous obtained licence to crenellate the manor-house on his estate, not far to the south of Alcester. Dugdale referred to a 'stately gatehouse of stone ... imbattled like a castle', and went on to say that Rous had 'a Commission to build the rest of his dwelling House here answerably, and to fortify it with strong walls of lime and stone, in like sort embattled'. The Rous family were succeeded by the Bromes, and in 1591 the property was sold by George Brome to Sir John Conway, the former Governor of Ostend and author of several devotional tracts. His family, which originated in Wales, had acquired the adjacent manor of Arrow by marriage earlier in the century, along with lands in Warwickshire and Worcestershire. His son was a soldier who went on the Earl of Essex's expedition to Cadiz in 1596, and later served as Secretary of State under James I and Charles I, before being raised to the peerage as Lord Conway in 1625. He acquired large estates in the north of Ireland and also in Wales, where he puchased Conway Castle from the Crown, and in 1628 he was made Viscount Conway. His son, the 2nd Viscount, intended to rebuild Conway Castle as his main residence, but the plan was abandoned because of the Civil War and he died in France in 1655. He was succeeded by his son, who was made Governor of three of the counties of Ulster in 1674 and also served for a time as one of Charles II's Secretaries of State. He took the decision to build a new house at Ragley, and it is his house which survives, though in a much-remodelled form, today.

Lord Conway's house was the most ambitious in late 17th-century Warwickshire. It was placed on a hilltop site to 'command the prospect', well away from the nearest village, and Kip's engraving of *c.*1698 shows that it was intended to be set in the middle of an arrangement of formal avenues, gardens and parterres: a completely controlled environment proclaiming man's mastery over nature and the nobleman's mastery over the landscape. Work was in progress by 1677, when Lord Conway told his cousin Sir Edward Harley that he was:

> ... playing the fool in laying out money upon building, having chiefly undertaken it because I find my grandfather [the 1st Lord Conway] designed to build here; yet I am not satisfied with myself. I have almost finished one side of the outbuilding and half the garden wall, which I am planting with fruit trees. Next year I hope to finish the other part of the outbuilding and the rest of the garden wall. I have also the model of the house designed.

Work on the house did not begin until 1680, and by this time there had been some modifications to the original design. The model referred to in Lord Conway's letter was probably made by 'Mr Holbert', who is first mentioned as builder of the house in 1679. He was almost certainly either Roger or William Hurlbut, one of the carpenters who had remodelled the state apartment at Warwick Castle (q.v.) a few years earlier; one of the Hurlbuts had already designed a stable block for Lord Conway at his house at Portmore, Co. Antrim, and William Hurlbut designed and built the Market House in Warwick in 1670. But in 1678 Lord Conway showed the model to the well-known scientist and amateur architect Roger Hooke, a friend of Sir Christopher Wren, and in the following year Hooke made a series of suggestions for improvements, some of which were carried out and some ignored. In its final form therefore the house owed something to Hurlbut, something to Hooke, and probably something to Conway himself.

The house contained two stories of equal height over a high basement or ground floor, like the 'rustick' of a neo-Palladian house, and attics in the roof. Hooke's main influence seems to have been on the plan, which, unusually among English houses of its date, was almost square. The layout incorporated several features derived from French domestic architecture, notably the provision of 'pavilions'

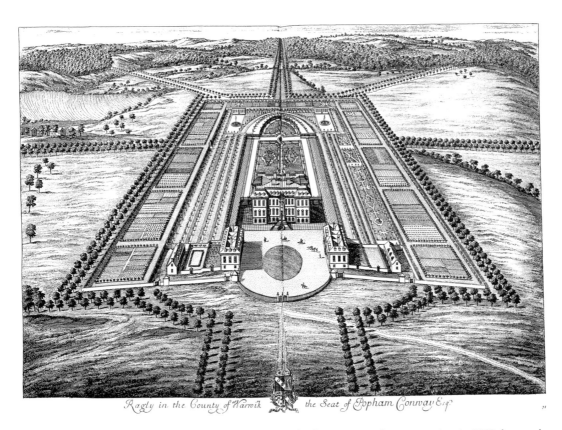

Ragly in the County of Warwik   the Seat of Popham Conway Esqr

120.   Ragley Hall, from Kip's *Britannia Illustrata* (1707). The house was under construction in 1677, but work was halted by Lord Conway's death in 1683 and it seems unlikely that the elaborate formal gardens were ever completed.

at the four corners, each of them containing an 'apartment' on each of the main floors made up of a drawing room, bedchamber, closet and back stairs (Plate X). Hooke claimed in 1680 that each apartment was self-sufficient, 'without all intermingling or running through one another and yet in the second storey you may go round the house through each of them'. The main axis of the house contained a very deep Hall and a Saloon, and on either side there were spacious staircases, a Library and a Chapel. Hooke made suggestions for the decoration of the Hall, which was to contain 'niches which may serve to receive statues, busts, vases or the like according to the most noble way of the Ancients and some of our better sort of modern buildings'. But these were not carried out, and there is no indication of what the other rooms were intended to look like.

There were also several changes of mind over the exterior. An elevation, probably by Hooke and now in the British Library, shows a rather awkward disposition of rectangular, oval and round-headed windows, with pediments over the central three bays and each pavilion, a broad staircase leading up to the front door and a balustrade and central cupola on the roof. As built, the more bizarre features were left out, and the house had a relatively conventional exterior, with walls of the local blue lias stone, sandstone dressings, hipped roofs and little in the way of external adornment, apart from a central pediment supported on a pair of giant half-columns (a device later used at Hanbury Hall, Worcestershire, and at Foxcote (q.v.). The house was approached through an open entrance courtyard, then a relatively novel feature in England, flanked by the outbuildings referred to in Lord Conway's letter of 1678, and closed on the far side by iron railings and gates.

167

Lord Conway died childless in 1683, only four years after being given an earldom, and the house was left an empty shell for more than 50 years, its elaborate formal gardens and parterres presumably never finished, contrary to the impression conveyed in Kip's engraving. Conway left the estate to his second cousin Popham Seymour, son of Sir Edward Seymour of Maiden Bradley (Wiltshire), a descendant of the powerful clan which had played such a large part in the politics of Tudor England. But Conway's widow continued living at Ragley, and in his will he instructed her and the trustees of the estate to finish the house 'out of the rents and profits of my estate in Ireland ... according to that model and design which I began and carried it on in'. It seems likely that his wishes were respected, at least so far as the walls were concerned, but the rooms were left undecorated, as Jeremiah Milles made clear when he visited Ragley in 1743: 'You ascend to the Hall, by a double flight of stairs, which is indeed a noble room, but has nothing except bare walls: on each hand are 2 rooms, one behind the other: and then on each hand a grand staircase. Behind the Hall is a Saloon with a room at each end. The form of the house above stairs is pretty much the same ... Behind this grand house is a small old irregular building, which is the present mansion house of Lord Conway'.

The Conway title was revived for Popham Seymour's brother and successor, and when Jeremiah Milles visited the house his son, the 2nd Lord Conway, was already contemplating making it habitable. The carpenter John Phillips (c.f. Alscot Park) was altering and reslating the roof in 1749, and references by him to 'setting the cornice' suggest that the present arrangement of the roof set behind a stone cornice and balustrade may date from this time, although alterations to the cornice were made 30 years later. Work on the interiors began in 1750, when Lord Conway was made Earl of Hertford (an old Seymour title), but it seems to have proceeded at a very leisurely pace, and in 1751 Hertford's cousin Horace Walpole wrote that the house was: '... but just covered in, after so many years. They have just begun to inhabit the naked walls of the upper story [sic]; the great one is unfloored and unceiled. The hall is magnificent, sixty by forty, and thirty-eight high ... The other apartments are lofty, and in quantity, though I had suspected that this leviathan hall must have devoured half the other chambers'. But when Bishop Pococke visited the house in 1756 he reported that the Hall had just been 'new modelled, and embellished with ornaments of stucco', and in the following year Horace Walpole (whose portrait by Reynolds hangs in the house), told one of his correspondents that the house 'has had a great deal done to it since I was there last. [Capability] Browne [sic] has improved both the ground and the water [the lake to the south-west of the house], though not quite to perfection. This is the case of the house; where there are no striking faults, but it wants a few Chute or Bentley touches. I have recommended some dignifying of the saloon with Seymours and Fitzroys, Henry the Eighths and Charles the Seconds. They will correspond well to the proudest situation imaginable'.

Lord Hertford did not take Walpole's advice over the decoration of the interior, and the Saloon was not made habitable for another twenty years. The main achievement of the 1750s was the decoration of the 'leviathan hall' to the designs of James Gibbs, with plasterwork by his collaborator Giuseppe Artari, who was working in the house between 1756 and 1760, and possibly by other craftsmen. Though Gibbs died in 1754 before work got under way, the essence of the scheme is his, with paired pilasters of the Composite order encompassing the room and a high coved ceiling above. In its essentially Baroque character the design looks back to some of Gibbs's interiors of the 1720s, like the Octagon at Orleans House, Twickenham (Middlesex), or the Saloon at Sudbrook Park, Richmond (Surrey), but Artari's embellishments, especially the cartouches between the paired columns and the wreaths of flowers under the coves of the ceiling, introduce an up-to-date note of the Rococo. The iconography celebrates British military and Imperial prowess — the decoration of the room began in the year of the outbreak of the Seven Years' War — with Britannia holding a spear in the central roundel of the ceiling, War and Peace over the fireplaces, heads of negroes and American Indians over the side doors, and military trophies on the coves.

There is equally fine plasterwork, possibly also by Artari, in the other rooms decorated in the 1750s. By now the 17th-century fashion for 'apartments' had gone out of fashion, and the rooms were intended for receiving guests and for more private use by the family. The Dining Room (now the Music Room)

121.   The Great Hall at Ragley Hall, looking west. The Baroque decorative scheme was designed by James Gibbs, but work did not begin until after his death in 1754. Giuseppe Artari was among the craftsmen responsible for the superb Rococo plasterwork in 1756–60.

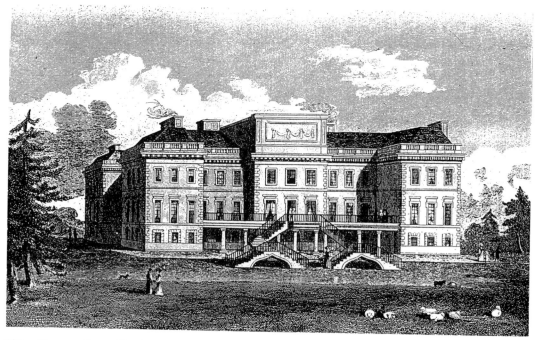

122.   The west front of Ragley Hall, drawing by T. Radcliffe, c.1830. The attic, colonnade and stairs are part of James Wyatt's alterations to the house in 1778-83, but the stairs were removed when the formal garden to the west of the house was laid out by Robert Marnock in the 1870s.

and the Breakfast Room, to the north of the Hall, came into the former category, the former with a Bacchic design over the fireplace and the latter with a representation of 'Leda and the Swan' on the ceiling. To the south was a more simply decorated room now used as the Study, and other family rooms. Only one of the rooms on the garden front was decorated at this time, the present Green Drawing Room, with another good plaster ceiling; it now contains a pair of splendidly extravagant Rococo mirrors in the Chinese Chippendale manner.

The other change to the interior came with the conversion of the old Library, to the north of the Hall, into a Dining Room and the removal of the library to the room on the opposite side of the Hall which had formerly been, or had been intended as, the chapel. At the same time Wyatt also re-sashed and lowered the windows on the main floor and designed (or possibly remodelled) the stable block to the north of the house, with the stables arranged around a semicircular courtyard. He was also responsible for altering the cornice and adding the Ionic portico to the entrance front (Plate X), which is

Having made the rooms on the east side of the house habitable, the Earl of Hertford, who had been Lord Chamberlain in 1766, paused before decorating the rest of those on the garden side, to the west. The work was undertaken, as the architect James Wyatt later wrote, 'for the express accommodation of His Majesty [George III] and His Family ... These works were so extensive and the completion of them so necessary to the comfort of the House that, had they not been put into the state I left them by a very extraordinary exertion, the Marquis's family alas could not have inhabited the house '. By the time work began, in 1778, taste had moved away from the Rococo to the more chaste neo-classical style introduced into England by Robert Adam and his contemporaries. Wyatt's style of interior decoration was every bit as delicate and refined as Adam's, as can be seen in the chimneypieces and ceilings of the Saloon and the rooms in the former 'apartment' to the north of it, now called the Ante-Room and the Mauve Drawing Room. The walls of these rooms were deliberately left unadorned to allow for the hanging of portraits and Old Master paintings, some of which still remain in the house.

reached by a semi-circular staircase with a splendid wrought-iron balustrade. Though the portico had the unfortunate effect of darkening the Hall, it served to emphasise the centre of what was otherwise a very long façade, and gave it an orthodox neo-Palladian appearance which belied its real age. There were also alterations to the garden front, notably the addition of an attic over the three central bays, and the building of a colonnade linking the two 'pavilions' at each end, with a curious arrangement of staircases allowing access to the Saloon. The stone came from local quarries, blue lias from Wixford and Temple Grafton and sandstone from Inkberrow. Meanwhile the gardens were further landscaped, and early 19th-century illustrations show tree-studded lawns surrounding the house on all sides.

By the time Lord Hertford died in 1794, a year after being made a Marquess, Ragley was at last fully decorated and furnished. His successors made some changes, but they were relatively minor. The 2nd Marquess was a friend of the Prince Regent — who was also on intimate terms with the Marchioness — and the room in the south-western corner of the house known as the Prince Regent's Bedroom contains a bed surmounted by a representation of the Prince's feathers, made when he first visited Ragley in 1796. The 2nd Marquess must have also been responsible for introducing the sumptuous red curtains and hangings and gilded furniture in the Saloon. The house was largely abandoned in the time of the 3rd and 4th Marquesses (1822-70); they both spent most of their time in Paris, where they built up the collection now known as the Wallace Collection, named after the illegitimate son of the 4th Marquess, and now displayed in the former Hertford House in the West End of London.

The 5th Marquess brought Ragley back into a habitable state in 1870-2, installing a new heating system and gas lighting, improving the kitchens and service accommodation, and refurnishing some of

123.   The Red Saloon at Ragley Hall. This room, at the centre of the garden front, was decorated by James Wyatt. But the French-style furnishings date from the time of the 2nd Marquess of Hertford, who entertained the Prince Regent at Ragley in 1794.

the rooms. His architect was a relatively obscure figure, William Tasker, who also built Park Hall at Salford Priors for his son, the future 6th Marquess, and he was largely responsible for the present appearance of the Dining Room and North Staircase. But the most important change was the creation of a formal garden on the west front by Robert Marnock, the designer of the rose garden at Warwick Castle (q.v.). This involved the removal of Wyatt's staircase and the building of terraces close to the house; despite some changes the garden still survives largely intact.

With the retrenchment which marked the history of most great estates in the 20th century, the future of Ragley Hall was more than once thrown into doubt. The Birmingham architect C.E. Bateman produced plans for drastically reducing the size of the house in 1930 (the designs can be seen there), and there were calls to abandon it completely after the Second World War, when it was used as a hospital. Instead the present (8th) Marquess, who lived after the War in a farmhouse on the estate, decided in 1956 to move back in, embarking on a long programme of redecoration and repair with the aid of Government grants, and opening the house to the public in 1958. He has left his mark by commissioning the artist Graham Rust to decorate the South Staircase Hall with Tiepolo-inspired murals of 'The Temptation', featuring members of the family as onlookers (1969-82) — something of which Horace Walpole might well have approved.

M.I. Batten, 'The Architecture of Dr. Robert Hooke', *Walpole Society* xxv (1936-7); BL, Add MSS 31323 (plan of house), 5238 (elevation), 15776 (Jeremiah Milles tour); Seymour-Conway papers in WRO (CR 114A); *Letters of Horace Walpole* (ed P. Toynbee) iii, pp.65-6, iv, p.174 ; *CL* 1/8 May 1958; *Archaeological Journal* cxxviii (1971), pp.230-3; J.M. Robinson, *The Wyatts* (1979), pp.73, 245; Ragley Hall guidebook (1984).

VIII   John Constable's painting of the entrance front at Malvern Hall in 1820. The picture was painted after the artist's second visit to the house, and shows the improvements to the grounds recently carried out by Henry Greswolde Lewis. They brought a degree of intricacy to the setting, in keeping with contemporary gardening practice.

IX   Packwood House from the south east. The garden in the foreground was created by Graham Baron Ash between the wars, and he also carried out a thorough remodelling of the late 16th-century house.

X   Ragley Hall from the south east. Two of the four corner 'pavilions' of Lord Conway's house can be seen, along with the portico added by James Wyatt in 1778. The house is built of local lias stone, with grey sandstone dressings.

SALFORD HALL

During the Middle Ages the manor of Abbots Salford was part of the possessions of Evesham Abbey, only a few miles away over the Worcestershire boundary, and in the 15th century one of the abbots, possibly Richard Hawkesbury (1467-77), built a country retreat here, part of which survives as the west wing of the present house. The ground floor is built of the local blue lias stone, but the upper floors are timber-framed, with close studding on the much-restored south gable end. This attractive building became the service wing of the present house, the rest of which, according to an inscription over the porch, was being built in 1602 (later incorrectly recarved as 1662). The builder was John Alderford, a Worcestershire man who was steward of the manor of Haselor, part of the possessions of Sir Fulke

124.   The north front of Salford Hall in 1954. The gable-end to the right of the porch is part of the timber-framed house of the 15th-century Abbots of Evesham. The rest of the house was built *c.*1602 by John Alderford. Since this picture was taken the house has been refurbished.

Greville. He married the daughter and heiress of Anthony Littleton, a younger son of a family from Frankley (Worcestershire) who bought the Abbots Salford estate from Sir Philip Hoby, the first lay owner. Alderford died in 1606, leaving the property to his daughter and her husband Charles Stanford; their names and the date 1610 appear on a bell, and may refer to the completion of the project.

The rebuilt Salford Hall consisted of three ranges around a narrow open courtyard. The west range is the medieval abbots' building, remodelled and extended with new chimneystacks and a staircase during the 16th century, possibly by Anthony Littleton; the north contains the Hall, entered through a projecting porch, with another projection containing a large mullioned and transomed window at the 'upper' end; and the east range, of three stories, originally contained parlours and a great chamber, with a long gallery on the top floor. The house is approached from the north through a long, low building which doubles up as gateway and barn. The north front is highly irregular, and highly picturesque, with the buildings gradually decreasing in size from the east wing, to the left, to the remains of the abbots' house to the right. The east face of the east wing has three projecting bays with large windows, overlooking what may once have been a formal garden, while on the other side there are tall brick chimneys and two tall gabled projections, one of them containing the main staircase and the other possibly closets and/or garderobes. Both this wing and the new hall range were built of blue lias stone, with Campden stone for the windows, and the roof-lines of both are enlivened with shaped Flemish-style gables of the type which was very popular in Warwickshire in the early 17th century.

Structurally, the house has changed very little since the early 17th century. The Stanfords, who lived there until the beginning of the 19th century, were Catholics and do not seem to have had either the wealth or the ambition to rebuild, or even to significantly remodel, a house which must soon have come to appear both old-fashioned and uncomfortable. In the early 18th century the former parlour at the east end of the hall was turned into a chapel, which was served by Benedictine monks from 1727. Robert, the last of the male Stanfords, died in 1789, and his widow left the house to Robert Berkeley of Spetchley (Worcestershire), who had requested it as a refuge for nuns from Cambrai in France. They had been installed five years before her death in 1812, and they stayed until 1838. In 1845 Robert Berkeley left the house to John Eyston of East Hendred (Berkshire), representative of another old Catholic family. He was living there in 1874, but the house was later turned into a farmhouse and most of the internal fittings were removed, except for some panelling and heraldic stained-glass windows of the early 17th century. It fell into dilapidation in the 20th century, but it was subsequently restored as a hotel, and considerable sums of money were spent on it by Best Western Hotels, the current owners, in 1987-8.

VCH iii, pp.156-7; *TBAS* xxi, pp.63-75; Aylesford Collection, ff.600-2.

SHUCKBURGH HALL

Shuckburgh Hall lies in the mysterious, empty part of south-east Warwickshire close to the Northamptonshire border. This was sheep-farming country, and the Shuckburgh family, who have been in continuous possession of the manor of Upper Shuckburgh since the early 13th century, were active sheep farmers in the early Tudor period. The site of a deserted village can be traced to the south of the parish church, which contains a splendid series of family monuments, and recent research has elucidated the formation of a park around their house, which stands in a fold of the hills, looking east over the quiet landscape. Their house was probably built, or rebuilt, of timber, in the late 15th or early 16th century, and some timber-framed gables can still be seen on the western side of the present building, which is constructed around four sides of a small internal courtyard. Some rebuilding in stone took place about a century later, possibly in the time of Anthony Shuckburgh, who was Sheriff of the county in 1585-6, or of his son John (d.1631), who held the same office in 1617-18. In 1666 the house

125. Shuckburgh Hall, drawing by Henry Jeayes, *c*.1790-1800. The late 17th-century east façade conceals an earlier timber-framed house. The parish church of Upper Shuckburgh is on the hill to the left.

175

had 22 hearths, making it one of the largest in Warwickshire; it then belonged to Charles Shuckburgh, whose father was made a Baronet in 1660 on the strength of his family's support for the Royalist cause during the Civil War.

The 2nd Baronet, who sat as M.P. for the county in 1698-1705, was almost certainly responsible for re-fronting the old timber house in brick towards the end of the 17th century. The first known view, in the Aylesford Collection, depicts a plain three-storied building, possibly on the site of the hall range of the earlier timber house, with stone quoins, a hipped roof, and slightly projecting wings; there is also a lower wing to the right. Celia Fiennes paid an unexpected call in 1697, having failed to find a suitable inn at Lower Shuckburgh — 'a sad village' — and was given a bed for the night. She recorded that

> ... the house stands within a good parke, the deer so tame as to come up near the gate which ascends steps to a Court of broad stone; the house looks very handsome built of brick and stone, good hall and large parlour and drawing roome well wanscoted, neately furnish'd and a little parlour on the other side with good pictures; the butlery kitchen and offices very convenient, two good staircases and 3 or 4 chambers very well furnish'd, tho' not very rich, but in generall all things were very well as any private Gentleman has whatever; he has severall good houses.

One of the rooms seen by Celia Fiennes survives today, with a late 17th-century plaster ceiling and some contemporary paintings on the ceiling and over the doors.

When Sir Charles's grandson Sir Stewkley Shuckburgh died unmarried in 1759 the estate passed to a cousin, whose nephew Sir George Shuckburgh, the 6th Baronet, carried out improvements to the grounds and built a new stable block after inheriting in 1773. A distinguished antiquary and scientist, he travelled in France and Italy, built an observatory at the Hall, arranged the family papers, and sat as one of the M.P.s for the county from 1780 until his death in 1804; his monument, by Flaxman, in the church, alludes to his scholarly interests. His brother Stewkley succeeded him and 'kept up the

126.   Shuckburgh Hall from the east. This side of the house was rebuilt in the 1850s.

mansion with great splendour', but in 1809 his daughter was shot by her jilted fiancé in a summer-house in the park, an event which, according to Deacon, 'brought on a melancholy and terminated his existence'; a willow tree was planted to mark the site of the summer-house.

Sir Stewkley Shuckburgh's son, the 8th Baronet, inherited a fortune of £40,000 through his wife, a daughter of the Earl of Pomfret. For a long time he visited Shuckburgh Hall only on rare occasions 'to pursue the amusement of turnery and other mechanical employments ... a suite of apartments being fitted up in the mansion with a complete set of laths, a forge and furnace, together with a very choice set of tools'. But he maintained an interest in the estate, and in 1844 he commissioned designs from the London architect Henry Kendall the younger, better known for his neo-Tudor remodelling of Knebworth House (Hertfordshire), for replacing the late 17th-century façade of the house with the present, much richer, Italianate frontage, covered in Roman cement and liberally embellished with bold architraves to the windows. An Ionic colonnade was also built across the entrance between the two wings, and the roof was hidden behind an urn-topped balustrade, while a tower, under construction in 1859, imparted a note of picturesque asymmetry.

William Holland of Warwick was employed as decorator in some of the rooms, starting with the Library and Dining Room in 1850-1, and he also played an important part in the thorough restoration of the parish church in 1849-54, supplying stained-glass windows and carrying out decorative painting. But in the final stages of the redecoration of the house he was aided by the little-known Warwick architect John Croft. Croft played a part in the redecoration of the Entrance Hall, with its splendidly extravagant neo-Jacobean wood-carving, in 1858-9, and he later designed cottages and the estate church at Lower Shuckburgh (1864) — an extraordinary example of high Victorian Gothic at its wildest. The gardens to the west of the house were also laid out with closely-planted trees. Since then there have been few changes. The *ensemble* of house and grounds still recalls the comfortable prosperity of a Victorian squire (the estate ran to 3,392 acres in 1883), and the Shuckburgh family are still in residence.

VCH vi, p.216; Aylesford Collection, f. 608; *Journeys of Celia Fiennes* (ed. C. Morris 1947), p.118; Colvile, pp.691-2; T. Deacon, *History of Willoughby* (1828), pp.80-1; Shuckburgh papers at WRO (CR 1248/Box 41); information from Christine Hodgetts.

STONELEIGH ABBEY

Stoneleigh Abbey was founded by Cistercian monks in 1154 on a secluded site close to the meandering River Avon, and the huge house — the largest in Warwickshire — still contains evidence of its monastic origin. The detached mid-14th-century gatehouse of red sandstone survives largely intact, and some of the structure of the monastic buildings, including the two Romanesque doorways, was incorporated after the Dissolution into a courtyard house which forms the core of the present building. The abbey was purchased in 1538 by Henry VIII's brother-in-law Charles Brandon, Duke of Suffolk, but neither he nor his two sons who followed him in quick succession ever lived there, and in the 1540s and '50s the site was leased to a farmer called Thomas Dadley, who may have lived in 'a fayre longe house buylded of a long range of stone and tymbre', with a hall and two chambers on the first floor and a 'cloiseter chamber' and buttery beneath 'in manner of a seller'. This presumably stood on the site of the east range of the present house, which still incorporates part of the medieval chapter house and the splendid vaulted undercroft of the monks' dormitory.

In 1561 the abbey, or what remained of it, was sold to two London merchants, Sir Rowland Hill, a Levant trader, and his former overseas agent Sir Thomas Leigh, a younger son from a Shropshire family who married Hill's niece and heiress and became Lord Mayor in 1558. Leigh's portrait, which still survives in the family collection, shows him as a wary-looking man in a merchant's furred gown and cap. He was certainly successful in providing for his children, building up a formidable landed estate which was divided after his death between his three sons, the eldest inheriting land in Gloucestershire and the youngest property in and around King's Newnham near Rugby, where he built a substantial house which disappeared without trace after passing in the mid-17th century to the Earl of Southampton and thence to the Montagus of Boughton (Northamptonshire). Stoneleigh, along with three neighbouring manors and an estate in Staffordshire, went to the middle son, Thomas, whose descendants held it until 1806, when it

127. The courtyard of Stoneleigh Abbey looking north east, drawing by A.E. Everitt, c.1850. The north range, to the left, stands on the site of the south aisle of the suppressed Cistercian abbey church. The late 12th-century doorway on the right of the early 17th-century east range originally led into the monks' chapter house.

passed to the Gloucestershire branch of the family. By the 19th century the Leighs, with nearly 15,000 acres, were the largest land-owners in Warwickshire.

Sir Thomas Leigh died in 1571, only 10 years after buying Stoneleigh, but his widow survived until 1603, giving her name to the almshouses in the nearby village. She seems to have moved into the patched-up remains of the monastic buildings, while her son built a new house at Fletchamstead (q.v.), not far away. He was made a baronet in 1611 and lived, in Dugdale's words, 'to a great age in much reputation, being *Custos Rotulorum* for the county, and in all publique employments of his time one of the superior rank'. He moved into Stoneleigh Abbey after his mother's death, and was almost certainly responsible for building, or rebuilding, the north and east ranges around the old cloister garth. An inventory taken after his death

128.   The north range of Stoneleigh Abbey in the 1820s. This range contained the Gallery of the early 17th-century house. The staircase was destroyed when the present north entrance to the house was created in 1836. The back of the west range of 1720 can also be seen.

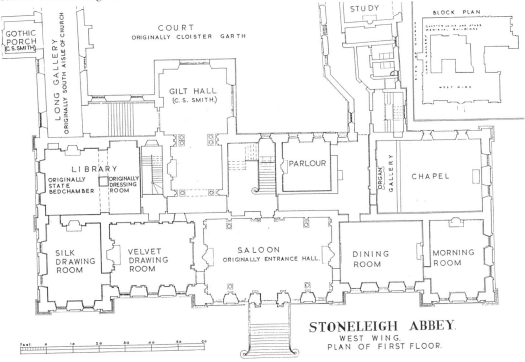

Plan of Stoneleigh Abbey, west range.

in 1626 lists many richly furnished rooms, but a rainwater head dated 1633 in the north range suggests that building continued, or was resumed, under his grandson and successor, another Thomas, who was raised to the peerage as Lord Leigh by Charles I in 1643.

With 70 hearths in the 1660s, the house was larger than any other in the county, but, judging by what remains, it was surprisingly plain. The east range, of Kenilworth stone, is a low two-storied building with a row of gables with balls at the top, and windows of the single mullioned and transomed type common in the early to mid-17th century. At the northern end there is a taller gabled building on the site of the south transept of the monastic church, with a mid-17th-century staircase inside, giving access to the north range, which occupies the site of the south aisle of the monastic church. This originally contained a Gallery at first-floor level, entered from the outside by two flights of stairs, probably also dating from the mid-17th century. The most important rooms, including the Hall, seem to have been in the west range, but they all disappeared when this was replaced in the 18th century.

A hipped-roof block containing a kitchen was built at the junction of the east and south ranges in the second part of the 17th century, but otherwise the house remained substantially unaltered until 1720, when the present west range was begun by the 3rd Lord Leigh. He had gone to Italy in 1711, the year after inheriting the estate, and soon afterwards he married a rich local heiress, Mary Holbech of Fillongley, a branch of whose family had recently rebuilt Farnborough Hall (q.v.). Her wealth helped

129. Stoneleigh Abbey from the south west. Francis Smith's west range, of 1720-6, is seen on the left, and to the right of it is the south range, rebuilt in the 1830s, the late 17th-century kitchen, and the conservatory of 1851. The formal garden between the house and the River Avon was laid out in the mid-19th century.

130.   The Drawing Room of Stoneleigh Abbey, *c*.1955. This was one of the rooms in the 'state apartment' in the west range and was decorated in the time of the 3rd Lord Leigh. The gilt chairs, which are now no longer in the room, were bought by Lord Leigh for the house.

finance the new building, which completely overshadows the rest of the house. The architect was Francis Smith, who had already designed several country houses in Warwickshire and the neighbouring counties. He undertook in 1714 to build a 170-foot façade in front of the old west range for £545, using grey sandstone from the estate, but by the time work began in 1720 a much grander design had been adopted and when the house was finished in 1726 six times that amount had been spent. Lord Leigh must, nevertheless, have approved of Smith's work, since he commissioned his portrait, holding a pair of compasses, which still hangs in the house. The design demonstrates Smith's strengths and his weaknesses as an architect. The strength lies in the impression of solid grandeur conveyed by the rectangular cliff-like façade with its giant Ionic pilasters and balustrade hiding the roof — favourite Smith motifs. The weakness is one of imagination. The façade is a trifle monotonous, with the same motifs endlessly repeated over too large an area. Smith's smaller houses are visually more satisfying.

Only a handful of the rooms in this gargantuan pile were decorated in the 3rd Lord Leigh's lifetime. They included an ante-room, a drawing room, a state bedroom and a dressing room, comprising a full-scale 'great apartment' to the north of the entrance hall, which occupied pride of place in the centre of the façade. These rooms — all of which have since changed their names — are lined with dark oak panelling, and all are adorned with giant Corinthian pilasters supporting a full entablature; some of the original furniture, including some superb embroidered chairs, still survives *in situ*. Behind the entrance hall (now the Saloon) is the main Staircase, of wood, with delicately turned balusters, probably by Thomas Eborall, one of Smith's regular collaborators. It was originally flanked by two smaller rooms overlooking the courtyard, and in the southern part of the new wing there were three more large rooms, one of which later became the Chapel and the others a dining room and breakfast room.

Work on decorating the house came to a temporary halt in the early 1730s. The Leighs were Jacobite sympathisers and shunned political life, so there was no pressure to entertain ostentatiously; as Britton later said, they 'never attended Parliament, and resided entirely at Stoneleigh, in eccentric seclusion ... Here the Lords Leigh passed their existence with rural sports for employment, quite indifferent to the public affairs of the world'. When work resumed in the time of the 4th Lord Leigh, who inherited in 1737, taste in interior decoration had changed, and the Chapel, which survives unaltered, contains excellent Rococo plasterwork of the kind found in several Warwickshire houses of the mid-18th century. The work was carried out in 1743-4 under the supervision of Francis Smith's son William, and the plasterer was John Wright, a Worcester craftsman who had worked with Smith a year earlier on the redecoration of the hall at Stanford Hall (Leicestershire). Wright was responsible for the swirling decoration of the ceiling with its 'IHS' monogram flanked by panels representing Hope and the Resurrection. At the northern end is a gallery, and from here Lord Leigh and his family could look down onto the members of the household sitting in their box pews — a typically Georgian arrangement which has survived unaltered.

The 4th Lord Leigh died in 1749, and a further hiatus ensued until his son and heir came of age in 1763. The 5th Lord then set about decorating the entrance hall (Saloon) and the staircase hall. He had intellectual interests, and the plaster panels on the walls of the Staircase Hall depict musical and scientific instruments, as well as the more conventional attributes of a country landowner; they were almost certainly carried out by John Wright's pupil Robert Moore of Warwick. William Smith prepared designs for the Saloon in 1745, but they were evidently too sober for Lord Leigh, and in the end a more elaborate scheme was adopted and carried out in 1763-5, possibly under the supervision of Timothy Lightoler, who certainly designed the opening in the form of a Venetian window on the landing at the top of the staircase. The design of the Saloon, which was originally divided into three by rows of Corinthian columns, would not have been beyond his capabilities, which were later demonstrated in his work at Warwick Castle (q.v.); he also designed a Rococo communion table for the Chapel, now in the Victoria & Albert Museum. But the main feature of the Saloon (Plate XI) is the magnificent Rococo plasterwork, some of the finest in Warwickshire, with six of the Labours of Hercules depicted in roundels over doors, two enigmatic representations of the Choice of Hercules over the marble chimneypieces, and the Apotheosis of the hero on the ceiling — a choice of subjects which must have reflected the classical interests of Lord Leigh. The identity of the plasterer still remains a mystery, but there are payments in the accounts to John Bastard of Marylebone for the marble chimneypieces, to Benjamin King for wood carving, and to the furniture makers and upholsterers Thomas and Gilbert Burnett of London. Together these craftsmen, both known and unknown, succeeded in creating one of the most beautiful rooms in Warwickshire.

The 5th Lord Leigh evidently entertained grandiose ideas for the further improvement of the house. There are designs by Timothy Lightoler or William Hiorn, who seems to have acted as contractor at Stoneleigh under Lightoler's direction, for a new library and music room to be built on the site of the Gallery in the north range, and for a new south range with a central portico. But these projects were abandoned when Lord Leigh went mad in 1767, and work on the house then stopped.

Lord Leigh died in 1787, and the house then passed to his unmarried sister, who lived there until her death in 1806. The estate then went to the Rev. Thomas Leigh of Adlestrop, head of the Gloucestershire branch of the family, whose cousin Cassandra Austen, the mother of the novelist Jane Austen, accompanied him on his first visit and recorded her impressions in a vivid letter:

> The house is larger than I could have supposed. We cannot find our way about it — I mean the best part; as to the offices, which were the Abbey, Mr. Leigh almost despairs of ever finding his way about them. I have proposed setting up direction posts at the angles ... At nine in the morning we say our prayers in a handsome chapel ... Then follows breakfast, consisting of chocolate, coffee, and tea, plum cake, pound cake, hot rolls, cold rolls, bread and butter, and dry toast for me. The house steward, a fine large respectable-looking man, orders all these matters. The gardens contain four acres and a half. The ponds supply excellent fish, the park excellent venison ... There is a delightful dairy, where is made

131.   The Chapel at Stoneleigh Abbey, looking south. The Chapel was decorated in 1743-4 under the direction of William Smith with plasterwork by John Wright. The box pews and other furnishings survive intact.

good butter, good Warwickshire cheese and cream ditto. One manservant is called the baker, and does nothing but brew and bake. The number of casks in the strong-beer cellar is beyond imagination.

Jane Austen must have had Stoneleigh in mind when she wrote about Sotherton in *Mansfield Park* (1814), with its old-fashioned rooms 'amply furnished in the taste of fifty years back', its walled gardens, and its chapel which, to the heroine Fanny Price, contained 'nothing more striking or more solemn than the profusion of mahogany, and the crimson cushions disappearing over the ledge of the family gallery above'. But, for all its solid grandeur and faded charm, the house failed to conform to contemporary demands for domestic comfort. Miss Berry, writing in 1810, called it 'one of the worst-contrived large houses of fourteen [actually thirteen] windows in front that I ever saw; most of the rooms are oak boxes, floored and lined with oak ... there is not even a pretence [*sic*] to a library in the house; and the present possessors, an old clergyman and his old sister are perfectly encumbered with the wealth to which they succeeded in a late period of life, and which obliged them to leave a comfortable parsonage, where they had passed their best years'.

The grounds, untouched by the landscape movement, also failed to conform to the contemporary taste for picturesque beauty. To remedy this defect Thomas Leigh had recourse in 1809 to the arch-improver Humphry Repton, who had already worked for him at Adlestrop. Some of the more extravagant recommendations in Repton's 'Red Book' were ignored, notably for adding a portico to the west front and a 'corridor' or colonnade with a conservatory and a low tower onto the south side of the house, overlooking the Avon. A proposal for labourers' cottages 'in the purest style of the wooden Gothic' was also set aside. But some important changes were made, chiefly by altering the course of the Avon to make it run nearer the house, and by making a new drive, which crosses the river by an impressive stone bridge designed by the engineer John Rennie in 1815, with new Grecian lodges on the present B4115 road. Trees were also planted, and views to the surrounding country opened up by the demolition of some of the existing walls and outbuildings shown in an estate plan of 1749 (others still survive to the east of the house). In this way the Stoneleigh landscape began to assume its present appearance.

132. The stables at Stoneleigh Abbey, drawing by J. Brandard, *c*.1830. The buildings were erected to the designs of C.S. Smith in 1815-20. The Riding House and coach houses were to the left of the neo-Tudor gatehouse, with the stables in the curved block to the right.

One of Repton's suggestions was to build a new stable block to the north of the house. This was finally carried out in 1815-20 to the designs of the local architect C.S. Smith. In accordance with the Romantic mood of the time, the stables were designed in the Tudor-Gothic idiom, recalling the medieval origins of the Abbey, and were built of red sandstone like that employed in the older buildings. They are laid out in a curved block on one side of a courtyard reached through a castellated gateway, with a spacious riding school on the opposite side, nearest the house — an effective composition which carries more conviction than most of Smith's architecture.

In his 'Red Book' Repton criticised the layout of the west range, which he thought was 'oppressed by the comparative great size of the hall', and suffered from the survival of rooms which had 'all the dignity together with the gloom of those Cedar Parlours occasionally mentioned in the works of Richardson, when society existed without the Music, the Pamphlet, or News Papers, of the present day'. With this kind of criticism in mind, James Leigh, who moved into the house after succeeding his uncle in 1813, called upon C.S. Smith to make a series of proposals for shifting the main entrance to the north (or gallery) range and creating a new Library. By the time work began in 1836, James Leigh was long dead, and it was his widow who supervised the making of this Library out of the fomer state bedroom and its adjoining closet, described by Cassandra Austen as 'an alarming apartment just fit for a heroine', with a 'high dark crimson Velvet Bed'; the remodelled room, divided by a wooden arch, still retains the furniture bought for the new purpose. The former entrance hall, shorn of four of its Corinthian columns, now became the Saloon, and a porch was built onto the north range, which was remodelled internally as an entrance hall. This was given a plaster vault, neo-Jacobean panelling (and a genuine Jacobean chimneypiece from Fletchamstead), installed by James Willcox of Warwick, and stained glass by Thomas Willement, who had recently supervised the internal remodelling of Charlecote (q.v.) in which Willcox was also involved. The removal of the floor of the Jacobean gallery meant that an internal staircase had to be built out into the courtyard, leading via a new Billiard Room and Inner Hall to the state rooms in the west range, and it is by this means that the main part of the house is entered today. The south range was rebuilt at about the same time, and work came to an end in 1839.

There have been few major changes since the 1830s. The Leigh peerage was revived in 1839 for James Leigh's son Chandos, a school-friend of Byron and an enthusiastic Whig, but neither he nor his successors felt the need to carry out major new building work. The ground between the south front and the river was laid out with formal terraces and a Classical conservatory, built to the designs of William Burn in 1851, thus creating a view which was celebrated in many Victorian photographs. And in 1858 a suite of upstairs rooms in the west range was redecorated in connection with a visit by Queen Victoria and Prince Albert *en route* to Birmingham for the opening of Aston Hall (q.v.) to the public. In the unctuous words of H.T. Cooke's *Guide to Warwick Castle*, the Queen 'graciously condescended to visit Stoneleigh Abbey for three days, and during that time, every one, both high and low, rich and poor, was entertained by the noble owner, in the most hospitable manner, so as to call forth, even from Majesty itself, expressions of congratulation'.

The west range of the house was damaged by fire in 1960, but fortunately most of the furniture and pictures were saved, and the main rooms were sensitively restored in 1982-4 and opened to the public. Meanwhile the Royal Agricultural Show was established in the part of the park to the east of the house in 1963. The ownership of the house was transferred by the current Lord Leigh to the Stoneleigh Abbey Preservation Trust in 1988, and in 1993 the architect Kit Martin prepared a scheme for converting most of the west wing into flats; it was hoped that the State rooms would be reopened to the public, but at the time of writing the final fate of the house still remained uncertain.

VCH, vi, pp 232-4; Leigh papers in SBT (DR18, DR671, DR823); Brewer, p.44; F.L. Colvile, *Stoneleigh Abbey* (1850); H.T. Cooke, *Guide to Warwick Castle, etc.* (1851 & later edns); W.A. Thorpe, 'Stoneleigh Abbey and its Furniture', *Connoisseur* cxviii (1946); G.H. Parks in *TBAS*. lxxix (1960-1); Andor Gomme in *Archaeological Journal* (1971) and *Antiquaries' Journal*, lxviii (1988), pp.265-86; *CL*, 13 & 20 Dec.1984; M. Batey, 'Jane Austen at Stoneleigh Abbey', *CL* 30 Dec 1976; M. Batey & D. Lambert, *The English Garden Tour* (1990); Stoneleigh Abbey guidebook 1984; N. Alcock, *People at Home* (1993), p.86.

STUDLEY CASTLE

This formidable grey stone pile was built in 1834-7 for Francis Lyttleton Holyoake Goodricke, a notorious *bon viveur* and rider to hounds. Unlike some of the other large 19th-century country houses in Warwickshire, it stands on a new site, and its construction marked the coming together of a substantial landed estate made up of smaller properties on the Warwickshire/Worcestershire border. Studley is a large parish, with several distinct estates, the most important of which in the early Middle Ages was that of the Corbizons, who founded an Augustinian Priory in the parish in the middle of the 12th century and built a castle or fortified house on a site next to the parish church. The old castle has long vanished, but a sprawling, L-shaped timber-framed house was built on the site in the 16th century, probably by a member of the Hunt family, who inherited the property by marriage in 1543. This attractive building, known variously as Corpsons, Church End House and Castle Cottages, still survives today.

The Castle manor was sold in the mid-17th century to Edward Phillips of Kings Norton (then in Worcestershire), and in 1693 it passed by marriage to another Worcestershire man, Humphry Lyttelton of Naunton. His descendants remained in possession throughout the 18th century, but when Phillips Lyttelton died in 1809 the property was inherited by a niece and her husband Francis Holyoake, a Wolverhampton banker. The Holyoakes had been lords of the neighbouring manor of Morton Bagot since 1641, but in the later 18th century they also acquired lands in Staffordshire and a house at Tettenhall, near Wolverhampton. With the inheritance of the Lyttelton property in Studley, the family now had a substantial estate in Warwickshire, including land in Studley, Morton Bagot and Great Alne.

But the event which lay behind the building of the present Studley Castle occurred in 1833, when Francis Holyoake's son inherited a massive fortune from his hunting crony Sir Henry Goodricke of Ribston (Yorkshire), the former Master of the Quorn. He then took the surname Goodricke, was made a Baronet in 1835, and set about enlarging the Studley estate, which amounted in 1847 to some 2,000 acres with an annual income of £3,377. This involved the enclosure of some common land, eliciting a curse from a local prophet of doom to the effect that 'whoever owned Studley Castle should die without owning an acre of land' — something which proved true.

The house was built by the contractors Grissell and Peto at 'an immense cost', estimated at some £120,000. It has a megalomaniac quality, which undoubtedly reflects the personalities both of the builder and of the architect, Samuel Beazley. Beazley was a playwright, with over 100 forgotten plays and two novels to his credit, and he also designed theatres, including the Theatre Royal in Birmingham, public buildings like the Reading Rooms and Royal Assembly Rooms at Leamington Spa, and castellated houses. Studley Castle, though outrageously unscholarly in its layout and detailing, has all the dramatic and pictorial qualities prized by the Romantic era. It stands on a hilltop, well away from the church and the old house, and it draws outrageously on the clichés of the architectural 'sublime'. The plan is symmetrical, as in the many 19th-century institutional buildings — prisons, hospitals and asylums — which the house uncannily recalls. Externally the dominating feature is a massive keep-like central block with an octagonal lantern tower, and from it the main block stretches out on either side, with castellated wings coming forward at right angles, adorned with corner turrets, oriel windows and shaped Jacobean-style gables: an extraordinary stylistic *pot-pourri*. One of these wings contained the service quarters, with bedrooms for bachelor guests on the first floor and servants' bedrooms at the top; the other was 'a complete house, intended for the residence of the Proprietor independently of visitors', complete with its own nursery and school-room. There is a red-brick stable block, built in a neo-Tudor style to the designs of G.O. Leicester, and to the south of the house a formal terrace and garden was laid

133.   The garden front of Studley Castle in 1897. The house was designed by Samuel Beazley in 1834–7. The Library was in the block in front of the central 'keep', with the Drawing Room to the right. The private wing is to its right.

out by one of the leading practitioners of the time, William Sawrey Gilpin, in a Loudon-esque style. Beyond was a newly-created park, since turned back to agriculture.

The heart of the house is the shadowy, top-lit Inner Hall in the central 'keep', approached through a carriage porch and Entrance Hall. It is surmounted by an octagonal lantern and lit by two-light windows of Norman character, with stained glass to impart the appropriate note of romantic gloom; a wooden gallery at first-floor level, reached by a spectacular staircase, gives access to the bedrooms. The Drawing room and Dining Room, on either side of the Inner Hall, have elaborate ceilings of a Regency-Gothic character, both of wood and plaster, and there is another Gothic ceiling in the octagonal Library. These rooms played host to a succession of shooting parties evocatively recalled by William 'Gumley' Wilson of Knowle Hall (q.v.): '... You breakfasted when you liked, took care of yourself all day long, and entered an appearance at dinner — which is my idea of "country house entertainment". I always hate breakfasting with ladies. I love a sulky breakfast with a newspaper, and, greatly as I admire the sex, I must say that they are better out of the way until lunch time'.

Studley Castle was a house for only 70 years. Sir Francis Goodricke may have become affected by the spirit of the place, for he became 'stern and gloomy' in the 1840s, and put it up for sale in 1847 after the collapse of the family bank, dying at Malvern in 1865. The estate was finally sold in 1863 to Thomas Walker, head of the Patent Shaft and Axletree Co. of Wednesbury (Staffordshire). He had already bought Berkswell Hall (q.v.), and he made Studley over to his son Thomas Eades Walker, who enlarged the estate and spent an estimated £80,000 on beautifying the grounds. Separate areas were given over to different types of plant, including an Italian Garden and a pinetum with 'an unrivalled collection of shrubs from all over the world', and beyond was a lake and suspension bridge and a collection of forest trees. But he too went bankrupt in 1890, and in 1897 the estate was again put up for sale, offering 'an opportunity ... to all classes ... of becoming landed proprietors at reasonable prices', as the sale catalogue put it.

The castle was bought by Samuel Lamb, who housed a notable collection of paintings there, including works by Etty and Maclise, but in 1903 it was sold again, with 340 acres, to Frances Evelyn, Countess of Warwick, and turned into a Horticultural College for women, which lasted until 1969. Some alterations were made to the building between the Wars, including the removal of the crenellation from the top of the central tower and the building of a new wing. In 1969 the house became a training centre for British Leyland, and it is now well maintained by the Rover Group, which uses it as a Marketing Institute and conference centre.

VCH iii, pp.178, 182; RIBA drawings, W1/22-3; G. Fleetwood Wilson (ed), *Green Peas at Christmas* (1924); BRL, Warw SC/674 (sales partics, 1847); WRO, EAC 23 (sale partics, 1897); D.M. Garstang, *The Early History of Studley in Warwickshire* (pamphlet in WRO).

XI   Stoneleigh Abbey, the Saloon. This magnificent room was originally the entrance hall, and the decoration was carried out in the time of the 5th Lord Leigh in 1763-5. The plaster panel over the chimneypiece depicts Hercules standing by an altar, the oval medallions over the doors show his Labours, and the Apotheosis of the hero is on the ceiling.

XII Upton House from Temple Pool, by Anthony Devis, *c*.1803. When the picture was painted the house belonged to the Earls of Jersey, who used it as a hunting seat. Since then the temple has been moved to the opposite end of the pool, and the gardens near the house have been extensively planted.

XIII Warwick Castle from the east, by Antonio Canaletto, 1752. Canaletto painted several views of Warwick Castle as it was in the time of the 8th Lord Brooke (later 1st Earl of Warwick). This one shows houses crowding close to the foot of the 14th-century Guy's Tower, to the right, and a walled entrance courtyard in the foreground, which was later swept away. (By permission of the Birmingham Museum and Art Gallery.)

144.   The State Bedroom at Warwick Castle, drawing by J.G. Jackson, *c.*1844. This room formed part of the 'state apartment' created for the 4th Lord Brooke in 1669-78. The bed was a gift from George III to the first of the Greville Earls of Warwick, and is still in the room.

century plaster Gothic vault. Yorke also noticed that the private apartments, on the site of the medieval service end to the east of the Hall, had been 'fitted up in the modern taste and sashed'. They were made up of a private dining room, library and bedrooms, and in 1754 the poet Thomas Gray recorded that Brooke, who was notoriously small in stature, had 'scooped out a little Burrough in the massy walls of the place for his little self and his children, wch is hung with Paper and printed Linnen, & carved chimney-pieces in the exact manner of Berkley-Square or Argyle-Buildings. What in short can a Lord do now a days, that is lost in a great old solitary Castle, but skulk about & go into the first old hole he finds, as a Rat would do in like case'.

The alterations to the interior were conceived in connection with an ambitious scheme for transforming the surrounding landscape. In 1749 the young 'Capability' Brown, then the little-known head gardener at Stowe (Buckinghamshire), was brought in to remove the 17th-century formal gardens — a process shown in the first of Canaletto's pictures of the castle — laying out the ground with lawns sloping down to the Avon, and planting the mound with shrubs; his activities prompted Horace Walpole to remark in 1751 that 'little Brooke, who would have chuckled to have been born in an age of clipped hedges and cockle-shell avenues, has submitted to let his garden and park be natural'. In 1753 Brown levelled the courtyard to allow for the introduction of the present drive leading up to the Hall, where the porch was rebuilt to his designs. Then, starting in 1755, he created the present Castle Park to the south of the river, encompassing both the former Temple Park, purchased by the 1st Lord Brooke, and large quantities of farmland, including a portion of Barford Common, which was enclosed in 1760. At the southern end of the park, overlooking the Avon and commanding a distant view of the Castle, is

Spiers Lodge, a Gothick confection built in 1748, possibly to the designs of Daniel Garrett, and later the rendezvous for amorous encounters between Edward VII and the then Countess of Warwick. The Duchess of Northumberland, who visited Warwick in 1752, was also impressed by the Dairy, which had 'Rooms for Maids, Cheese and Keeper in all 11 Rooms'.

Lord Brooke was made Earl of Warwick in 1759 after the demise of the Rich family, who had held the title since the time of James I. He celebrated his advance in the peerage in 1764 by building a new Dining Room onto the courtyard side of the Hall, next to the Chapel; the Cedar Room then became a drawing room. The Dining Room is an early example of Jacobean-revival decoration, with panelling and plasterwork, by Robert Moore, deliberately designed to evoke the age of the 1st Lord Brooke. The architect was Timothy Lightoler, who had settled in Warwick in the early 1750s and married a local carpenter's daughter. At about the same time mullioned windows were introduced onto the courtyard side of the private wing, giving the whole of the courtyard front a castellated, Tudor-Gothic appearance which it has retained to the present day. Lightoler was also responsible in 1764-6 for building a new stable block (the present visitors' entrance), supplanting the 1660s block, which was removed, along with sundry old houses, to allow a better view of the east front (Plate XIII) — another example of the growing appreciation of the older parts of the castle.

Further changes occurred in the time of the 2nd Earl of Warwick, who succeeded his father in 1773. He was an avid art collector, filling the state rooms with Old Master pictures, and introducing fashionably neo-classical ceilings and chimneypieces, notably in the Green Drawing Room, which has a ceiling modelled on a plate in Robert Wood's *Ruins of Palmyra* (1753). Miss Berry, visiting the castle in 1807,

145.   The courtyard of Warwick Castle looking south west, drawing by Henry Jeayes, *c.*1786. The crenellated block on the left contains Timothy Lightoler's Dining Room of 1764. The entrance to the Chapel can be seen to the right, and above it the Spy Tower. The 'Warwick Vase' stands in the middle of the courtyard, but was removed to its new home in the Greenhouse soon after the drawing was made.

was impressed by the cabinets, Boulle furniture and *pietra dura* tables on display — some of them still on view — but wrote dismissively about the 'modern' chimneypieces, 'all in expensive marble, in the worst taste, of about thirty years ago'. But the 2nd Earl's most spectacular purchase occurred when his uncle Sir William Hamilton, British ambassador at Naples and husband of the now more famous Emma — formerly the Hon. Charles Greville's mistress — sold him the celebrated 'Warwick Vase', a huge Roman bowl dug up near Tivoli in 1770-1. It was first placed in the courtyard, and was seen there in 1775 by John Byng, who wanted to cast it into the River Avon or present it to the church as a font. But it was later removed to a new Greenhouse built in 1786-8 to the designs of a local mason William Eborall on an open site to the west of the castle overlooking a broad expanse of lawn (the original has been sold to the Burrell Collection in Glasgow, but a replica has recently been made).

The 2nd Earl also re-routed the main Warwick-Banbury road further to the east of the castle, building a new bridge (1788-93) in place of the decayed medieval one, and planting trees along the margin of the new road. The castle was now approached by a spectacular new drive cut through the sandstone rock, which deposited the visitor without warning in front of the 14th-century towers: an exercise in the deliberate evocation of the 'sublime' which impressed the Prussian Prince Pückler-Muskau in 1826:

146.   The Great Hall at Warwick Castle looking north west. The Hall dates in its present form from a reconstruction by Anthony Salvin in 1872-5. The doorway on the left leads into the 'state apartment', that on the right to the Dining Room. The 'Kenilworth Buffet' is on the right, and sundry pieces of armour bought by the 4th Earl of Warwick are on display.

From a considerable distance you see the dark mass of stone towering above primaeval cedars, chestnuts, oaks and limes ... A ruined pier of a bridge, overhung with trees, stands in the middle of the river, which ... forms a foaming waterfall and turns a mill ... Lofty iron gates slowly unfold to admit you to a deep hollow way blasted in the rock, the stone walls of which are tapestried with the most luxuriant vegetation ... Suddenly, at a turn of the way, the castle starts from the wood into broad open daylight, resting on a soft grassy slope; and the large arch of the entrance dwindles to the size of an insignificant doorway between two enormous towers.

The 2nd Earl's increasing financial troubles put an end to further improvements, and in 1802 he was declared bankrupt, the estate being put into the hands of trustees. By this time the castle had already become a favourite resort for visitors in search of the venerable and romantic, and the housekeeper, Mary Hume, allegedly paid off some of the most pressing creditors out of the accumulated tips from visitors; according to West, writing in 1830, it was 'not uncommon to see from five to ten carriages loitering in front of the porter's lodge at the same time'. Nevertheless, some of the family estates had to be sold and for some 50 years the castle remained largely untouched, save for the refurbishment of some of the private apartments and the remodelling of the Hall in 1830 after the late 17th-century plaster ceiling fell in; it was replaced by a new medieval-style tie-beam roof, designed by Ambrose Poynter, and at the same time a marble floor was introduced and hot-air heating installed.

The succession of the 4th Earl in 1853 signalled a new phase of improvements both to the castle and the grounds. An enthusiast for medieval antiquities who, in the words of his daughter-in-law, 'loved every stone of the castle', he employed Anthony Salvin, the doyen of castle restorers, to enlarge the private apartments in 1856-8, and to restore the Watergate Tower and refenestrate those parts of the river front which still retained their Georgian sash windows in 1863-6; today the windows on this side of the castle are virtually all Victorian. Two years later, in 1868, he called in the well-known garden designer Robert Marnock to lay out a new formal rose garden (recently restored) to the east of the castle, and in the following year Marnock designed a new formal garden in front of the conservatory housing the Warwick Vase. Finally, after a disastrous fire which gutted the Hall and private apartments in 1871, Salvin was employed once again to supervise the reconstruction, which was structurally complete by 1875. He was responsible for the present appearance of the hall, with its sandstone walls, Gothic arches at the end adjoining the private apartments (based on the discovery of evidence of the arches leading to the medieval service quarters), huge canopied fireplace and heavy hammer-beam roof of pitch pine; the ponderous, though undeniably impressive, effect is enhanced by the collection of armour, much of it bought by the 4th Earl, and by the presence of the gargantuan 'Kenilworth Buffet' by William Cookes of Warwick — a major *tour de force* of the 'Warwick school' of craftsmen.

The private apartments were also redecorated by a variety of hands, and in their present form they provide an interesting anthology of late-Victorian taste in interior design. The most impressive of these rooms is the Library, created out of two earlier rooms and richly decorated in the neo-Renaissance manner by C.E. Fox in the 1870s, but there are also rooms in the neo-Jacobean taste incorporating old panelling purchased, along with other items, by the antiques dealer Samuel Pratt of New Bond Street, from whom Lord Warwick had been buying armour and other items since the 1850s. The architect T.E. Colcutt worked at the castle for the 5th Earl at the end of the century, and he may have been responsible for the French 18th-century style Drawing Room, the most recent of the rooms now seen by visitors.

By this time landlords like the Earls of Warwick, who depended largely on agricultural rents, were suffering from the effects of the nationwide depression in farm prices. The fabric of the castle was well maintained for most of the 20th century, but there was little or no building, and for long periods of time the Earls forsook Warwick completely. The sale of the castle by the 8th Earl to Madame Tussaud's in 1978 put an end to the steady attrition of works of art sold to raise money, and ensured a much-needed inflow of cash. Today, in their capable hands, the castle attracts more visitors than any other English country house in private hands, and the building, gardens and contents are probably in a better state of preservation than they have been for many generations.

CL, 30 May/ 6 June 1914, 22 Feb 1979, and 2/9/16/23 Dec 1982; *VCH* viii, pp.458-464; Edmondson, *History of the Greville Family* (1766); Frances, Countess of Warwick, *Warwick Castle and its Earls* (1903); Leland ii, pp.40-1; Warwick Castle archives at WRO (CR1886); G.W. Legg (ed), *Short Survey of Several Counties*, 1634, p.73; Hist MSS Comm *Portland* ii, pp.290-1 (tour of Thomas Baskerville); *Journeys of Celia Fiennes* (ed. C. Morris 1947), p.116; *Beds. Hist. Rec. Soc.* xlvii (1968), p.138 (journals of Philip Yorke); Percy letters at Alnwick Castle, *ex. inf.* H.M. Colvin (alterations by Daniel Garrett); *Correspondence of Thomas Gray* (ed. P. Toynbee & L. Whibley 1938), pp.408-9; *Letters of Horace Walpole* (ed. Toynbee, iii, p.66); D. Buttery, *Canaletto and Warwick Castle* (1992); *CL* 31 Jan 1974 (travel journal of Duchess of Northumberland); *Torrington Diaries*, p.102; *Journal and Correspondence of Miss Berry* (ed. Lady Lewis 1866), pp.316-7; Puckler-Muskau, *A Regency Visitor* (ed. E.M. Butler, 1927), pp.119-128; West, *History & Directory of Warwickshire* (1830), p.664; H.T. Cooke, *Guide to Warwick Castle, etc* (1851 & later edns.); Warwick Castle, Ltd, guidebooks to Warwick Castle and gardens (1991, etc.).

WARWICK PRIORY

The site of the Priory of St Sepulchre, on the northern edge of Warwick, was bought in 1546 by Thomas Hawkins, otherwise known as Thomas Fisher. Reputedly the son of a Warwick fishmonger — hence the name — he went into the service first of the Duke of Somerset and then of John Dudley, later Earl of Warwick and Duke of Northumberland, and gradually accumulated a substantial estate of lands formerly belonging to the Church. And 'being thus enrich with such ample possessions', in Dugdale's words, 'he pull'd to the ground this Monastery and raised in the place of it a very fair House ... which, being finished about the 8. year of Queen *Eliz.* reign, he made his principall seat, giving it a new name (somewhat alluding to his own), *viz*: Hawkyns Nest, or Hawks Nest, by reason of its situation, having a pleasant grove of loftie Elmes almost environing it'. He also built a second large house in the depths of the country at Bishop's Itchington (q.v). It is not clear what the Warwick house looked like at first, but it seems probable that it was built around a courtyard, and it certainly played host to Queen Elizabeth when she paid a surprise visit to the gout-ridden Fisher in 1572.

Fisher died in 1576, but his eldest son Edward quickly ran through the fortune accumulated by his father and sold the Priory estate in 1582, finally ending his days in the Fleet Prison. The new owner was a lawyer, John Puckering, who later became Lord Keeper of the Great Seal. His son Thomas, who

147.   Warwick Priory from the south, from an estate plan of 1711. The Jacobean hall range separates the two court-yards, with the lower buildings to the left possibly representing part of the house built by Thomas Fisher after 1546.

succeeded him in 1596 and was made a Baronet in 1612, was probably responsible for rebuilding the east or hall range of Fisher's house in the form which it retained until its demolition in 1925; the date 1620 was inscribed on a stone gateway in the courtyard (since removed), and may refer to the alterations.

The new hall range was built of local grey sandstone, with strapwork ornament over the bay windows and the porch, and a row of six curved gables crowning the roofline — a popular feature in Jacobean Warwickshire. The porch was placed slightly off-centre, and led into a screens passage, with a two-storied Hall to the right and a parlour to the left, lit by two projecting bay windows. Over the parlour there was a great chamber, reached by a finely carved oak staircase, and there was also a gallery which contained a collection of portraits of 'great Learned remarkable men in Europe' when George Vertue visited the house in 1737. The rooms were richly decorated, and there was a particularly elaborate arrangement of stalactite-like pendants hanging from the flat ceiling of the Hall. The first known illustration of the house, from an estate plan of 1711, also shows three ranges of lower buildings enclosing an entrance courtyard in front of the Hall range, probably a survival from Thomas Fisher's house; the southernmost of these ranges is the only part of the house to survive today. A taller range, which looks as if it was remodelled in the mid- to late 17th century, stretched back from the southern end of the Hall, and behind it there were outbuildings. With 36 hearths in 1663, the house was one of the largest in the county.

Sir Thomas Puckering died in 1636, and is commemorated by an impressive monument by Nicholas Stone in St Mary's Church, Warwick. The Priory, which John Evelyn dismissed in 1654 as a 'melancholy old Seat', then passed to his daughter and from her to a cousin, Sir Henry Newton, who took the name Puckering and represented Warwickshire in Parliament from 1661 to 1679; he was presumably responsible for laying out the formal gardens shown in the 1711 view. He died in 1700, leaving the estate, which included the manor of Lillington, to his widow, and in 1709 her niece sold it to the Warwickshire-born Henry Wise, royal gardener in the reign of Queen Anne, subject to the life interest of Lady Bowyer (d.1727), the last of the Puckerings.

Henry Wise opened up the entrance to the house by demolishing the west range of the front courtyard, replacing it by iron gates. He also laid out a formal parterre to the south of the house, with

148.   The hall range of Warwick Priory, drawing by W. Niven, 1874. This part of the house was built *c.*1620 by Sir Thomas Puckering. The Hall was to the right of the entrance. Part of the building was re-erected in the U.S.A. after the demolition of the house in 1925.

149.   The Hall at Warwick Priory in 1910. The plaster ceiling dates from the time of Sir John Puckering, but the furniture and pictures were all introduced by Thomas Lloyd after 1865.

a terrace commanding a panoramic view of Warwick Castle and St Mary's Church. A drawing by Canaletto, dating from 1748 or 1752 (now in the Yale Centre for British Art at New Haven, Connecticut), shows lawns bisected by a wide pathway, with urns on the lawns and a female statue on the terrace, closing the vista from the house. A plan of the grounds by Wise also shows formal avenues to the north and west, and a semi-circle of closely-planted trees to the east, but it is uncertain how much of this arrangement was ever carried out. By 1788 the formal layout had in any case disappeared, to be replaced by a more 'natural' landscape of lawns and clumps of trees which has lasted to the present day.

Henry Wise died in 1738, and his son Henry Christopher Wise extended the old south range, overlooking the garden, with a substantial, though plain, two-storied building, which was completed in 1745. The original intention, according to Ward, was to demolish the remainder of the house, but this did not happen, and some of the rooms in the new building were still empty when Ward compiled his notes in the early 19th century. Externally, the new building resembled the almost contemporary Farnborough Hall (q.v.). It was entered from the east, and contained a suite of new reception rooms 'having every convenience for a family of respectability', including a Library 'very beautifully wainscotted and ornamented with carving' and a Staircase Hall 'ornamented with rich cornices and figures in plaster' (the staircase itself was removed to Frankton Manor in 1926). The craftsmanship was in the Rococo taste favoured in Warwickshire in the mid-18th century, and a Rococo Gothic window was also inserted into the southern wall of the Hall and a Gothic aviary built in the grounds.

The Wise family ceased to live at the Priory in the early 19th century, and in 1809 there was a sale of the furniture. The house was then let to a succession of tenants. The Rev. Henry Wise, who inherited from his brother Matthew Blackett Wise in 1810, was Rector of Offchurch and lived in the

211

150.   The garden front of Warwick Priory, early 19th-century watercolour by an unknown artist. The hall range can be seen above the conservatory formed out of the south range of the 16th-century house. To the right is the wing added by Henry Christopher Wise and completed in 1745.

parsonage there, and in 1851 his son Henry Christopher Wise sold the Priory and grounds after they had been cut off from the rest of the estate by the building of the main Oxford to Birmingham railway line. Later, in 1861, he built a new house at Woodcote (q.v.) with the proceeds of the sale, and this then became the family home.

The purchaser of the Priory was a Mr. Scott, who sold it in 1865 to Thomas Lloyd, a member of the well-known banking family from Birmingham. Soon afterwards he carried out another spate of improvements, including the removal of rendering from the outside of the Hall range and the remodelling of the main interiors with new stone chimneypieces, new (or renewed) wood panelling, and armorial stained glass. The house was also sumptuously refurnished, and the walls lined with portraits, tapestries and Old Master paintings. But in 1910 Lloyd's son put the house up for sale, and in 1925 the fittings were removed and the shell of the house sold to an American, A.W. Weddell, who later became his country's ambassador to Spain. He demolished the main body of the building and re-erected part of it, along with the early 17th-century staircase, in Richmond, Virginia, where it still survives as Virginia House; a writer in *The Architect* (25 Oct 1925) thought that the episode showed 'greed on the part of the seller, and vanity, ostentation, and bad breeding on the part of the purchaser'. The grounds were sold to Warwick Corporation in 1935, and became Priory Park, leaving the remaining part of the house — the south range of Thomas Fisher's courtyard — to linger on in increasing disrepair until 1972, when the site was taken over by the Warwick County Record Office. A new building containing a search room, offices and storerooms was then built on the site of the hall range of the former house, and the south range is now used as a store and caretaker's residence.

Dugdale, pp.457-8; *VCH* viii, pp.438-40; BL, Add MS 29264, ff. 63-74; WRO, CR 26/2(2) (estate plan 1711); *Walpole Society* xxx (1955), p.81 (Vertue notebooks); WRO, EAC 157/1-2 (sale partics. 1910, 1925); D. Green, *Gardener to Queen Anne* (1956); A.W. Weddell, *Description of Virginia House* (1947); information from Michael Farr.

In redesigning the house, Blore abandoned the castellated idiom in favour of a neo-Tudor style which evoked the origins of the estate in the early 16th century. The house was T-shaped, and the main reception rooms — Drawing Room, Billiard Room and Library — were placed in a south-facing range, three stories high, with a tower flanked by ogee-shaped turrets at the centre. They looked out onto a formal garden, and behind there was a longer range containing the Dining Room and the more private rooms, reached by a corridor which also led to the service quarters. The most impressive of the interiors was probably the top-lit Staircase Hall, something which later appeared at Blore's other Warwickshire house, Merevale Hall (q.v.). Elsewhere, there was a profusion of neo-Tudor carving and some furniture by the young A.W.N. Pugin; late 19th-century photographs also show what appears to be a distinguished collection of works of art. Lord John Russell, the future Prime Minister, apparently thought that Weston was 'the most convenient, the best arranged, the handsomest and most picturesque modern house that he had ever seen'.

When Sir George Philips's son died in 1883 the estate went by marriage to the 3rd Earl of Camperdown, who left it in 1918 to his steward Henry Warriner. Warriner did not live in the house, and his son demolished it in 1934 after the discovery of dry rot, many of the contents having already been sold. But the stables, by Trubshaw, still survive, and three of Blore's attractive lodges still act as landmarks along the Oxford-Stratford road.

Dugdale, p.584; *Life and Times of Anthony à Wood* (ed. A. Clark) iii 1894), pp.97-103; *Walpole Society*, xxiv (1936), p.140 (Vertue notebooks); *Walpole Society* xvi (1927-8), p.62 (Horace Walpole's visits to country seats); WRO, CR 1381/1 (Sir George Philips's MS autobiography); WRO, CR 456/25 (building accounts); BL, Add MS 42036-7 (Blore drawings); RIBA drawings J2/24, K5/74; M. Warriner, *A Prospect of Weston* (1978).

WROXALL ABBEY

When the Benedictine nunnery of Wroxall was suppressed the property, described as 'a proper little house in good repair', was bought by Robert Burgoyne, a Bedfordshire man who took an active part in closing down and despoiling the monasteries. He died in 1545, but his son was living at Wroxall in 1580, and he was responsible for making a house out of the monastic buildings. He retained the north aisle of the monastic church, which still survives as the parish church, with a brick tower of 1663-4, and he also kept the partly timber-framed south and east ranges of the monastic buildings, including the former chapter house, parlour, refectory and kitchen. These became the service quarters of the house, which was given a new west-facing hall range, probably by Robert Burgoyne, Sheriff of the county in 1597, or by his son Roger, who succeeded him in 1613 and served as Sheriff in 1631. It was built of brick and consisted of a central hall block, two stories high, flanked by projecting wings lit by canted bay windows. There were curved gables over the ends of the wings and over the two-storied porch, which led into a screens passage at the south or 'lower' end of the hall; the porch was matched at the 'upper' end by a gabled projection with a large window lighting the high table. The new building was clearly a handsome one, and it is unfortunate that it no longer survives.

An estate plan of 1714 shows four avenues converging on the house, which still partially survive, and there is also an early 18th-century walled garden, probably laid out by one of the last of the

156. Wroxall Abbey from the west, drawing by Thomas Ward, c.1800. This part of the house was built either by Robert Burgoyne or by his son Roger, who succeeded him in 1613. To the left is the tower of the former monastic church, which still survives.

220

157.   The east front of Wroxall Abbey. The present house was built for James Dugdale in 1866-8 to the designs of Walter Scott. It stands a little to the west of the site of the former house.

Burgoynes. They split their time between Wroxall and their estate at Sutton (Bedfordshire) until 1711, when there was a failure of male heirs. The Wroxall estate was bought in 1713 by the 79-year-old architect Sir Christopher Wren on behalf of his son, another Christopher Wren, who married the widow of the last of the Burgoynes and settled at Wroxall, where he compiled the memoir of his father which was later published under the name *Parentalia*. The main part of the house seems to have been little altered in the 18th century, except for some minor work in the south and east ranges, but greater changes took place after the architect's great-great-grandson Christopher Roberts Wren returned from 10 years in India in 1812. He reoccupied the house after a long period of letting, and employed the Birmingham architect Joseph Bateman to remodel the front of the house and to modernise the interior. A new central porch had been built by 1820, when the house was illustrated by Neale, and there was also a new breakfast parlour made out of the former great chamber over the hall, with a window leading out onto a balcony over the porch, and a summer parlour in the south range of the former monastic buildings. But the drawing room, to the left of the hall, and the dining room, to the right, still retained their original Elizabethan or Jacobean oak panelling and carved armorial chimneypieces. And when Maria Edgeworth visited the house in 1820 she was most impressed by 'all the little dens of nuns cells, now servants rooms and cloisters and refectory, now offices and chapel and turrets and stairs without end'.

Further changes to the grounds and surrounding estate were made by Chandos Wren Hoskyns, an enthusiastic agricultural improver who married Christopher Roberts Wren's daughter and succeeded him in 1828. But in 1861, after inheriting a Herefordshire estate which also needed large expenditure, Hoskyns sold Wroxall to James Dugdale, a banker and mill-owner from Lancashire. In 1866-8 the new owner totally demolished the house, which was said to be badly drained and structurally unsound, and employed a Liverpool architect, Walter Scott, to replace it with the present house on a new site slightly to the west, from which point it could command a better view over the pastoral countryside. It is a large red-brick building with Gothic details and the obligatory array of gables and tall chimneys. But though it was designed to support a full-scale Victorian country-house establishment, with a substantial service wing and stable block, it gives the impression of being a somewhat over-sized version of a large suburban villa of the period. There is some good stained glass by T.K. Drury in the Staircase Hall, with vignettes of the early history of the estate, and some impressive chimneypieces survive in the main reception rooms, which overlook the gardens. They were created at the same time as the house was being built, with terraces, glades and a profusion of rhododendrons typical of the period.

James Dugdale also left his mark on the estate. He employed Thomas Garner to restore the church, which is now separated from the house by the foundations of the former monastic buildings, and he rebuilt the village, with its school of patterned brick (1863) and its estate cottages of the same date. All this has remained largely unchanged. Dugdale died in 1876, and 1936 the house was leased by his descendants to The Laurels School for girls. The school, now Wroxall Abbey School, purchased the whole estate in 1963, and it now maintains both the house and the gardens in excellent order.

J.W. Ryland, *Records of Wroxall Abbey and Manor* (1903); Neale; BL, Add MS 29265, f.7; Aylesford Collection, f.738; Maria Edgeworth, *Letters from England*, pp.218-9; B. Bourke, *The Laurels and Wroxall Abbey* (1972).

with avenues converging on the house. John Newsham died in 1724 and his son James, who was, in Thomas Ward's words, 'very profuse and extravagant', sold the estate, with its 10 farms, to the Earl of Ilchester in 1764. It was later sold again to Robert Knight, Earl of Catherlough (c.f. Barrells Hall), who leased the house and estate to a grazier. Knight's illegitimate son, another Robert Knight, fixed his main residence at Chadshunt in preference to Barrells in the 1830s, and a plain, rather featureless, stuccoed house resulted from rebuilding carried out in 1841-6. Knight died in 1855, leaving the estate to his daughter, who had married Edward Bolton King of Umberslade (q.v.), and at the end of the 19th century it belonged to their son Captain Edward Raleigh King, who seems to have carried out further alterations to the house.

BL, Add MS 29264, ff.241-4; W. Bray, *Sketch of a Tour into Derbyshire and Yorkshire* (1783), p.40; SBT, DR 622/42 (Robert Knight's account book).

CHADWICK MANOR

A red-brick neo-Jacobean house built on a new site in 1875 for Richard Ramsden, a soap manufacturer, to the designs of an unknown architect. Externally the main features are the shaped gables and the crenellated tower over the entrance; inside, there is a galleried entrance hall, and the grounds were well supplied with rhododendrons and Wellingtonias. The house was sold in 1900 to J.A. Watson, and was sold again, with 732 acres, in 1931. It later became a hotel.

WRO, EAC 36 (sales partics, 1931).

CLAVERDON HOUSE

Claverdon was one of the estates of the Earls of Warwick in the Middle Ages, but in 1568 the manor was bought by Sir John Spencer of Wormleighton (q.v.), who settled it in 1586 on his younger son Thomas. Thomas built 'a very fair house' on land leased from the Dean and Chapter of Worcester, 'and for the great Hospitality he kept thereat', according to Dugdale, he 'was the Mirrour of this County'. It was inherited in 1636 by his great-nephew Sir William Spencer of Yarnton (Oxfordshire), who died in 1647; three years later it was described as

168.   The stone tower at Claverdon, drawing by James Saunders, *c*.1810-30. The mysterious tower still survives, but the timber-framed building attached to it has vanished. (By courtesy of the Shakespeare Birthplace Trust.)

'a Fair Mansion House built with Timber', with a hall, parlour, dining room and 20 other chambers, from which the panelling had been removed by Lady Spencer. It seems to have been demolished at the end of the 17th century, but a tall late 16th-century stone tower, possibly built as a lodge or 'banqueting house', still survives, to which a low timber-framed structure was once attached; traces of garden terraces were also visible in the 19th century. The Spencers' estate was sold in 1716 to Andrew Archer of Umberslade (q.v.), but it was split up in the mid-19th century, with some of the land being purchased by Darwin Galton, son of Samuel Galton, a Birmingham banker, who had already acquired land in the parish. The Galtons built a new house called Claverdon Leys, and this was replaced in 1958 by a 'luxuriously appointed ranch-style residence'.

Dugdale, p.823; *Parliamentary Survey 1649*, Worcestershire Hist. Soc. (1924), p.221; Aylesford Collection, f.122; WRO, EAC 2433/33/124 (sale partics, Claverdon Leys); typescript history of Claverdon by D.G.Wheler-Galton 1934 (copy in WRO).

CLIFFORD CHAMBERS MANOR (in Gloucestershire until 1931)

The monks of Gloucester had a grange at Clifford Chambers in the Middle Ages, and the revenues were appropriated to support the chamberlain of the Abbey — hence the suffix to the village name. A timber-framed farmhouse was built there in the late 15th or early 16th century, and was later remodelled with a massive central chimney stack. The manor was leased to the Rainsford family after the Dissolution of the Monasteries, and in 1562 Charles Rainsford bought it. The family suffered financially for supporting the King in the Civil War, and in 1649 Henry Rainsford sold the estate to a lawyer, Job Dighton, whose family came originally from Lincolnshire. His son Henry (d.1687) or his grandson Richard (d.1738) was presumably responsible for building the present red-brick manor-house, fronted by a set of iron gates which provide a pleasing termination to the village street. The house was built next to the old farmhouse, possibly on the site of an earlier house erected by the Dightons, and consists of a hall block and two wings, with tall windows on the ground floor, high chimneys, and a hipped roof covered with stone slates. The Hall extends the full height of the house, and originally contained the main staircase with twisted balusters of wood. The estate passed by inheritance to the Rev. Arthur Annesley, Rector of Clifford, in 1807, but was sold in 1865 to the Wests of Alscot Park (q.v.). Arthur Annesley's grandson, the Rev. Francis Annesley, bought the house back in 1890, but it was sold again in 1903 to John Gratrix. He employed the architect Tudor Owen to remodel the west wing of the main house, with a new Library and Dining Room, and further alterations were carried out, especially to the gardens, by the next owner, Edward Douty in 1909-17. When he died, his widow married Lt-Col. G.B. Rees-Mogg, and in 1918 she called in Edwin Lutyens to rebuild and extend the house after a fire. Few changes were made to the already Lutyens-like façade, apart from a slight increase in the height of the roof. But the main rooms were remodelled in a neo-Georgian fashion, and the former medieval farmhouse at the back of the house, which had suffered most in the fire, was rebuilt on a larger scale as a guest wing. There were also changes to the gardens. The house was sold after Mrs. Rees-Mogg's death in 1949, and the guest wing was demolished in the 1950s.

CL 4 /11 Aug 1928; NMR, sale partics 1989; P.H. Bagenal, *Clifford Manor* (1914); *VCH Gloucestershire* vi, pp.209-10.

COTON HOUSE, Churchover

The Dixwell family took over from Kenilworth Priory as lords of the manor of Coton in the 16th century, and on the death of Sir William Dixwell in 1757 the estate passed to his nephew William Grimes. The present house was built on a new site in about 1784 by his son Abraham Grimes, almost certainly to the designs of Samuel Wyatt. It is a chaste neo-classical villa clad in smooth ashlar stone, with a main façade enlivened by a curved projection in the middle and windows set within relieving arches; there are some good neo-classical chimneypieces inside, but the main feature is the splendid top-lit staircase with an iron balustrade. A substantial service wing has been demolished, but the brick stable block still survives. The estate, of 1,974 acres, was sold in about 1870 to Francis Arkwright, M.P. for East Derbyshire, and the house remained a private residence until 1948, when it was bought by British Thompson Houston Ltd., as a hostel for apprentices. It was sold to the Post Office in 1970, and was re-opened as its Management College in 1971. It has since been refurbished, and new buildings have been erected in the grounds.

VCH vi, pp.62-3; J.M. Robinson, *The Wyatts*, p.256; Brewer, p.80; NMR photographs; information from Coton House Management College.

169.   Clifford Chambers Manor in the 1930s. The brick façade dates from the late 17th century, when the Dighton family owned the estate.

170.   Coton House. The house was built for Abraham Grimes, *c.*1784, probably to the designs of Samuel Wyatt.

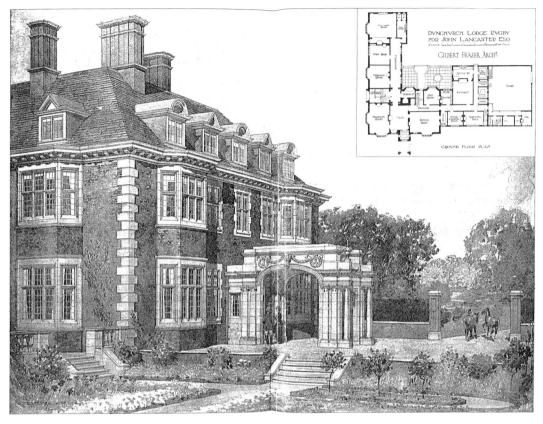

171.   Dunchurch Lodge, from *Building News* (1908). The neo-Georgian house presides over the impressive gardens laid out by T.H. Mawson.

DUNCHURCH LODGE

An accomplished house of 1908, built for a coal-owner, John Lancaster, to the designs of Gilbert Fraser of Liverpool. Lancaster's father had bought and lived at the adjacent Bilton Grange (q.v.), but moved to a house on the site of Dunchurch Lodge when Bilton Grange became a school; he kept a pair of clogs in a glass case on the drawing room mantelpiece 'to remind him of his early struggles as a collier, and to prove to all and sundry that he was the proud conqueror over early untoward circumstances'. The present L-shaped house, of red brick with stone dressings, is designed in a free version of the 'Queen Anne' style, and the extensive gardens were laid out with terraces and walled enclosures by the celebrated garden designer Thomas Mawson. The house is now used as a management college by G.E.C.

Building News xcv (1908), p.689, xcvii (1909), p.754; T.H. Mawson, *Life and Work of an English Landscape Architect* (1927), p.149, and *The Art and Craft of Garden Design* (1926), pp.380-6.

EATHORPE HALL

A plain two-storied red-brick house of 1759, largely built by the Rev. Thomas Vyner, Rector of Frankton (d.1766). He was a descendant of William Vyner (d.1639), a younger son from a Gloucestershire family, who became steward to the 1st Lord Brooke and bought the Eathorpe estate. The five-bay parsonage-like house was expanded to its present size either by Thomas Vyner's son, a Prebendary of Canterbury and 'one of the most accomplished horsemen that ever steered a hunter across country', or by his younger brother Robert, who succeeded him in 1804, married an heiress and farmed Eathorpe on 'a very extensive scale'. He died in debt in 1823, after which the property was let, and in 1858 his son Robert, another enthusiastic sportsman, sold the estate to Samuel Shepheard, founder of Shepheard's Hotel in Cairo; it was later sold again to the Earl of Clonmel, whose descendants lived there until the 1930s. Since then there have been more sales, most recently in 1986.

BL, Add MS 29264, f.211; *Vyner Family History* (1887); M. Bird, *Samuel Shepheard of Cairo* (1957); NMR, sales partics 1986.

EDGBASTON HALL

The Middlemore family, lords of the manor since the 14th century, were Catholic recusants, and their house, which had 22 hearths in 1666, was burned by a Birmingham mob at the time of the Glorious Revolution in 1688 to prevent it being used as a 'sanctuary and refuge for Papists'. The estate passed by marriage in 1661 to Sir John Gage of Firle (Sussex), and, again by marriage, in 1686 to Thomas Belassys of Newburgh (Yorkshire), later Viscount Fauconberg. He did not rebuild the house, which was shown on an estate plan of 1701, and in 1717 he sold the estate of 1,700 acres to the Staffordshire-born Sir Richard Gough, an East India merchant and M.P. for the rotten borough of Bramber (Sussex). He immediately began building a plain foursquare house of brick to replace the old one, probably to the designs of Francis or William Smith of Warwick, and he created

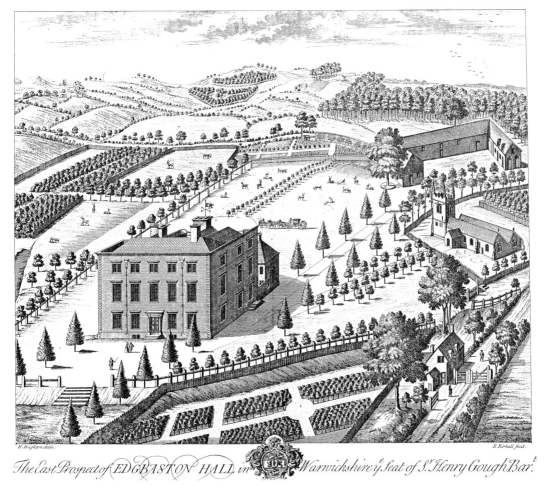

The East Prospect of EDGBASTON HALL *in Warwichshire y Seat of S.ʳ Henry Gough Bar.ᵗ*

172. Edgbaston Hall, drawing by Henry Beighton, *c.*1730. The house was built by Sir Richard Gough soon after he bought the estate in 1717. It still survives, as does the parish church to the right, despite the suburban expansion which Sir Richard's descendants promoted.

a park and repaired the church slightly later. The house still survives, as does the delicately-carved wooden staircase which is the most notable feature of the interior. Sir Richard's son Henry was made a Baronet in 1728, and in 1740 he married Barbara Calthorpe, heiress of estates in Norfolk, Hampshire and elsewhere. There were some internal alterations by the Hiorn brothers in 1751-2, and the park was landscaped by 'Capability' Brown in 1776 for the 2nd Baronet, who inherited in 1774 and was given a peerage as Lord Calthorpe in 1796. The Goughs ceased to live at Edgbaston in 1783, and the Hall was leased to a succession of tenants, starting with the physician and botanist William Withering (d.1799). But the Goughs held onto the estate, which was developed in the first half of the 19th century as one of the finest of all Victorian middle-class villa suburbs. Sir Charles Barry carried out some alterations of a very minor nature to the Hall in 1852, which became a golf club house after the departure of the last private resident in 1932.

Dugdale, p.895; *VCH* vii, pp.67-8; *TBAS* xxxix (1913), pp.5-35; Dartmouth papers at Staffordshire Record Office, *ex. inf* Professor Andor Gomme; R. Brown (ed.), *The Architectural Outsiders* (1985), p.211; Stroud, *Capability Brown;* Aylesford Collection, f.326; D. Cannadine, *Lords and Landlords* (1980), pp.83-91;

EDSTONE HALL

Thomas Somerville, of Somerville Aston (Gloucestershire), married the heiress of the Edstone estate *c.*1460, and his descendants lived at Edstone until 1745, when the property was sold to Robert Knight of Barrells (q.v.), later Lord Catherlough; the last of the Somervilles was William (d.1742), a now-forgotten poet whose main claim to fame was *The Chase*, published in four volumes of blank verse in 1735. At the end of the 18th century the estate, along with the plain, unpretentious manor house, was sold by the trustees of Knight's illegitimate son, Henry Raleigh Knight, to H. Mills, presumably a relative of Charles Mills of Barford (q.v.), M.P. for Warwick, who bought land in the parish of Wootton Wawen in 1802. In 1827 it was sold again by Charles Mills to John Phillips, a barrister from Droitwich who had married the heiress of Hanbury Hall (Worcestershire). According to his monument in Wootton Wawen church, Phillips decided after his wife's death to take up 'the more calm enjoyments and not less useful life of a country gentleman', and in 1829 he moved into the 'newly erected' house at Edstone, which Hannett says was begun by Mills. This was an impressive, if somewhat severe, building in the Grecian style, faced in smooth sandstone ashlar, with a porch in the form of a Doric temple-front and a Doric colonnade along one of the side elevations. Phillips died in 1836, leaving the estate to his daughter Mary, who married Darwin Galton (c.f. Claverdon House), and for much of the rest of the 19th century the house was leased to tenants. It later passed to Mary Galton's younger sister, who lived at Ardencote in the parish of Claverdon, and then to her cousin Frederick Griffiths. He sold the estate of 2,015 acres in 1920 to William Fieldhouse, a partner in the Griffin Foundry, Birmingham, and a local philanthropist. Fieldhouse had already built Austy Manor, a neo-Jacobean house of 1912 by the Stratford-Birmingham road, and Edstone House was sold in 1928 and turned into a hotel before being demolished in about 1930, save for a Grecian lodge at the entrance to the drive. The present Edstone House was built in 1936 to the designs of Francis Yorke of Birmingham. It is a substantial brick building with a Cotswold slate roof and a long curved façade, and in 1979, when it was offered for sale, it boasted 18 bedrooms, five bathrooms, a sun lounge and a music room lit by stained-glass windows.

VCH iii, p 200; W. Cooper, *Wootton Wawen* (1936), pp.67-75; Hannett, p.46; BRL, SC/196 (Austy Manor), SC/682 (Edstone); NMR, sales partics 1979.

ELMDON HALL

The first known house at Elmdon was built, according to Dugdale, by a lawyer, John Boteler or Butler, son of Richard Boteler of Solihull, during the reign of Henry VIII. He inherited the manor by marriage to the heiress of the Hore family, and had his coat of arms carved on a 'great beame' of his new house. The estate was sold *c.*1570 to the Mayne family, and they and their descendants remained in possession until 1760, when it was sold to Abraham Spooner, a Birmingham iron manufacturer, with mills at Erdington and elsewhere. He built the present parish church in 1780-1, and four years later, in 1785, he began a new house on an adjacent site, overlooking a landscaped park and lake. It was a square stone building with a Doric colonnade on the entrance front, a vestigial temple-front articulating the garden front, and a curved projection on one of the side elevations; neo-classical severity also seems to have been a feature of the interior, judging from the few illustrations which have survived. Abraham Spooner was succeeded in 1788 by his son Isaac, a leading Birmingham banker, but after Isaac's son was killed by a falling tree in 1834 the estate, which comprised the whole of the parish, was

181. Little Wolford Manor in the 1930s. The porch, with the coat of arms of the Ingrams, dates from 1671. It leads into the early 16th-century hall, and to the left is a restored 16th-century range with close-studded timberwork on the upper floor.

LITTLE WOLFORD MANOR

A picturesque old house of stone and timber, originally built by the Ingram family, who lived at Little Wolford from at least the 14th century. The oldest part of the house is the stone hall range, which dates from the early 16th century, and was probably built by John Ingram (d.1541), bailiff to Sir William Compton of Compton Wynyates (q.v.). The Hall is entered through a screens-passage and is still open to the roof, though the roof itself dates from the 20th century; there is heraldic glass of 1557, and the porch is dated 1671. A stair-turret projects from the former 'upper' end of the Hall, and from here a wing once projected forward, but this has long been demolished. A second wing, however, survives at the 'lower' end, with a stone ground floor and a first floor of close-studded timber; this dates from the 16th century, but has been much altered. After the death of Mary Ingram, the last of her line, in 1824, the hall range was used as the village school and the remaining wing turned into cottages. The building later fell into a sorry state, and was purchased in 1840 by Sir George Philips of Weston (q.v.), who turned part of the house into the manor farm, while retaining the hall range as a village hall and Nonconformist meeting-house. The house was bought between the Wars by Sir Robert Hilton, a steel and electrical magnate, and he spent large sums of money in restoring the house and installing new chimneypieces, panelling and other features from threatened houses elsewhere; he also added a new drawing room. In 1954 the house was bought by Cyril Bradshaw, a collector of antique furniture.

VCH v, pp.213-7; *CL*, 10 April 1920; *Antique Collector*, April 1957.

LONGBRIDGE HOUSE, Warwick

The oldest part of this irregular house is a 16th-century timber-framed wing, which appears to represent the hall range of a house mentioned in an inventory of 1616. It was built by a member of the Staunton family, who had land at Longbridge from at least the mid-15th century. They were a branch of the Stauntons of Staunton (Nottinghamshire), and they remained in possession until just before the First World War. A staircase was built in the early 17th century, and a five-bay wing with a hipped roof was added in the late 17th or early 18th century; there were further alterations after a fire *c.*1810, and a barrel-vaulted ballroom was added early in the 20th century. The house is now uncomfortably close to an interchange on the M40 motorway.

VCH viii, p.435; NMR, sales partics 1985.

LOXLEY HALL

A mainly 19th-century house standing next to the unspoiled 18th-century parish church on the site of a grange of Kenilworth Priory, parts of which are said to survive in the cellars. The Forster family had a house here in the late 17th century, but the oldest visible part of the present building is a plain two-storied stuccoed range which was obviously built, or rebuilt, in the early 19th century. By then the manor had passed through a series of female inheritances and had then been bought by a Stratford banker, who sold it to the Dewes family of Wellesbourne (q.v.) after his bank collapsed in 1800. John Milward was living in the house in 1845, and he was succeeded by James Cove Jones, who employed a little-known architect, T.T. Allen, to add a large north-facing red-brick range in about 1868, with a patterned roof; Allen must also have designed the gabled entrance range on the south side. The Cove Jones family sold the house and estate, which encompassed most of the parish, in 1914, and in 1928 the house was bought by Major C.H. Gregory-Hood with the proceeds of the sale of Stivichall Hall (q.v.) near Coventry. It remains the home of the Gregory-Hood family today, and looks out onto a well-maintained garden dotted with post-Second World War sculptures of surprising shapes and materials.

VCH iii, p.129; White, *Directory of Warwickshire* (1874).

182.   Loxley Hall. The wing on the right dates from the early 19th century, but the gable-ended portion of the house to the left is part of the alterations carried out by T.T. Allen for James Cove Jones, *c.*1868.

industrialist who had bought the estate of 760 acres in 1867, and had built a new church (by F. Preedy 1874-5) and numerous estate cottages. He then gave the house to his daughter and her husband Dominic Gregg, and they employed N. Fletcher of London to lay out the grounds. The house is an irregular red-brick gabled building with tall chimneys and mock half-timbering in the style of the 'Domestic Revival'; the architect is unknown. It was sold in 1921 to Thomas Lonsdale, and remained in his family until 1953, when it became a hotel. The estate was broken up in 1921, and the house was turned into flats in the late 1970s.

VCH iii, p 97; BL, Add 29265, f.90; WRO, CR 2683/3; EAC 449 (sales partics 1953).

UPPER SKILTS *see* **Skilts.**

WATERGALL HOUSE

A house was built here by a member of the Rayney family, who came into possession of the manor by marriage in 1639. It was enlarged by John Mead, a Londoner who bought the estate in the early 1720s, and a view in an estate survey of 1722 shows a five-bay house, probably of the late 17th century, which had obviously been extended and heightened at a later date; there were formal gardens and iron gates placed on the axis of the main entrance. The estate was subsequently bought by the Leighs of Stoneleigh, and was demolished in 1815.

Dugdale, p.329; WRO, Z.141/3 (view in estate plan).

WEDDINGTON HALL

A house may have been built here by Thomas Grey, Marquess of Dorset, at the end of the 15th century, close to the site of a deserted village on the banks of the River Anker, but the manor came into the hands of the Crown after the Wyatt rebellion of 1554 and was granted in 1562 to Humphrey Adderley, Master of the Queen's Wardrobe. His descendants lived at Weddington for the next 150 years in a house which had 15 hearths in 1666, but the male line died out in the mid-18th century and the property then passed to a cousin, Amice Bracebridge, who married George Heming of Jamaica. Their son, the Rev. Samuel Bracebridge Heming, sold it to Lionel Place after inheriting in 1804, and Place employed Robert Lugar to rebuild the house in the castellated style

192.   Weddington Hall, drawing by Robert Lugar, *c.*1811. The irregular, castellated house was designed to exploit the picturesque potential of the site and at the same time to convey a romantic sense of the past.

made popular by John Nash, a style which Lugar believed was 'peculiarly suitable ... in a well-wooded country'. The skyline was enlivened with crenellated turrets, and the remodelled house contained a new Dining Room and Drawing Room, along with a service courtyard entered through a castellated gateway; the result looks more attractive in Lugar's seductive drawing, published in 1811, than in the few surviving photographs. Trees were also planted, a flower garden laid out, and roads were diverted to enhance the sense of seigneurial seclusion. Inside, the rooms were decorated in the sparse style characteristic of the period; they were arranged around a central, top-lit staircase. The house, sometimes called Weddington Castle, later passed through several hands before being bought by a local builder after the First World War, turned into flats, and demolished in 1928. The estate then fell victim to the northern expansion of Nuneaton.

VCH iv, pp.179-80; R. Lugar, *Plans and Views of Buildings* (1811), pp.10-11; NMR photos; A.F. Cooke, 'Weddington' (typescript in WRO).

WELLESBOURNE HALL

A pleasing late 17th-century brick house of seven bays and two stories, situated on the edge of the village, with a hipped roof, stone quoins and the three central bays recessed in the manner of Honington Hall (q.v.). It was built on the site of an earlier manor house by Robert Boyce (d.1714), and was sold *c.*1748 to John Dewes, who married Anne Granville, the sister of the amateur artist Mrs. Delany. Mrs. Delany recorded alterations to the house in a letter written in 1750, and she also designed two shell-work chimneypieces there; the present Adamesque plaster ceilings seem to have been introduced in the 1760s or '70s. Since then there have been few major changes, either internal or external, apart from the addition of a conservatory (since demolished) *c.*1800. The Dewes family changed its name to Granville on inheriting Calwich Abbey (Staffordshire), and Wellesbourne Hall was let for much of the 19th century. The house remained in the family until 1922, and has since changed hands on several occasions.

R. & P. Bolton, *A Wellesbourne Guide* (1989 — copy in WRO); Burke i(1), pp.191-2; Mrs. Delany, *Life and Correspondence* i(2), pp.558, 573; NMR, sales partics; WRO, EAC 192.

WESTON-IN-ARDEN HALL, Bulkington

A plain though well-proportioned late 16th- or early 17th-century manor house of red sandstone, with a three-gabled façade like that of Little Compton Manor (q.v.) and some contemporary and earlier wood panelling inside; there were eight hearths in 1666. The manor belonged to the Lords Zouch in the 16th century, but it was sold to Humphry Davenport, who sold it in his turn to Sir Christopher Yelverton (d.1612); it is not clear which, if any, of these men built the house. In the second half of the 18th century the Hall was the home of the sculptor Richard Hayward, who supplied some of the chimneypieces for Arbury Hall (q.v.), and also made the font (1789) and a monument to his parents in Bulkington parish church. A wing was added in 1893, when the house belonged to F.A. Newdigate. The house later became a school, but since 1970 it has been a hotel.

VCH vi, pp.48-51, 56; Aylesford Coll, f.720; Kelly, *Directory of Warwickshire* (1940).

WESTON-UNDER-WETHERLEY HALL

The only visual record of this once-magnificent house is a drawing in the Aylesford Collection, taken from a painting of 1635 by Wenceslas Hollar, formerly in the possession of the Throckmorton family. It shows the entrance front of a large timber-framed building, probably arranged around a courtyard, with ogee-shaped cupolas at each end and flanking the entrance, and a detached gatehouse, also of timber. The builder, according to Dugdale, was Sir Edward Belknap (d.1521), 'a man of great note, [who] had his residence here and new built the Mannour house, one of the fairest structures of timber that I have seen, on several parts whereof his Arms are cut in wood'. He was 'a man of much publique action', who served as a Squire of the Body to Henry VII and Henry VIII and became Custodian of Warwick Castle in 1502 and subsequently Chief Butler of England. He bought the Weston estate in 1501, and later carried out an extensive programme of sheep-farming inclosures on another of his estates at Burton Dassett. He died without male heirs, and the manor was finally bought in 1557 by two lawyers, Sir Edward Saunders and Francis Morgan; Morgan's son married Saunders's daughter and heiress, and Weston then became their home. It passed by descent to Thomas Morgan, a Roman Catholic who was killed at the Battle of Newbury in 1643, and for a time the family chaplain was the Father Huddleston whom later received Charles II into the Church on his deathbed. There were then several absentee owners, one of whom, Lord Clifford of Chudleigh (Devon), demolished the house in the 1730s. It had vanished without trace by the early 19th century, but the antiquary Thomas Ward, who was Vicar of Weston, found the foundations,

193. Weston-in-Arden Hall, drawing by W. Niven, 1872. The late 16th- or early 17th-century house was enlarged some 20 years after this drawing was made.

194. Weston-under-Wetherley Hall, drawing by Henry Jeayes from a lost original of 1635 by Wenceslas Hollar. In its heyday the early 16th-century house built by Sir Edward Belknap must have been one of the grandest in Warwickshire, but it was demolished in the 1730s.

269

together with the moat, fish ponds, and a lodge or summer-house on a nearby hill. Another, much smaller, farmhouse called Weston Hall was built near the site in the 18th century.

Dugdale, p.297; *VCH* vi, p.252; Aylesford Collection, ff.772-4; BL, Add MS 29264, ff.174-7.

WHITLEY ABBEY, Coventry

Despite its name, this large late 16th- or early 17th-century stone house did not stand on a monastic site, and until the 19th century it was known as Whitley Hall. The builder was probably Bartholomew Tate, M.P. for Coventry, who inherited the manor from Ann Longvile in 1574, or his son Sir William Tate (d.1618), who succeeded him in 1601. There was a main hall block and two projecting wings facing north towards the City of Coventry, only a mile or so away; one of the wings was much longer than the other, and there was a two-storied porch and an array of curved and pinnacled gables to enliven the roof-line. Sir William Tate's son sold the estate in 1627 or 1628, and the garden front was remodelled with a hipped roof at some time in the late 17th or early 18th century. The house subsequently passed to a barrister, Francis Wheler, and he may have been responsible for creating a landscaped park with an ornamental lake formed out of the River Sherbourne in the valley below. His daughter and heiress married the 2nd Viscount Hood, son of the famous Admiral Hood, and he employed Sir John Soane to carry out a series of changes to the interior in 1810-12. Though less extensive than first envisaged, they involved a considerable rearrangement of the interior and the addition of a new service wing; funds seem to have been fairly limited, and the spatial flights of fancy for which Soane is famous were largely eschewed. Under the new arrangement the porch led into the Hall, centrally placed and divided by piers, with a groin-vaulted Drawing Room and main Staircase to the left, leading into the Library in one of the wings; to the right was the Dining Room and Lord Hood's Study, beyond which was the service wing, at an angle to the main building. The 4th Viscount Hood sold Whitley to Edward Petre, a grandson of Lord Petre, in 1867, and Petre carried out further alterations in 1879, after a fire had destroyed most of the west wing five years earlier. He also added a Catholic Chapel next to the east wing in 1867-8, and laid out new ornamental gardens with rockwork, rhododendrons, and a 'mimic waterfall' by the lake; he may also have remodelled the garden front with the neo-Jacobean gables shown in early photographs. In 1879 the house was described as 'one of the most convenient and attractive mansions in the county'. It was sold by Petre's son in 1920, and then remained unoccupied until its demolition by Coventry Corporation in 1953. A comprehensive school by the City architect Arthur Ling now stands on the site, and won many plaudits from architectural critics in its early days.

VCH viii, p.88; Aylesford Collection, ff.726-8; Sir John Soane's Museum, xxv.2; Neale; W.G. Fretton, *Whitley and its Groves* (pamphlet 1879; copy in Coventry City Library); NMR photos.

WOLSTON PRIORY

The Carthusian priory of Wolston was bought after the Dissolution by Roger Wigston, a lawyer and commissioner for the surrender of the monasteries, whose forebears were wealthy wool merchants from Leicester. He or his son probably built the gabled red sandstone house, which may incorporate parts of the monastic buildings, and some of the notorious Marprelate Tracts were printed there in 1589. The house has gables, mullioned and transomed windows and a three-storied porch, but there is a large stack of four chimneys where the service end ought to be, suggesting that it was left unfinished, or partially demolished at some later date. The estate passed from the Wigstons to the Warner family, from them to Sir Peter Wentworth, who was taxed for 13 hearths in 1666, and then to the Wilcox family.

Dugdale; *VCH* vi, p.274.

WOODCOTE, Leek Wootton

The Mallory family had land in the manor of Woodcote in the 17th century, and in the early 19th century Robert Mallory carried out improvements to the existing house which enabled Field to describe it in 1815 as 'a handsome modern dwelling'. When he died in 1821 the property passed to his daughter Harriet, who married Osman Ricardo, and they sold it in 1851 to Henry Christopher Wise, who already owned a substantial estate in the area. His family had profited from the expansion of Leamington Spa, and after considering schemes for remodelling the old house he opted for building a new one, which superseded Warwick Priory (q.v.) as the main family seat. It is a large neo-Elizabethan building of local sandstone, built to the designs of John Gibson in 1861-2; the rooms are arranged around a central Staircase Hall, and the elevations are plainer than might be expected, with ornament confined to some strapwork cresting over the bay windows, and an impressive array of tall chimneys. Wise's son was succeeded in 1888 by a cousin, Maj-Gen Sir George Waller, whose son lived

195.   Whitley Abbey, drawing by J.P. Neale, *c.*1821. The north or entrance front of the late 16th- or early 17th-century house is shown, seemingly little altered by Sir John Soane's internal remodelling for Lord Hood in 1810-12.

196.   Woodcote, from *Building News* (1874). John Gibson built the house for Henry Christopher Wise in 1861-2, not long after he had sold Warwick Priory, the old family seat.

at Woodcote until his death in 1947. The house became the headquarters of the Warwickshire Constabulary in 1949, and has since been extended.

S.E. Longland, *Notes on the History of Leek Wootton* (1935, revised 1977; copy in WRO); *VCH* vi, p.169; Field, p.345; WRO, CR 26/2(5), /5(5); *Building News*, 7 Aug 1874.

WOOTTON HALL, Wootton Wawen

This handsome stone house was built in 1687 by Francis Smyth, 2nd Viscount Carrington, a Roman Catholic who married a daughter of the Marquess of Powis and had his arms carved on the pediment. His father, a prominent Royalist, was given the Carrington peerage by Charles I, but was murdered by his valet in 1665. He was a descendant of John Smyth (d.1540), a Baron of the Exchequer who acquired an estate in Wootton by marrying the heiress of the Harewell family. The Smyths expanded their possessions in the parish in the 16th century, and the will of Francis Smyth (d.1629) mentions a lodge in the park; their house, which almost certainly stood on the site of the present one, had 21 hearths in 1666. The present house is an L-shaped building of stone with a pedimented entrance front of nine bays, two stories and a hipped roof, and a long three-storied wing with a large Venetian window; two other ranges were said to have been recently pulled down in 1789. The Carrington title died out in 1706, and the Wootton estate later passed to a cousin, Francis Smith, and then by marriage in 1758 to Peter Holford, whose daughter married Sir Edward Smythe of Acton Burnell (Shropshire). Wootton Hall was used for a time by the Prince Regent's secret wife Mrs. Fitzherbert, a Roman Catholic and a cousin of the Smythes, and in 1813 a Catholic chapel with an impressive Grecian interior was built at the back of the house by Catherine, Lady Smythe. For most of the 19th century the house was used as a dower house, or was leased out, and there were consequently few alterations, but in 1904 the estate was sold to George Hughes of Birmingham, and it was probably he who was responsible for re-decorating the interiors in a variety of fashionable Edwardian styles, neo-Jacobean for the staircase, French Rococo for one of the drawing rooms, and neo-Georgian for the bedrooms. The house was sold to Robert Darley Guinness in 1912 and was later turned into flats.

W.Cooper, *Wootton Wawen* (1936), pp.37-40; W. Camden, *Britannia*, ed. Gough ii (1789), p.342; Hannett, p.45; WRO 195/90/2 (album of early 20th-century photos).

197.   Wootton Hall in the 1930s, showing the entrance front of 1687 to the right, with the arms of the 2nd Lord Carrington over the pediment. It is two stories high, but the wing to the left has three stories.

WORMLEIGHTON MANOR

In the 15th century Wormleighton belonged to the Montfort family of Coleshill (q.v.), but three years after the execution of Simon Montfort in 1495 it was bought by William Cope, Cofferer of the Household to Henry VII. He dispossessed 60 people to create sheep pasture, married a daughter of John Spencer of Hodnell, another prominent livestock farmer, and in 1506 sold the manor to her cousin John Spencer, son of William Spencer of Snitterfield. Spencer built a new house of brick near the parish church in 1516-9 to replace what was described as a 'sory thached hows' in the valley below, and lived there with a household or 'family' of 60 people. The main survival of this once-splendid building is a tall two-storied crenellated block with large mullioned and transomed windows, lighting what may once have been the parlour and great chamber; this block formed part of a courtyard shown in an estate plan of 1634, but the remaining buildings, including the Hall, have gone. John Spencer's descendant Robert was given a peerage as Lord Spencer in 1603, and he built an impressive gatehouse of local brown stone, with the date 1613 carved on it. It is a formidable structure, with a tall tower to one side of the main round-arched gateway, which has coats of arms carved

198.   The gatehouse at Wormleighton Manor, built by the 1st Lord Spencer in 1613.

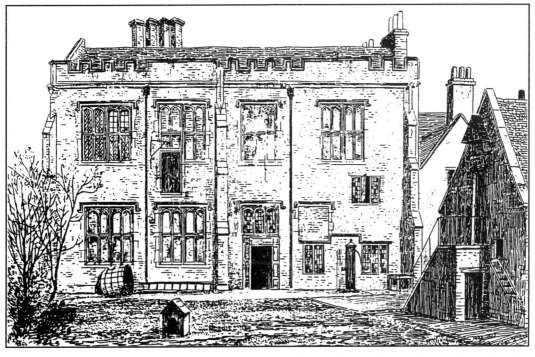

199.   Wormleighton Manor, drawing by W. Niven, 1877. It shows what may be the parlour and great chamber wing of the house built by John Spencer in 1516-19.

above it. The house served as Prince Rupert's headquarters before the Battle of Edge Hill, but Dugdale wrote in his diary that in 1646 it was 'burnt by his Majesties forces of Banbury, to prevent the Rebells making it a garrison'; nevertheless, there were still 15 hearths in 1666. After the Civil War the Spencers abandoned Wormleighton for their other family seat, at Althorp (Northamptonshire), but they retained control of the estate, as can be seen from the well-preserved cottages built in the village in the 19th century. The manor house then became a farmhouse.

H. Thorpe, 'The Lord and the Landscape', *TBAS* lxxx (1962), pp.51-71; *VCH* v, pp.218-20; P. Tennant, *Edgehill and Beyond* (1992), p.218; WRO, Z 176/1/2 (estate plan 1634).

INDEX

The names of all known architects, craftsmen and families are listed. Public or corporate owners of houses are listed more sparingly, and in most cases the names of individual owners are subsumed within those of their families. Figures in **bold** refer to the entry for each house, figures in *italics* indicate the numbers of the illustrations.

Adam, Robert, xxii, 67, 68, 156
Adams family, 224
Adderley family, xxiii, of Hams Hall, 106-7; of Fillongley, 224; of Weddington, 267-8
Addison, Joseph, 228
Addyes family, 256
Adlestrop (Gloucs), 182, 184
Admington Hall, **223**
Akroyd, James, xxiv, 244
Alcott, John, 14
Alderford, John, 173, 232
Allen, R.R., 254
Allen, Rev. Thomas, 31
Allesley Park, **223-4**, *158*
Alscot Park, xvii, xxi, xxii, **1-5**, 30, 31, 82, 168, *1-3*
Alston family, 5, 243
Althorp (Northants), 154
Alton Towers (Staffs), 35
Alveston House, xx, 51, **224**; Manor, **224**
Ancaster, Dukes of, 101, 103
Anderson, Sir Edmund, xix, 9
Annesley family, 238
Ansell, Colonel, 256
Ansley Hall, **6-8**, *4-5*; church, 7, 8; Coal and Iron Co., 8, 260
Ansty Hall, **224**
Antrobus, Sir Edward, 248
Apperley, C.J., 228
Arbury Hall, xvii, xix, xx, xxi, xxiii, xxvi, 3, **9-15**, 163, 164, *Frontispiece, 6-9*
Archer family, Lords Archer, xxi, 101, 189-91, 238
Arden family, xviii, 39, 106, 261
Ardencote, 242
Arkwright, Francis, 238
Arlescote House, 162, **224**
Armstead, H.H., 84
Armstrong, Charles, xxv, 231
Arnold, Col. Stanley, 227
Artari, Giuseppe, xxii, 168
Arton, George, 160
Ascott (Bucks), 98
Ash, Graham Baron, xxv, 27, 160, 161
Ashburnham House, Westminster, 231
Ashdown House (Berks), 59
Ashorne Hill House, xxv, 138-9, **225**
Assers, Edward, 152
Astley Castle, xviii, 10, **16-17**, *10-11*; church, 16

Astley family, 16
Aston, Sir Walter, 231
Aston Hall, xviii, xix, xx, xxiv, **18-20**, 185, *12-15*; church, 39
Atherston Hall, 22, **225**
Austen: Cassandra, 182, 185; Jane, 182, 184
Austy Manor, 242
Aylesford, Earls of, xxi, xxvi, 152-7, 255, 260
Aylesford Collection, xxvi

Baddesley Clinton, xviii, xxiv, **23-7**, 161, *16-18, I*; church, 24
Baddesley Ensor, church, 133
Baginton Hall, xviii, xxi, **28-9**, *19*
Bagot: Sir William, 28; family, 261
Baker, William, of Audlem, 22
Baldwin, Martin, xxi, 255
Baraset, xxiv, **225**
Barcheston, tapestry works at, 216
Barclay, Henry, 136
Barford Hill House, xxiv, xxv, **226**
Barford Manor, xxiii, **226**
Barnsley, Sidney, 107
Barrells Hall, xxii, xxiii, **30-2**, *20-1*
Barrington Court (Somerset), 43
Barry, Sir Charles, 242
Bartoli, Domenico, 157
Barton Manor, Barton-on-the-Heath, **227**
Bassingburn, Warin de, 16
Bastard, John, 182
Bateman: C.E., xxiv, 94, 172, 249; Hugh, 94; Joseph, 221
Batoni, Pompeo, 44
Bearstead: 2nd Lord, xxv, 193-5; Lady, 195
Beauchamp: family, 97, 138, 141, 200-2, 226, 227, 237, 247, 264; Richard, Earl of Warwick, 28, 100; Sir William, Lord Bergavenny, 223; Giles de, 227
Beauchamps Court, Alcester, **227**
Beaufort, Lady Margaret, 126
Beaufoy family, 101, 243
Beaumont: Guillaume, 29; family, 200
Beazley, Samuel, xxiv, 186
Beech, James, 232
Beecham, Sir Thomas, 52; Adrian, 52
Belassys, Thomas, *see* Fauconberg, Viscount
The Belfry Hotel, see Moxhull Hall
Belknap, Sir Edward, 268
Bentley family, 252

Bereford, Edmund de, 250
Berkeley: Lords, xx, 235; Robert, of Spetchley (Worcs), 174; Elizabeth, 235
Berkswell Hall, 187, **227**
Berry Hall, xxiii, xxv, **227**, 248, *160*
Berry: Miss Mary, 54, 102, 184, 206; Thomas Aloysius, 231
Bertie, Lady Mary, 101
Besant, Francis, 139
Bettes, John, 9
Bicknell, Julian, 195
Biddulph family, 229
Bidlake, W.H., 94, 191
Billesley Manor, xviii, **33-4**, *22*; church, 33
Bilton Grange, xxiv, xxv **35-7**, 240, *23-5*
Bilton Hall, xix, **228**, *161*
Bingham, Sir Richard, 134
Binley church, 61
Bird family, 227
Birdingbury Hall, xix, **229**, *162*; church, 229
Birmingham: Corporation of, 22, 261; Co-operative Society, 140; Theatre Royal, 186; St Philip's church (cathedral), 189
Bishop's Itchington House, 209, **231**
Bishopton, Sir John, 234
Bledisloe House (Gloucs), *see* Coates Manor
Blickling Hall (Norfolk), 19
Blockley, Thomas, 22, 68, 263
Blomfield, Sir Reginald, 159
Blore, Edward, xxiv, 62, 120, 132, 218, 219
Blow, Detmar, 33
Blyth Hall, **231**, *163*
Bodiam Castle (Sussex), 125
Bois, H.G., 34
Bolingbroke, Henry St John, Lord, 30
Bonn, Leopold & Major Walter, 147
Bonomi, Joseph, xxiii, 31, 156, 157, 265
Bordesley Hall, 231
Borgnis, Giovanni, 157
Boteler (or Butler) family, 242
Boughton family, xix, 35, 232; of Bilton Hall, 228; of Cawston, 235; of Lawford Hall, 250
Boultbee family, 265
Bourton Hall, Bourton-on-Dunsmore, xxv, **231-2**
Bowyer, Lady, 210
Boyce, Robert, 268
Brace, Alan, 265
Bracebridge family, xviii; of Atherston Hall, 225; Thomas, 6; Abraham, 22, 225; Amice, 267
Bradford, Earls of, *see* Bridgeman family
Bradshaw, Cyril, 253
Brailes House, 218, **232**
Bramcote Hall, **232**
Brandon Hall, xxiv, **232**, *164*; Cottage, *see* Brandon Hall
Brandon, Charles, Duke of Suffolk, 9, 178
Brett, John, 262
Brettingham, Matthew, 155
Bretts Hall, Ansley, 6, 7
Bridgeman family, 39-41, 122, 228
Bridgens, Richard, 22
Britton, John, xxvii

Brome family, xviii, 23-4, 166
Bromley family, xxi, 28-9, 247-8
Bromley-by-Bow (Middlesex), Old Palace, 33
Bromwich: Thomas, 4; Henry of, 38
Brooke, Lords, *see* Greville family of Warwick Castle
Broom Court, 145, **232**
Brown, Lancelot ('Capability'), xxii, 44, 60, 61, 62, 67, 69, 149, 153, 154, 168, 205, 242
Brown family, of Radford Semele, 262
Brownsover Hall, xxv, 199, **232**, *165*
Brueton, Horace, 124
Bryant: George, 225; Colonel, 245
Buccleuch, Dukes of, 236
Buckingham, Dukes of, 126, 127, 231, 263
Buckland House (Berks), 79, 80
Budbrook, church, 98
Bulkington, church, 268
Bumstead, William, 192
Burdett family, 232
Burgoyne family, 220-1, 249
Burn, William, 157, 185
Burnaby, Sir Richard, 258
Burnett, Thomas & Gilbert, 182
Burton Agnes Hall (Yorkshire), 39
Burton family, 262
Burton Dassett, 268
Bury family, 227
Bushell, William, 79
Bushwood Hall, xviii, 19, **234**
Buxton, Christopher, 70
Byng, John, 54, 62, 69, 127, 130, 154, 157, 207

Caldecote Hall, xxiv, **234**, *166*; John, 250
Calthorpe, Lords, *see* Gough family
Caludon Castle, xviii, xx, **235**
Cambridge, Queens' College, 126
Camden, William, 24
Camperdown, Earl of, 219
Canaletto, Antonio, 89, 91, 204, 205, 211
Canning family, xxi, 95-6
Canonbury House, Islington (London), 75
Capesthorne (Cheshire), 29
Carew, George, Earl of Totnes, 50-1
Carey, Lord, 118
Carhampton, Earl of, *see* Luttrell, Simon
Carlile, James William, 266
Carrington, Lords, 249, 272
Castle Ashby (Northants), xix, 74, 76
Castle Bromwich Hall, xx, xxi, **38-41**, 59, 217, *26-8*; church, 41
Catesby family, xviii, 234, 250
Catherlough, Robert Knight, Earl of, 30-1
Caversham Park (Berkshire), 59
Cawston House, **235-6**, *167*
Chadshunt House, **236-7**
Chadwick family, 143-4; Manor, **237**
Chamberlain, Richard, 16, 17
Chamberlayne family, 266
Chambers, Sir William, 7, 131
Chance, Arthur, 245
Chantrey, Sir Francis, 218

Charlecote, xviii, xix, xx, xxii, xxiv, xxvi, 9, 26, **42-7**, 69, 217, *29-33, II*
Charles I, 118, 162
Charles II, 152
Charnley family, 259
Chastleton House (Oxon), 39, 217
Chatwin, J. A. & P. B., xxvi, 227, 247, 264
Chesham, Lord, 193
Chesterfield, Earls of, 98
Chesterton House, xx, xxiii, **48-9**, 66, *35*; church, 48; windmill, 48, *34*
Chetwode, Sir John, 8
Chetwynd family, 245-6, 255
Child, Francis & Robert, 192
Chippendale, Thomas, 4
Cibber, Caius Gabriel, 48
Civil War, xx, 20-1, 74, 118, 127, 149, 152, 162, 203, 234, 238, 255, 274
Clarence, Duke of, 202
Clarendon, Earls of, *see* Villiers family
Clark: George, 205; Thomas, 155
Clarke: Edward, 84; Sir Simon, 145, 232
Claverdon House, xix, **237-8**, *168*
Claverdon Leys, 238
Clifford of Chudleigh, Lord, 235, 268
Clifford Chambers Manor, xxv, **238**, *169*
Clinton: family, 53; Geoffrey de, 113, 115, 125; William, Earl of Huntington, xviii, 125, 202; Sir Thomas, 23; John de, 126
Clonmel, Earl of, 241
Clopton House, **50-2**, 214, *36-7*; family, 50-2, 261
Clutton, Henry, xxiv, 133, 215
Coates Manor, Cirencester (Gloucs), 107
Cobb, John, 4, 149
Cobham, Lord, 149
Cockayne family, 260
Cockerell, Samuel Pepys, 252
Colcutt, T. E., 208
Coleshill Hall, xix, **53-5**, 86, *38-9*; church, 53, 54, 106
Collier & Plucknett, 257
Combe family, 213
Combe Abbey, xix, xx, xxi, xxii, xxiii, xxiv, xxv, xxvi, **57-63**, *40-6*
Combrook, 69
Compton: family, xviii, xix, xxvi, 72-6; Sir William, 72-4, 127, 223; Rev. B., 225
Compton Verney, xvii, xviii, xxi, xxv, 46, **64-70**, 252, *47-50*
Compton Wynyates, xviii, xix, xx, xxiv, xxvi, **71-6**, *51-4, III*; church, 74
Constable, John, 120, 123-4
Conway Castle, 166
Conway family, Earls of Conway, xix, xx, 166-8
Cookes, William, xxiv, 5, 208
Cooksey family, 245
Cooper, Richard & Manasses, 224
Cope: John, 119, 120; William, 273
Corbin family, 247
Corbizon family, 186
Corby Castle (Cumberland), 96
Coton House, **238**, *170*

Cottingham, L.N., 62
Couchman, Henry, 14, 155, 156
Coughton Court, xvii, xviii, xx, xxvi, **77-80**, *214, 55-57, IV*
Coventry family, Earls of Coventry, 264-5
Coventry: County Hall, 260; Priory, 109, 258, 259; White Friars' church, 236, 258; Whitmore Park, 258
Coventry and Oxford Canal, 11
Crace, J.G., 36
Craddock-Hartopp family, 94
Craggs, James, 236
Cranfield, Lionel, Earl of Middlesex, xx, 245, 255
Craven family, Earls of Craven, xix, 58
Cresswell, H. Bulkeley, 236
Croft: John, 177; William, 81
Croome Court (Worcs), 154, 264
Crowdy, Arthur, 33
Cullen, Sir Rushout, 192

Dadley, Thomas, 178
Dance, Major Cyril, 250
Daniell, William, 152
Danvers family, 192
Darlington, James, 255
Dashwood: Francis, 119; Sir Francis, 145; Samuel, 189
Davenport: Humphry, 268; John, 79, 214; Rev. Walter, 29
Deene Park (Northants), 43
D'Eivile family, 196
Delany, Mrs. Mary, 82, 198, 268
de Largilliere, Nicholas, 79
Denbigh, Earls of *see* Feilding family
Derby, St Helen's House, 106
Dering, Edward Heneage, 27
Devereux, family, of Castle Bromwich, 38-9, 243; Lady Dorothy, 82; Sir Edward, 39; Sir George of Sheldon, 263; Sir William, 130
Devis, Anthony, 192
Dewes: family, 198; Rev. John, 249
Dietterlin, Wendel, 20, 24
Digby: family, of Coleshill, xix, 53, 54, 255, 263; of Meriden Hall, 255; Sir Everard, 78
Dighton family, 238
Dilke: family, xix, xxvi, 127-9, 159; Sir Thomas, 127
Disraeli, Benjamin, 84, 106
Ditchley Park (Oxon), 225
Dixwell family, 238
Donellan, Captain, 232
Dormer family, xxiii, 31, 98
Douty, Edward, 238
Downing (Flintshire), 151
Drury, T.K., 222
Duddeston, manor house, 19
Dudley: Lady Alice, 250; Ambrose, Earl of Warwick, xix, xx, 118, 152, 203; John, Duke of Northumberland, xix, 57, 115, 202, 209; Robert, Earl of Leicester, xix, xx, 98, 115-7, 235, 250; Sir Robert, 118
Duffour, Joseph, 149
Dugdale family, of Blyth Hall and Merevale, xxiii, xxvi, 131-3, 231; Sir William (historian), xxvi, 24, 131, 166, 189, 231, 232
Dugdale, James, of Wroxall Abbey, 221, 222

Dunchurch Lodge, xxv, 36, **240**, *171*
Dutton, --- (joiner), 255

Eardley-Wilmot, John, 227
Eathorpe Hall, **240-1**
Eborall: Thomas, 181; 'the smith', 191; William, 207
Edgbaston Hall, xxi, **241-2**, *172*
Edgcote (Northants), 110
Edge Hill: Battle of, 118, 145, 224; Tower, 162-3, *118*
Edgeworth, Maria, 22, 221
Edstone Hall, xxiv, **242**
Edward VII, 206
Edwards, William, 101
Egerton, Sir Thomas, 127
Eglington: Samuel, 69, 260; Joseph, 260
Eliot, George, 11, 14, 224
Elizabeth I, xix, 9, 43, 46, 54, 115, 117, 135, 203, 209
Elizabeth, Princess (the 'Winter Queen'), 58
Elland, Harry, 70
Elmdon Hall, 5, **242-3**, *173*
Emmett, Major Robert, 139
Emscote Hall, **243**
Erdington Hall, xxiii, 22, 152, **243**, *174*
Essex, Robert, Earl of, 39, 82, 130, 166
Ethelfleda, 'Lady of the Mercians', 200
Ettington Park, xvii, xviii, xxi, xxiii, xxv, xxvi, 54, **81-7**, 199, *58-62, V*
Etty, William, 188
Evans, Thomas & William, 82
Evelyn, John, 210
Everitt: A.E., xxvii, 80; G.A., 121
Evesham Abbey (Worcs), 173
Eyston, John, 174
Eythrope Park (Bucks), 98

Fairfax-Lucy family, *see* Lucy
Farmer family, 260
Farnborough Hall, xvii, xx, xxi, xxii, xxvi, **88-91**, 110, 112, 198, 211, *63-66*
Fauconberg, Viscount, 241
Feilding family, xix, 148-51
Fenwick, Henry, 165
Ferrers: family, of Baddesley Clinton, xx, 24-7; Henry de, 81; Sir John, of Tamworth Castle, 106; Sir Thomas, of Tamworth Castle, 134
Ferrers of Chartley, Lords, 38, 130
Ferrers of Groby, Lords, 24
Fetherston family, of Packwood, xx, 128, 158-60
Fetherston-Dilke family of Maxstoke, *see* Dilke family
Field, George, 122
Fieldhouse, William, 242
Fielding: George & Robert, 249; Henry, 165
Fiennes, Celia, 176, 204
Fillongley Hall, xxiv, 107, **244**
Finch: family, *see* Earls of Aylesford; Hon. Charles, 261
Fisher family, of Packington Hall, xix, 127, 152
Fisher, Thomas, of Warwick Priory, xix, 209, 231
Fisher, Thomas, of Caldecote Hall, 234, 249
Fitton, Mary and Anne, 9
Fitzherbert, Mrs., 272
Flammock, Sir Andrew, 101
Flaxman, John, 176

Fletchamstead Hall, 178, 215, **245**
Fletcher, N., 267
Flint, Thomas, 223
Flitcroft, Henry, xxii, 266
Foljamb, Francis, 11
Folliott, 3rd Lord, xxi, 92, 250
Fonthill Abbey (Wiltshire), 45
Foremark Hall (Derbyshire), 232
Forest Hall, Meriden, 157
Forster family, 254
Fortescue, Rev. Francis, 224
Four Oaks Hall, xx, xxi, 10, **92-4**, *67-8*
Fox, C.E., 208
Foxcote, xvii, xxi, **95-6**, 110, 166, *69*
Frankton Manor, 211
Fraser, Gilbert, 240
Freeman, John, 110
Freville family, 134
Fulbrook Castle, xviii, 44, 73
Fullerton family, 266

Gage, Sir John, 241
Galton family, 238
Garland, Charles Tuller, 138-9, 225
Garner, Thomas, 222
Garrett, Daniel, 204, 206
Gaveston, Piers, 102
Geast, Richard, 231
George III, 170
George IV, 171
Gibbons: Grinling, 10; William & Thomas, 141
Gibbs, James (architect), xxii, 66, 67, 168
Gibbs family, 109
Gibson, Sir Isaac, 59, 60
Gibson, John, xxiv, 46, 69, 104, 270
Giles, ---, of Derby (architect), 247
Gillott, Joseph, xxv, 227, 247
Gilpin, William Sawrey, 106, 187
Gladstone, William Ewart, 106
Glicksten, Martin, 34
Gloucester Abbey, 238
Goddard, R. & G., of Leicester, xxiv, 234
Goldicote House, **245**
Goldie, E., xxvi, 225
Gooch, Sir Thomas, 33
Gooder family, 28
Goodricke, Sir Francis Lyttleton Holyoake, xxiv, 186, 187, 245
Goodwin family, 224-5
Goodwin, William, 162
Gordon, Bentley, 252
Gore, John, 110
Gouge, Edward, 39, 40, 59, 60, 89
Gough family, xxi, 241-2
Gower, George, 9
Granville family, 268
Gratrix, John, 238
Graves, Richard, 30
Gray: John, 63; Thomas, 102, 205
Great Alne: parish, 186; Manor, **245**
Greatheed family, xxi, xxiii, xxiv, 101-4

Gregory (later Gregory-Hood) family, xxii, 254, 266
Grendon Hall, **245-6**, *175*
Gresley, Rev. Thomas, 94
Greswolde: family, 120, 122, 249, 262; Humphrey de, 124
Greville family, of Beauchamps Court and Warwick Castle: Lords Brooke & Earls of Warwick, xix, xx, 127, 203-8, 223, 227, 243, 255, 263; Sir Fulke, 1st Lord Brooke, xix, 64, 119, 173-4, 203; Fulke, of Knowle Hall, 119; Hon. Charles, 207
Greville family of Milcote, xx, 224, 227, 234, 245, 255
Grey family, xviii, xxiv, 16, 263, 267
Grey de Ruthin, 19th Lord, 232
Greys Mallory, 194
Griffiths, Frederick, 242
Grimes family, 238
Grimshaw: Hall, xviii, xxv, **247**, *176*; family, 247
Grimsthorpe (Lincs), 103
Grissell and Peto, Messrs., 186
Grove Park, xxiii, xxiv, **97-9**, *70-1*
Guernsey, Lords, *see* Aylesford, Earls of
Guinness, Robert Darley, 272
Gundry, H., 199
Guy of Warwick, 100
Guy's Cliffe, xxi, xxiii, xxiv, xxvi, **100-5**, *72-6*; chapel, 100, 102, 103; 'Saxon Mill', 102

Hacket family, 250, 256, 257
Hagley Hall (Worcs), 93, 149, 163
Hakewill, Henry, xxiv, 69, 90, 157, 198, 226, 258, 263
Hale End Hall, **247**
Hales: John, 258; family, of Snitterfield, 264
Ham House (Surrey), 109
Hamilton: Sir Richard, 199; Sir William, 207; Emma, 207
Hammond, Lieutenant, 117-8
Hampton, Viscount, 236
Hampton-in-Arden Manor, xxiii, **247**
Hampton-on-the-Hill, church, 98
Hams Hall, xxiii, xxv, **106-7**, 244, *77*
Hampstead Marshall (Berks), 58, 59
Hanbury Hall (Worcs), 95, 166
Hanslap family, 266
Hanwell, W. (plasterer), 14
Harding, William & William Judd, 225
Hardman, John, 36, 227
Harefield (Middx), 9, 10, 11
Harewell family, 272
Harington, John, 57, 58
Harlech Castle (Wales), 125
Harman, John, 256
Harris, Mrs. Leverton, 252
Harrison: Thomas (mason), 78; Oswald, 107; Thomas (architect), 218
Harrowfield, J. (gardener), 82
Harvington Hall (Worcs), 79, 80
Haseley Manor, xx, xxv, **247**, *177*
Hastings family, 223
Hatch Court (Somerset), 231
Hatfield House (Herts), 19
Hatton, church, 248
Hawes, William & Ursula, 249
Hawkesbury, Abbot Richard, 173

Hawkesworth, Colonel, 118
Hawkins, Thomas, *see* Fisher, Thomas
Hayward, Richard, 14, 266, 268
Heath: Arthur, 147; Richard, 152
Heber-Percy, Captain, J.R., 104
Heming: Dempster, 234; George & Rev., S.B., 267
Henman & Cooper, architects, xxvi, 256
Henry III, 115
Henry V, 115
Henry VII, 126
Henry VIII, 72-3, 115, 127, 135, 152, 202
Henwood Hall, xxiii, **248**
Hereford, Viscounts, *see* Devereux family
Hertford, Marquesses of, *see* Seymour-Conway family
Hertford House, London, 171
Herthill family, 28
Hewlett, Alfred, 248
Hiatt, William, 69
Hibbert, John Washington, xxiv, 35-6
Hill: Sir Rowland, 178; family, 249; Richard, of Little Kineton, 252
Hillfield Hall, **249**
Hilton, Sir Robert, 253
Hiorn: William and David, xxii, 242, 266; David, 11, 12, 44, 154, 263; William, 12, 44, 67, 89, 94, 155, 182, 191
Hitchcox, William, 12, 163
Hobcraft, John, 149
Hoby, Sir Philip, 174
Hodgson, Arthur, 52
Hogarth, William, 89
Holbech: Mary of Fillongley, 180; Thomas, of Fillongley, 255
Holbrook Grange, **250**
Holdsworth, Edward, 54
Holford, Peter, 272
Holkham Hall (Norfolk), 155
Holland, William, xxiv, 86, 177, 199, 234
Holland Corbett family, 223
Hollar, Wenceslas, xxvi, 65, 268
Holman, C.B., 96
Holte family, xix, xx, 19-22, 243-4
Honiley Hall, xxv, xxvi, **249**; church, 249
Honington Hall, xviii, xx, xxi, xxii, 2, 31, 51, 92, **109-112**, 146, *78-81, VI*; church, 109
Hood: Lords, xxii, 270; Henry Alexander, 266
Hooke, Robert, xxi, 166-7
Hopper, Thomas, 4
Horder, Percy Morley, xxvi, 165, 194, 195
Hore family, 242
Horton, Colonel, 223
Hoskyns, Chandos Wren, 221
Howard, Philip, 96
Howitt, William, 52, 74
Howman, Rev. George, 259
Huddleston family, 96
Hudson, William, of Warwick, 101
Hugford family, 243, 248
Hughes, George, 272
Hume: A., 35; Mary, 207
Hunt, G.H., 245
Huntingdon, Earl of, *see* Clinton, William

Hurlbut, Roger and William, xxi, 159, 166, 204
Hurley Hall, **249**
Hutchinson, Henry, 82, 83, 84
Hyde: Lawrence, Earl of Rochester, 118; Alexander, Bishop of Salisbury, 109

Idlicote House, **249-50**
Ilchester, Earl of, 237
Iliffe, William, 224
Inchcape, Earl of, 236
Ingram family, 253
Irnham, Lord, *see* Luttrell, Simon

Jackson, Gilbert, 139
Jago, Richard, 2, 30, 69, 154, 163
James, Henry, xvii, 75
James I, 118, 119, 148, 203
Jeayes, Henry, xxvi
Jeffray family, 264
Jennens: Humphrey, xxiii, 152, 243, 260; family, 157, 243
Jensen, Gerrit, 40
Jersey, Earls of, *see* Villiers family
Jesson family, 92, 250
John, King, 113
John of Gaunt, Duke of Lancaster, 115
Johnson, Henry, 260
Joliffe, Charles, 245
Jones: Inigo, 155; James Cove, 254; Kitty Lloyd, 195; Sir Thomas, 255; William, 110, 112
Jordan, John, 213
Juxon family, 250-2

Keble, Henry, 216
Keene, Henry, 12
Keighly-Peech, Henry, 249
Kelway, Robert, 57
Kendall, H.E., xxiv, 177; J.H., xxiv, 199, 215
Kenilworth Castle, xvii, xviii, xix, xx, xxiv, 43, 98, **113-8**, 126, 127, *82-5, VII*; Priory, 115, 152, 238, 249, 252
Kent, William, 155
Kettlewell, Rev. John, 54
King: Benjamin, xxii, 12, 69, 149, 153, 155, 182, 191, 266; Edward Bolton, 191, 237
Kingsbury Hall, xviii
Kirby Hall (Northants), 43
Knebworth House (Herts), 177
Knevitt, Henry, 262
Knight family, xxii, 30-2, 237, 242
Knightley family, 260
Knights Hospitaller, 263
Knights Templar, 262
Knottesford, John, 224
Knowle Hall, **119-21**, 187, *86-7*

Ladbroke Hall, **250**
Ladbroke, Sir Robert, 249
Ladkin, Edward, 189
Laguerre, Louis, 39
Lamb & Co., of Manchester, 227
Lamb, Samuel, 188
Lancaster, John, 36, 223-4, 240
Lane, Richard, 224

Laneham, John, 117
Langley Hall, xxi, 92, **250**
Langley Park (Norfolk), 110
Lattimer, William, 40
Lawford Hall, **250**, *178*
Lawley, Sir Francis, 136
Leamington Spa, xxiv, 102, 259, 263, 270; Assembly Rooms, 186; *Manor House Hotel*, 263; Reading Rooms, 186
Leasowes, The (Worcs), 30
Lee, Sir Robert, 33
Legge, Heneage, 22, 249
Leicester, Earl of, *see* Dudley, Robert
Leicester, G.O., 186
Leigh: family, of Stoneleigh, xix, 178-85, 267; Charles, of Birdingbury, 229; Sir Egerton, of Brownsover, 232; Juliana, of Kings Newnham, 10
Leland, John, xvii, 28, 73, 100, 115, 135, 202, 227
Lethaby, W.R., 94
Lewis, Henry Greswolde, xxii, 120, 122-4, 262
Light, Walter, 162
Lightoler, Timothy, xxiii, 153, 182, 206
Lingen, Thomas, 161-2
Lipscomb, George, 69
Lisle family, 256
Little family, 258
Little Compton Manor, xxv, **250**, *179*
Little Kineton House, **252**, *180*
Little Wolford Manor, **253**, *181*
Littleton, Anthony, 174
Lizours, Sir John, 141
Lloyd family, of Welcombe, 52, 213, 214; Sampson, 231; Thomas, 212
Lobb, Joel, 44
London, George, 11, 41, 59
Longbridge House, **254**
Longleat (Wiltshire), 117
Longvile, Ann, 270
Lonsdale, Thomas, 267
Lough Fea, co. Monaghan, 84
Loveday, John, 29, 64, 66, 89, 225
Lovell, James, 149, 163
Lowe, John, 1
Loxley Hall, **254**, *182*
Lucy family, xviii, xix, xxvi, 42-7, 263
Ludford family, 6-8
Lugar, Robert, xxiv, 232, 268
Luttrell, Simon, Lord Irnham and Earl of Carhampton, xxi, 92
Lutyens, Sir Edwin, xxv, 238
Luxborough, Henrietta, Lady, xxii, 30-1, 102, 191; Lord, *see* Catherlough, Earl of
Lydiard Park (Wiltshire), 149
Lyght, Walter, *see* Light
Lygon, William, 247
Lynall, Henry, 122
Lyttelton: George, 163; Humphry, 186

Macky, John, 152
Maclise, David, 188
Mair, George, 215
Malchair, John Baptist, 156

Mallory Court, 194
Mallory family: of Newbold Revel, 145; of Woodcote, 270
Malvern Hall, xxii, 120, **122-4**, *88-9, VIII*
Manton, Lord, 70
Mappleborough Green, church, 164
Marmion family, 134
Marnock, Robert, xxv, 172, 208
Marow family, 227
Marriett, Richard, 1
Martin: Edward, 10; Kit, 185
Mauduit, William, 201
Maunton, John, 68
Mavesyn Ridware (Staffs), 143
Mawson, Thomas, xxvi, 240, 264
Maxstoke Castle, xvii, xviii, xix, xxvi, 52, 117, **125-9**, 159, 202, *90-3*; Priory, 125
Mayne family, 242
Mead, John, 267
Melford Hall (Suffolk), 43
Melvin, Sir Martin, 34
Merevale Hall, xvii, xxiii, xxiv, xxv, xxvi, **130-3**, 219, *94-7*; Abbey, 130
Meriden Hall, xxi, **255**; Heath, 157
Middlemore family, 241
Middleton Hall, **134-7**, *98-100*; church, 134
Middleton Park (Oxon), 192
Milcote House, xx, **255**
Miller: Sanderson, xxi, xxii, 12, 89, 112, 153, 154, 162-5, 192, 198; William, 63
Milles, Jeremiah, 168
Mills: John and Matthew, 33; family, of Barford, 226; H., of Edstone, 242
Milward, John, 254
Minton, Messrs., 36, 199
Moillett, John Lewis, 264
Moland, Richard, 265
Montague family, Dukes of Montagu, 178, 236
Montfort: family, of Coleshill, 53, 273; Simon de, Earl of Leicester, 155, 201
Moor Hall, xxvi, **255-6**
Moore, Robert, xxii, 2, 4, 12, 30, 44, 67, 69, 94, 102, 153, 163, 182, 191, 198, 206, 263, 266
Morant, George, 244
Mordaunt family, xxii, 196-9
Moreton Hall, xvii, xxv, xxvi, **138-40**, 225, *101*
Moreton Paddox, xxv, xxvi, **139-40**, *102-3*
Morewood family, 250
Morgan family, 235, 268
Morris: --- (builder), 102, 103; Roger, 154
Moseley Hall (Worcs), 231
Morton Bagot, 186
Motion, Andrew, 193
Mount Greville, *see* Milcote House
Mowbray, Lord, 235
Moxhull Hall, **256-7**, *183-4*
Muntz family, 191
Murdak family, 64
Murray, J.W., 247
Myers, George, 36

Nash, John, 162

Neale family, 223
Needham, Joshua, 190
Nesfield: William Andrews, xxv, 63, 132; William Eden, 62, 63, 247
Neville, Richard, Earl of Warwick, 202
New Hall, **141-4**, *104-6*
New House, Coventry, 92, **258**, *185*
Newbold Comyn, **258-9**
Newbold Pacey Hall, **259**
Newbold Revel, xxi, 29, 112, **145-7**, *107*
Newby, Thomas, xxiv, 215
Newdigate (or Newdegate): family, of Arbury, xxi, xxvi, 6, 9-11, 15; Sir Roger, xxi, xxii, 3, 8, 11-14, 17, 153; Francis, of Astley, 17; Col. F.W. of Allesley, 224; F.A., of Weston-in-Arden, 268
Newnham Paddox, xix, xxi, xxii, xxvi, **148-51**, 154, 163, *108-10*
Newsam, Charles, 224
Newsham family, 236-7
Newton, Sir Henry, 210
Newton family, 32
Niven, W., xxvii
Noel, Hon. B.O. & B.P., 257
Norman, Samuel, 4
North: Lord, 66; Roger, 109
Northampton, Marquess of, *see* Compton family
Northumberland, Duchess of, 206
Northwood House (Isle of Wight), 215
Norton, Lords, *see* Adderley family, of Hams Hall and Fillongley
Noseley (Leics), Chapel of St Mary, 234

Odingseles family, 125
Okeover, Rowland Farmer, 260
Offchurch, parsonage, 212
Offchurch Bury, **259-60**, *186*
Ogilby, Col. Robert, 140
Old Stratford, manor, 213
Oldbury Hall, **260**
Olton Hall, 120, 121
Orleans House, Twickenham (Middx), 168
Osterley Park (Middx), 192
Overbury, Sir Nicholas, 227
Owen: Alfred, 144; Archdeacon, 82; Tudor, 238
Oxford: Ashmolean Museum, 11; Balliol College chapel, 74; Magdalen College, Addison's Walk, 228; New College hall, 115; Radcliffe Camera, 110; St Mary the Virgin, porch, 40; University College, 12-13

Packington Hall, xvii, xxi, xxii, xxiii, xxiv, xxvi, 14, **152-7**, *111-14*; church, 157; Old Hall, 152
Packwood House, xviii, xix, xx, xxv, 27, **158-61**, 162, *115-17, IX*
Paestum (Italy), 123
Palmer: Benjamin, 120; family, of Ladbroke, 250; --- (joiner), 255
Panini, Giovanni, 89, 91
Pantasaph (Flintshire), church, 151
Park Hall: Castle Bromwich, xviii, 39; Salford Priors, 172
Park House, Moxhull, *see* Moxhull Hall
Park House, Snitterfield, 215, 265

Parker: Aldwyn, 105; Francis, 15; Henry, 109-10; Sir Hugh, 109
Partheriche, John, 52
Peach, Samuel, 249
Peake, Robert, 54
Peel: Sir Frederick, xxiii, 247; John, 136; Sir Robert, xxiii, 247, 250
Peers family, 224
Pennant, Thomas, 155
Percival, Thomas, 155
Percy family, 104
Perks, Rev. William, 31
Perritt, William, xxii, 89, 112
Peterley (Bucks), 98
Peto, Harold, xxv, 232
Petre, Edward, 270
Pettifer, James, 204
Peyto family, xx, 48-9, 66
Philips: Sir George, xxiii, 215, 218, 253; Mark, 215, 265; Robert, 215, 265
Phillips: Edward, of Kings Norton, 186; Edward, of Whitmore Park, 258; John (craftsman), xxii, 2-3, 168; William Garrick, 8
Phyffers, Theodore, 74
Pickford, Joseph, xxiii, 106, 266
Pierce, Edward, 39, 59
Pipewell Abbey (Northants), 35, 235
Piranesi, Giovanni Battista, 156
Pitt, William the elder, 163
Place, Lionel, 267
Plymouth, Lord, 191
Pococke, Bishop, 166
Polesworth Abbey, 260
Pollen, Francis, 98
Ponce, Nicholas, 157
Pooley Hall, xviii, **260-1**, *187*
Pope: Alexander, 54, 89; Thomas, 250
Portman, Hon. Claude (Lord), 245
Portmore, Co. Antrim, 166
Potter, Joseph, 245
Poynter, Ambrose, 208
Pratt: Roger, 59; Samuel, 208
Preston, John, 235
Preston-on-Stour: church, 3; village, 5
Prew, Thomas, 263
Price: Mrs. Cromwell, 29, 248; Sir Uvedale, 157
Prichard, John, xxv, 84, 85, 86
Priestley Riots, 231
Prinsep, Robert, 234
Puckering, 209-10
Puckler-Muskau, Prince, 104, 207
Pudsey family, xxi, 92, 250
Pugin, A.W.N., xxv, 35-6, 219
Purefoy family, 234
Pype Hayes Hall, **261**

Radbrook Manor, 110, **261-2**
Radcliffe family, 24; Daniel, 245
Radford Semele Hall, **262**; Manor House, 262
Radway Grange, xix, xxii, 12, **162-5**, *118-9*
Ragley Hall, xvii, xix, xx, xxi, xxii, xxv, xxvi, 95, 110, **166-72**, 189, *120-3*, X
Rainsford family, 238
Raleigh family, 88
Ramsden: Charles, 146; Richard, 237
Ranelagh Gardens, Chelsea, 112
Ray, John, 135-6
Rayney family, 267
Rees-Mogg, Lt.-Cpl. G.B., 238
Rembrandt van Rijn, 156
Rennie, John, 184
Repington, Sir John, 225
Repton, Humphry, xxv, 32, 184, 185
Reynolds: Edwin, 161; Sir Joshua, 168
Ricardo, Osman, 270
Rich family, 206
Richard III, 126, 202
Richmond Palace (Surrey), 77
Rickman, Thomas, 22, 41, 82, 83, 84
Rigaud, Jean Francois, 156, 157
Robbins, Thomas, 112
Roberts: Henry, 224; Thomas, 110
Robinson, P.F., 258
Roche family, 38
Rollason-Walker, W.H., xxvi, 138-9
Rose, Joseph, 67, 157
Rous, John, 100, 166
Rugby School, 234
Ruskin, John, 84
Russell: Lord John, 219; John (architect), 258
Rust, Graham, 172
Ryland family, of Sherbourne and Barford, xxv, 226, 263
Ryland family, of Moxhull, 257
Rysbrack, John Michael, 4

Sacheverell family, 141-3; Rev. Dr. Henry, 142
Sackville, Richard, Earl of Dorset, 255
St George, Howard, 225
St John's House, Warwick, **262-3**, *188*
St Marie, Dunchurch Road, Rugby, 35
St Martin's School for Girls, Solihull, 124
St Sepulchre's Priory, Warwick, *see* Warwick Priory
St Vincent's School for Girls, 199
Salford Hall, **173-4**, *124*
Salter, John, 189
Salvin, Anthony, xxiv, 208
Samuel, Walter, *see* Bearstead, 2nd Lord
Sanders, John, 249
Saunders: Sir Edward, 268; Capt. James, xxvii
Scott: Sir George Gilbert (architect), 84, 90, 199, 234, 263; Lord John, 236; Mr., of Warwick Priory, 212; Sir Walter, xxiv, 22, 44, 118, 200; Walter (architect), 222
Seddon, J.P., 32, 84
Segrave, John, 235
Seymour-Conway family, 168-72
Shakespear, George, xxii, 2-3
Shakespeare, William, xxiv, 44, 46, 50, 213
Shaw: James Frederick, xxv, 231; Richard Norman, 63
Sheldon family, xix, xx; of Weston, 216-18; of Brailes, 232; of Skilts, 264
Sheldon tapestry maps, 216, 217, 218
Sheldon Hall, **263**

Shenstone, William, 30, 31, 163, 162, 191
Shepheard, Samuel, 241
Sherborne Castle (Dorset), 54
Sherbourne Park, xxv, 226, **263**; church, 263
Sherlock, Rev. Thomas, Bishop of London, 33
Shirley family, xviii, 81-7
Shrewsbury: 15th Earl of, 98; 16th Earl of, 35
Shrubland House, **263-4**, *189*
Shuckburgh family: of Shuckburgh Hall, xviii, xix, xxvi, 175-7, 252; of Bilton Hall, 228; of Bourton Hall, 231; of Birdingbury, 229
Shuckburgh Hall, xviii, xxiv, xxvi, **175-7**, *125-6*
Shuckburgh, Lower, 176, 177
Siddeley, Sir John, 1st Lord Kenilworth, 118
Siddons, Mrs. Sarah, 102
Simpson, Hon. John Bridgeman, 228
Skilts, xix, **264**
Skipwith family, xxi, 145-6; Sir Grey, 112, 146
Skyllington, Robert de, 115
Smith: Charles Alston, 263; C.S. (architect), xxiv, 45, 82, 98, 185; Francis of Warwick (architect), xxi, 29, 66, 145, 181, 189, 241, 255; Gustavus Thomas, 245; John, 101; William, of Warwick (architect), xxi, xxii, 66, 120, 182, 189, 241; William, 79
Smith-Ryland family, 226, 263
Smyth family, of Wootton Wawen, 272
Smythson, Robert, 203
Snape, John, 93
Snell, W. & E., 133
Snitterfield House, xx, **264-5**, *190*
Soane, Sir John, xxii, 31, 122-3, 124, 270
Somerset, H.C.H., 33
Somerset and Richmond, Mary, Duchess of, 57
Somerville: Thomas, 242; William, 30, 242
Southampton, Earls of, 178, 250
Spencer family, xix, 237, 273-4; Sir John, Lord Mayor of London, 74
Spicer, William, 117
Spiney (or Spineto), Guy, 77
Spooner family, 242, 247; William, 248
Springfield House, xxiii, **265**
Stafford family, *see* Buckingham, Dukes of
Standbridge, John, 44
Stanford, Charles, 174
Stanford Hall (Leics), 182, 189
Stanley, Charles, 110
Starkey, Col., 165
Staunton family, 254
Steavens, Thomas, 1
Steinitz, Charles, 86
Stivichall Hall, xxii, 254, **266**, *191*
Stokes, Adrian, 16
Stone: Sir Benjamin, xxvii; John, xx, 48; Nicholas, 48, 64, 210
Stoneleigh Abbey, xvii, xx, xxi, xxii, xxiii, xxiv, xxv, 145, 162, **178-85**, 190, 245, 258, *127-32, XI*
Stoneythorpe Hall, **266**
Stoughton family, 262-3
Stowe (Bucks), 149, 205
Stratford family, 6, 130-1, 231
Stratford-upon-Avon: Clopton Bridge, 50; Guild Chapel, 50; parish church, 51; the College, 213, 266
Strathmore, Earl of, 234
Strawberry Hill (Middx), 9
Street, George Edmund, 84
Studley Castle, xxiv, **186-8**, *133*; Horticultural College, 188; Priory, 186
Suckling, Sir John, 255
Sudbrooke Park, Richmond (Surrey), 168
Sudbury Hall (Derbys), 92, 204
Suffolk, Dukes of, *see* Grey family; Brandon, Charles
Sunrising House, 193
Sutton (Beds), 221
Sutton Coldfield: church, 256; manor, 141; Moat House, 92; Park, 92-3

Talman, William, 189
Tamworth Castle (Staffs), 26, 106, 134
Tanworth, church, 189
Tasker, William, 172
Tate: Bartholomew & Sir William, 270; H. Burton, 34
Taylor: --- (builder), 102, 103; Edward, of Ansty Hall, 224; of Bordesley Hall, 21, 244
Temple Grafton Court, **266-7**; church, 167
Temple Park, Warwick, 205
Tewkesbury Abbey (Gloucs), 250
Thelsford, Friary, 42, 226
Thomas: Rev. William, xxvi, 3, 66, 152; William, of Leamington (architect), 262
Thoresby Hall (Notts), 145, 189
Thornbury Castle (Gloucs), 77
Thorpe, John, 20
Thorwaldsen, Bertel, 106
Throckmorton family: of Coughton, xviii, xx, xxvi, 77-80, 229, 247; of Haseley, 29, 247, 262
Tollemache, Hon. Wilbraham, 122
Tompion, Thomas, 40
Totnes, Earl of, *see* Carew, George
Townsend family, 110, 112
Townshend, Henry, 234
Tracy, Charles Hanbury, 33
Tree: A.M., 139, 225; Ronald, 225
Trevelyan, Sir George Otto, 215, 265
Trollope, George & Sons, 46
Troman, David, 124
Trubshaw: James, 218, 219; Richard, 229, 245
Trussell family, xviii, 33, 228

Ullenhall, church, 32
Umberslade Hall, xxi, 29, **189-91**, *134*
Underhill family, 81, 249
Upton House, xvii, xxv, xxvi, **192-5**, *135-7, XII*

Vanbrugh, Sir John, 64, 103
Van Dyke, Sir Anthony, 149, 217, 228
Van Nost, John, 190
Vansittart, Rev. Edward, 223
Vassalli, Francesco, 89
Verney family, Lords Willoughby de Broke, xviii, xx, 49, 64-70, 252
Vertue, George, 53, 54, 64, 210
Veysey, Bishop John, 141, 255

Victoria, Queen, 22, 185
Villa Borghese, Rome, 45
Villiers family: Earls of Clarendon, 118; Earls of Jersey, 192
Virginia House, Richmond (USA), 212
Vyner family, 240

Wade, Herbert, xxv, 249
Walker: Sir Edward, 52; M. Eyre & Harewood, A.W. architects, 34; Thomas, 187, 227; Thomas Eades, 187; William, 84
Wallace Collection, London, 171
Waller, Maj.-Gen. Sir George, 270
Walpole, Horace, 9, 11, 30, 149, 168, 205, 217, 218
Walton Hall, xvii, xxii, xxiii, xxv, xxvi, 84, **196-9**, *138-40*; village, 199
Ward family, of Barford, 226; Rev. Thomas, xxiii, xxvi, 52, 120-1, 214, 226, 268-9
Ward, John (later Ward-Boughton-Leigh), of Brownsover, 234
Ward, Kendrick & Reynolds, *see* Reynolds, Edwin
Warde, Charles Thomas, 52, 214-15
Waring family, 227
Warmington Manor House, 88, 224
Werner family, 270
Warriner family, 219
Warton, Thomas, 7
Warwick: Bridge, 207; County Record Office, 212; *Lord Leicester Hotel*, Jury Street, 189; Market House, 166; rebuilding of (1694), xxviii; St Mary's church, 92, 100; Shire Hall, xxi
Warwick Castle, xvii, xviii, xix, xx, xxi, xxii, xxiii, xxiv, xxv, 119, 126, 162, 182, **200-8**, 268, *141-6, XII*; Dairy, 206; estate, 194; Greenhouse, 207; Spiers Lodge, 206
Warwick, Earls of, *see* Beauchamp family; Dudley family; Greville of Warwick Castle; Neville, Richard
Warwick, Frances Evelyn, Countess of, 188, 216
Warwick Priory, xix, 139, **209-12**, *147-50*
'Warwick Vase', xxi, 207, 208
Warwickshire College of Agriculture, 140
Washington family, 162
Watergall House, **267**
Watson, J.A., 237
Watson, William, 79
Watt, James, xxiv, 22
Webb: John, 82, 151; Richard, 245; family, of Sherbourne, 263
Weddell, A.W., 212
Weddington Hall, xxiv, 106, **267**, *192*
Welcombe, xxiv, 52, **213-15**, *151-2*
Wellesbourne Hall, 198, **268**
Wentworth, Sir Peter, 270
West: James, xxii, 1-4, 30, 160; family, xxv, 4-5, 238
Westbury Court (Gloucs), 43-4
Westminster Abbey, 12, 14, 119
Weston House, xxiii, xxiv, xxv, 132, **216-19**, *153-5*
Weston-in-Arden Hall, **268**, *193*
Weston Park (Staffs), 41
Weston-under-Wetherley Hall, xix, **268-70**, *194*; Hall Farm, 270
Whalley, Bernard, 33
Wheatley family, 227
Wheler: Sir Charles, 229; Francis, 270

White: Edward, 140; John, 41
Whitehall family, 260
Whitehall, Palace of, Banqueting House, 48
Whightwick, John, 260
Whitford, Thomas, 79
Whitley Abbey, xxii, **270**, *195*; School, 270
Whitley Hall, *see* Whitley Abbey
Whitmore Park, *see* New House
Whitmore, William, 69
Wiggin, Sir Charles, 112
Wigley, Edward, 124
Wigston: Roger, 270; Sir William, 57
Wilcox: Jonathan (carpenter), 39, 59, 60; family, 270
Wilkins, William, 68
Wilkinson, William, 144
Willcox, James, of Warwick, xxiv, 46, 86, 185
Willement, Thomes, 46, 185
Willes: Edward, 249; family, 258-9
Williams: F.E. & F.W.G., 124; Thomas, 84
Willington: William, xix, 19, 216, 249; family 249
Willoughby family, Lords Middleton, of Middleton, 134-6
Willoughby de Broke, Lords, *see* Verney family
Wilmot, Robert, 227
Wilson: Robert, 121; Sir William (architect), xxi, 10, 40, 92, 250; Rev. William, 120; William 'Gumley', 120, 121, 187
Wilton House (Wiltshire), 139
Winckworth, John, 258
Winde, William, xx, 39, 59, 60, 61
Windsor Castle, 82; Dean & Chapter of, 224
Wingfield Castle (Suffolk), 161; George, 54
Wingfield-Digby family, 54
Wise family, 210-2, 263-4, 270; Henry, 41, 210, 211; Jacob, 248; Matthew, 263
Withering, William, 242
Wollaton Hall (Notts), 135
Wolston Priory, **270**
Wood: Anthony, 109, 217; Arthur and Edward, 146-7; Richard Henry, 231
Woodcote, xxiv, 212, **270-2**, *196*
Woodley House, Kineton, 70
Woodmen of Arden, 157
Woodward family, 95, 110, 262; Edward, xxi, xxii, 2, 3; Edward (son), 82; John, 245
Woolcot, George, 244
Wootton Wawen Hall, **272**, *197*; church, 31, 242
Worcester Cathedral, 224, 237
Wormleighton Manor, xviii, xix, xx, **273-4**, *198-9*
Wren, Sir Christopher, xxi, 10, 39, 92, 221; family, 221
Wright: John (plasterer), xxii, 31, 182, 191; Sir Nathan, 234
Wroxall Abbey, 20, 217, **220-2**, *156-7*
Wyatt: Benjamin Dean, 45; James, xxii, 106, 170; J.H., 151; Matthew Digby, 74; Samuel, 238
Wynne, Charles, 260

Yelverton: Sir Christopher, 268; Sir Henry, 232
Yorke: Francis, 242; Philip, 204, 205
Young, William, 248

Zouch, Lords, 268
Zucchi, Andrea, 67, 68